Catholics in Interreligious Dialogue: Studies in Monasticism, Theology and Spirituality

Catholics in Interreligious Dialogue: Studies in Monasticism, Theology and Spirituality

edited by
Anthony O'Mahony and Peter Bowe, OSB

GRACEWING

First published in 2006

Gracewing
2 Southern Avenue, Leominster
Herefordshire HR6 0QF

All rights reserved. No part of this publication may be reproduced, stored in a retrieval system, or transmitted in any form, or by any means, electronic, mechanical, photocopying, recording or otherwise, without the written permission of the publisher.

Compilation and editorial material © Anthony O'Mahony
and Peter Bowe, OSB, 2006
Copyright for individual chapters resides with the authors

The right of the editors and the contributors to be identified as the authors of this work has been asserted in accordance with the Copyright, Designs and Patents Act 1988.

UK ISBN 0 85244 640 3
ISBN 978 0 85244 640 9

Typesetting by
Action Publishing Technology Ltd, Gloucester, GL1 5SR

Contents

Preface vii
*by Archbishop Michael L. Fitzgerald,
President, Pontifical Council for Interreligious Dialogue,
Vatican City (On 15 February 2006, Archbishop Fitzgerald
was appointed as Apostolic Nuncio in the Arab Republic of
Egypt and Delegate to the Organization of the League of
Arab States)*

Introduction xi
by Anthony O'Mahony and Peter Bowe, OSB

Part One: Monastic Interreligious Dialogue

Chapter 1   Monastic Interreligious Dialogue:
a History   3
Pierre François de Béthune, OSB

Chapter 2   Contemporary Witness, Future
Configuration: Monastic Interreligious
Dialogue   10
Peter Bowe, OSB

Chapter 3   Thomas Merton's Dialogue: The
Quest for a Normative Christianity   26
Eoin de Bhaldraithe, OSCO

Part Two: Catholic Encounters with Islam

Chapter 4   Charles de Foucauld (1858–1916):
Silent witness for Jesus 'in the face
of Islam'   47
Fr Ian Latham, LBJ

Chapter 5	Between Christendom and Islam: The Martyr Mystic Christian de Chergé and the Atlas Cistercians in Algeria *Jean Olwen Maynard*	71
Chapter 6	Thomas Merton's Encounter with Islam *Agnes Wilkins, OSB*	97
Chapter 7	Francis and the Sultan: A Model for Contemporary Christian Engagement with Islam *Steven Saxby*	120
Chapter 8	'Our Common Fidelity to Abraham is What Divides': Christianity and Islam in the Life and Thought of Louis Massignon *Anthony O'Mahony*	151

Part Three: Christian Dialogue with Asia

Chapter 9	Monastic Interreligious Dialogue in India: Henri Le Saux, OSB (Abhishiktananda) and Bede Griffiths, OSB Cam *Judson B. Trapnell*	193
Chapter 10	Through a Glass Darkly: the Jesuit Encounter with Buddhism in Tibet *John Flannery*	217

Notes on Contributors 242
Index 247

Preface

Archbishop Michael L. Fitzgerald +

It is perhaps not incorrect to date organized interreligious dialogue from the Second Vatican Council and its Declaration *Nostra Aetate*. There had, of course, been a number of pioneers, people such as Louis Massignon and Jules Monchanin, Henri Le Saux and Thomas Merton, who had an open attitude towards other religions. Yet the encouragement 'to enter with prudence and charity into discussion and collaboration with members of other religions' (*Nostra Aetate*. 2) was something new. The Secretariat for Non-Christians, later to become the Pontifical Council for Interreligious Dialogue, was created by Paul VI precisely to spread this new spirit throughout the Catholic Church.

The important contribution of monasticism to interreligious dialogue was recognized right from the beginning, although it was not until 1974 that official backing was given to the efforts being undertaken, particularly in the Benedictine family. It was in that year that Cardinal Pignedoli, the President of the Secretariat, wrote a letter to Abbot Primate Rembert Weakland. Three points can be emphasized in connection with this letter.

The first point is that there is a need for contemplative life if the Church in a particular area is to find its full expression. This has been seen as particularly important in Asia, with its long tradition of prayer and its search for the Absolute, and where the Church is often considered more as an Non-Governmental Organization (NGO), suitable for responding to humanitarian needs, but not a prayerful organization and even less a school of prayer.

Secondly, there is the realization that monastics can build bridges to other religions. As Pignedoli put it, 'if we tried to approach Buddhism and Hinduism without monasticism, we would hardly be considered religious'. Christian monastics find themselves in harmony with monks and nuns of other religious traditions, because the monastic vocation expresses something that is fundamental in the human person, namely, the thirst for God, the thirst for something greater than oneself.

In the third place one can point to a cross-fertilization between Catholic monasticism and the Pontifical Council for Interreligious Dialogue. The Council has encouraged monastics to establish relations with the monasticism of other religious traditions. At the same time the Council has been influenced by the experience of monastics. The document produced in 1984, *The Attitude of the Church towards the Followers of Other Religions*, lists the dialogue of religious experience as one of four forms of dialogue. It is unlikely that this would have been mentioned if monastics had not started to reach out to others in this way.

The main efforts of monastic interreligious dialogue have been directed towards Buddhism. This is natural since Buddhism sets great store on monasticism and monastic life is still flourishing in all three traditions of Buddhism, Theravada, Mahayana and Vajrayana (Tibetan). Yet it has been possible to reach out to other religious traditions too, establishing contact with Hindu *sanyasin* and Muslim *Sufis*. This is surely to be encouraged, since it can lead to spiritual emulation. As the document *Dialogue and Proclamation* (1991) states:

> Interreligious dialogue does not merely aim at mutual understanding and friendly relations. It reaches a much deeper level, that of the spirit, where exchange and sharing consist in a mutual witness to one's beliefs and a common exploration of one's respective religious convictions. (n°40)

The chapters in this volume, dealing with history, theology and actual experience, will surely help to make monastic interreligious dialogue better known. At a time when there is so much need for understanding among people belonging to different religions, may these studies stimulate that exchange at the deeper level which leads to an experience of harmony, and even of a certain unity. Our conflict-ridden world is longing for this.

Introduction

Anthony O'Mahony and Peter Bowe, OSB

The American Catholic theologian David Tracey has stated: 'we are fast approaching the day when it will not be possible to attempt a Christian Systematic Theology except in serious conversation with the other great ways.'[1] However such conversation is not the exclusive preserve of theologians as the chapters in this book bear witness to. The origin of this book was the collaboration between the Centre for Christianity and Interreligious Dialogue, Heythrop College, University of London and the English-speaking Commission of the Monastic Interfaith Dialogue in Britain and Ireland, which was affiliated to DIM (*Dialogue Interreligieux Monastique*) for a colloquium held in 2002 entitled, 'Monasticism and Interreligious Dialogue: Theological and Mystical Encounters'.

The wide-ranging and engaging essays gathered for publication bear witness to the success of that meeting. By bringing together experience and reflection, this colloquium demonstrated how important, indeed, essential, is this kind of work for dialogue. What was especially noteworthy was the kind of collaboration that is possible when people from various backgrounds contribute their various approaches to dialogue. They witness to the depth of theological reflection that contemporary Christian monastic and scholarly communities are engaged in as the religious traditions seek to understand and relate to each other in a global context. It is hoped that our collective thoughts will resource and stimulate the conversation between Christianity and other faiths and within the Christian community itself.

Note

1 David Tracey, *Dialogue with the Other: The Interreligious Dialogue,* Louvain, Peeters, 1990, p. xi.

Part One

Monastic Interreligious Dialogue

Chapter 1

Monastic Interreligious Dialogue: A History

Pierre François de Béthune, OSB

To give context to the monastic encounter with other faiths, some historical clarifications may be helpful in understanding the place of 'Monastic Interreligious Dialogue' (MID) in the 'dialogical movement' (as I like to call our engagement). The way things happened is a good illustration of this specific kind of dialogue. In a broader context this study will also show the fundamental evolution in ways of thinking among Christians during the last fifty years.

In fact, we must speak here of a revolution rather than an evolution. When we look at the attitude of the Church in this field fifty years ago, we must recognize that we have witnessed a real revolution in ways of thinking. To illustrate this here, let me tell an anecdote. In 1928 my monastery of Saint André, in Belgium, founded a monastery in China. The initiator of this new monastery was Father Jehan Jolliet, a monk of Solesmes, a great admirer of Chinese culture. Very soon young Chinese men asked to join the community and one day, during recreation, a novice who had been previously in a Buddhist monastery told about his life there. He commented especially on some remarkable similarities between the two monastic traditions. Father Jolliet was extremely irritated when he heard of this comparison of Christian monasticism with a heathen way of life. The same day he threw the novice out of the monastery.

One could thus have a great esteem for Chinese culture

and at the same time a great fear of any contact with Chinese religion. There was a fundamental fear of the so-called *communicatio in sacris,* because the other spiritual traditions were considered as devilish. If some element seemed nonetheless beautiful it was explained as a manifestation of Satan disguised as an angel of light (2 Cor 11,14).

This attitude had been firmly established for many centuries and yet it was totally changed in a few years. The role of monks or spiritual men has been important for this achievement. We think here of some pioneers like Swami Abhishiktananda, Bede Griffiths, Louis Massignon, Thomas Merton. Other speakers will give an account of how they performed this revolution in ways of thinking, not without great difficulties, as we can see in Abhishiktananda's diary.

They were very isolated and even suspect, but their experience and their intuition were slowly accepted in the new context of the Second Vatican Council. It is in this new context that the MID commissions were created. Let us now see how this new organization was established.

* * *

At the beginning of the 1960s the Benedictine and Cistercian Congregations wanted to collaborate in order to help their new monastic foundations in Africa, Latin America and Asia. A Secretariat was set up in 1960 to help them. It was called 'Aide a l'Implantation Monastique' (AIM), (Aid for monastic foundations). The same letters, AIM, are now read as 'Alliance for an International Monasticism'. In fact many new monasteries were founded after World War II. This time the new monasteries wanted to have better contact with the countries where they were settled. Here also a great change had already occurred. Christian monasteries had existed in those countries since the nineteenth century, but they were as islands of western culture in the midst of them. I remember a tourist leaflet in Japan showing the places of interest in the northern island of Hokkaido and among them the Trappist monastery of

Hakodate where 'you can feel as if you were in Normandy' according to the text, – and in fact the picture showed a neo-gothic building of dark brick with a deep green meadow with cows reared for making a renowned Trappist cheese. But the new foundations needed much deeper inculturation.

To help those new foundations the AIM Secretariat held congresses where they could discuss their main concerns with experts. The first pan-Asiatic congress (1968) was held in Bangkok, Thailand. This congress is well known because it was during this meeting that Thomas Merton met his untimely death. Thomas Merton's commitment to interreligious dialogue became clear to everybody; this was the unforeseen consequence of the sad event of his death. At the same time Father Jean Leclercq, an important Benedictine scholar who also participated in this congress, discovered Buddhist monasticism in Bangkok and became eager to continue intermonastic contacts.

He organized the next pan-Asiatic congress – on the search for God in every religion – in Bangalore (India) in 1973. Many experts came from Europe, Asia and America to speak on the topic. But in his final speech the Abbot Primate, Dom Rembert Weakland, noted that only very few of them were monks or nuns and he expressed his wish that this study should be continued in the monasteries so that they could give advice on interreligious dialogue to the AIM Secretariat.

One year later Cardinal Pignedoli, President of the Vatican Secretariat for Non-Christians (now called 'The Pontifical Council for Interreligious Dialogue') sent an official letter to the Abbot Primate. This letter, written by Mgr Piero Rossano with the advice of Father Cornelius Tholens, invited monks and nuns to engage in interreligious dialogue in their monasteries, because 'monasticism can be like a bridge between Christian and other spiritualities'.

Following this official invitation contact was made with various monks and nuns in Europe and North America in order to develop a monastic way of interreligious dialogue. Two meetings were finally planned, one in Petersham,

Massachusetts, USA, and another in Loppen, Belgium, during the summer of 1977. Two sub-commissions of the AIM were then created which met for the first time in 1978. The American commission was called 'North American Board for East-West Dialogue' (NABEWD). The European committee was first called 'Commission pour le Dialogue Interreligieux Monastique' (DIM), but we prefer now to adapt this name to the various countries; in the UK it is called 'Monastic Interfaith Dialogue' (MID). The same acronym was later also adopted in America (North American MID).

The new commissions developed various projects to sensitize monks and nuns to this new dimension of Christian life, to help them come to a better discernment in this field and also to organize encounters with Buddhist or Hindu monastics in their monasteries or in Christian monasteries.

I shall not go on with a chronological description of their achievements. Let it suffice to mention that MID commissions have been autonomous since 1994. They are no longer sub-commissions of AIM. Abbot Primate Jerome Theisen recognized that dialogue is a specific attitude, not to be confused with the concern of establishing Christian monasteries in the East. (Both initiatives must nonetheless be enterprises undertaken in common accord.) It will be interesting to study how reflection on the task of MID has evolved. Here also we can see how initial fear has given place to admiration.

In the mind of many founders of the MID commissions, the term 'monastic' was initially understood as somehow restrictive: the interreligious dialogue to which monks and nuns were called was focused on the 'monastic' sphere, i.e. the ways and customs of monasteries, leaving aside the more theological approaches of other religions, because monks were supposed to be unable to master this difficult field. In this sense some explicit texts show that the old fear still remains. They express the conviction that a real encounter at the level of spiritual experience still seemed too dangerous.

But precisely those spiritual experiences, made possible

by the new organization, invited monks and nuns to be more and more confident. After only a few years it appeared clear that, for instance, the 'East-West Spiritual Encounters', jointly organized by Japanese Buddhist and European Christian monks were, for most of the participants, a strong incentive to move further and more profoundly towards spiritual sharing of the common monastic vocation.

Monastic interreligious encounters are now recognized as something specific, a kind of existential dialogue, from faith to faith, a dialogue of religious experience. However, monks do not have a monopoly of this kind of dialogue! That is very evident. Yet they are in the best place to continue along this line. To summarize the precise nature of this kind of intermonastic dialogue, which monks have moved towards, I should say that it first concerns a specific encounter. This could be a stay in a monastery (or a sacred place of another religion), an exchange with a monk or nun of these traditions or simply the practice of a spiritual method developed there, like yoga or Zen meditation that can be practised in a monastic cell. This encounter is experienced as an understanding, a shared awareness or agreement, based on the discovery of so many similarities in life and spiritual ideals, in spite of there being significant differences. More than a bridge, the monastic ideal here is like a tunnel which ensures unseen communication between monks of different traditions.

This dialogue at the level of religious experience is essentially an 'intrareligious dialogue', to use the expression of Raimundo Panikkar. It consists of accepting and questioning of a religious experience developed in another tradition. Thus, the way a Buddhist monk commits his whole life to searching for the Truth requires us to re-evaluate our own commitment on the monastic path. In this way we welcome into our spiritual life elements coming from elsewhere. There follows, therefore, dialogue and even debate in our own spiritual life. In fact, such an exchange does not only take place at the frontiers of our religious life, in the 'inter' or neutral space which separates us; it can be fulfilled only in a truly intra-religious dialogue.

Let us notice in passing that at this level the demands of dialogue are all the greater. When Father Le Saux (Swami Abhishiktananda) makes his own the experience of the Vedantic *advaita* he is not substituting this experience for his Christian experience (that would remain a series of two monologues); nor is he making of it a recovered Christian *advaita* (which would most certainly make dialogue empty). In order to achieve dialogue the two sides of the exchange should be firm and solid, just as to build a bridge the two foundations must be solid. Regular monastic life can ensure, on one side, this solidity and depth in spiritual commitment. It is still necessary that in meeting another tradition, the other side should be completely serious and profound.

This approach may seem rather odd, even Utopian. It may even trouble those who have never had anything to do with such experiences. However, it is only about extending an entirely classic tradition, that of hospitality, always very much honoured in monastic surroundings, particularly the Benedictine. One of the most beautiful chapters of the Rule of Saint Benedict is devoted to it. Over the last few years we have discovered that the model of hospitality applies very well to interreligious exchange. Indeed all traditions insist that hospitality is sacred, for each time we welcome a stranger, it is – mysteriously – one sent from God that we receive.

Interreligious hospitality is, it seems to me, the best way of meeting a believer of another religion. This is for two reasons. Firstly, his approach through hospitality, as we have experienced it, offers an environment for verbal exchanges. In this existential context words and explanations can come into their own. Secondly, what characterizes hospitality is precisely that it is always designed for strangers. They are warmly welcomed, but with respect for their otherness, with no intention of ignoring their difference or of exploiting them.

The convictions which the partners in such a dialogue hold are hospitable truths, truths which allow the warm welcoming of the truths of others. These experiences of hospitality also make it possible to go beyond the abstract terms which too often still burden the theology of interreligious dialogue as, for example, the expression 'implicit membership of the Church'.

However, one cannot be content with rough-cut experiences. They must be considered and referred to the whole body of the theology of dialogue, for reflection is essential if the 'dialogical movement' is to make progress. But the contribution of monks and nuns to this movement is specific. They are not called upon to say very much, but their encounters preceding or following the discussions – what one might term paradoxically the dialogue of silence – can do much to help provide the unutterable and purely religious dimension of this important meeting with the other spiritual traditions to which we are all invited nowadays.

At the end of one of the Spiritual Exchanges with Japanese monks, when we asked them to describe in a few words their most important experience, I remember one who said:

> I have been in the Trappist monastery of Belle Fontaine for three weeks. Life is hard there. They get up very early in the morning. There is much work, little food, much silence and only a few moments of encounter. But I have seen much joy on the faces of the monks: Where does this joy come from?

I don't remember how we answered this question, but I am sure that this Buddhist monk returned to his own monastery with an important interreligious experience. It is a good example of intermonastic dialogue.

That is where we are at this moment. We have been able to take part in a remarkable evolution in ways of thought in the Church and we have come out onto a vast field of spiritual and religious discovery. But we know well that this is only a beginning.

Chapter 2

Contemporary Witness, Future Configuration: Monastic Interfaith Dialogue

Peter Bowe, OSB

The purpose of this chapter is to try to put monastic interfaith dialogue into some perspective at this present time and to pose some questions for the future. First, in what situation does dialogue find itself today in the monastic world, and to what point have the seminal figures of the twentieth century brought us so far? What has been learned from the experience up to now? And where does it seem to be leading?

Where are we now?
Today an understanding seems to be growing of what may be termed a *monastic archetype*[1] or *monastic phenomenon*,[2] something shared by monks and nuns with all humanity, which may be described perhaps as a basic quality of desire for God, an authentic spiritual search, which men and women in all walks of life and faith traditions may follow. For some it involves a degree of separation, renunciation and detachment usually in the context of a community and under a Rule and a director – in fact some type of formal way of life. For others, the 'lay' monastics perhaps, it is simply the inner direction and commitment of the heart. And indeed there are those who question whether monasticism, a concept so diversely understood, can be thought

of as an archetype at all, a psychological force exercising its own power. They would prefer to speak only of a monastic *paradigm* or *ideal* or *model*, the image or symbol or manifestation of a deep inner reality.[3] So we may conclude with Jean Leclercq that:

> Monasticism is not only a deep, primitive, archetypal structure of the religious man lying in the depths of the collective unconscious of all peoples but also a utopian model, a certain special realization of the religious ideal, a dimension of human life and society.[4]

The outcome of this is that what we call *monastic* interfaith dialogue, that openness to the monastic spirit of a monk or nun or indeed any person of another faith, can be a way for everyone who recognizes within himself this monastic archetype. Particularly of course for monks and nuns, but for others too, to participate in such dialogue turns out to be an authentic way to live one's vocation. Dialogue helps us to assimilate and deepen our own tradition, and so to gain spiritual enrichment. Dialogue arises naturally from welcoming strangers, from practising a contemplative form of prayer and from personal commitment to the search for God.

A monastery is well placed for dialogue. Monastic dialogue should be natural for 'people of silence' as monks have been called.[5] Raimundo Panikkar has noted that the monastic way provides for a stripping away of forms and so does deep dialogue.

> Christian encounter with other religions requires a very special asceticism, the stripping off of all external garbs and forms to remain alone with Christ, with the naked Christ, dead and alive on the Cross, dead and alive within the Christian too who dares such an encounter with his non-Christian brother ... (This) immediate contact with Christ (...) carries him beyond – not against – formulae and explanations.[6]

A monk's own tradition enables him to enter into another monastic tradition and be received there on his own terms.

For, according the Desert Fathers, the work of monks is discernment – the conditions of their life should help them be people possessed of discernment and so predisposed to listening and to dialogue.

Monks – and all can be monks – are able to be more than usually concerned, as has been said of Buddhist monks, with the soundness of the question put rather than with the pertinence of the response given. Monks of all traditions and faiths live with the great questions of life before them: suffering, love, liberty, encounter with the Absolute, and they all share their silence before the mystery. This makes monastic life a privileged place for interfaith dialogue.[7]

What has the Christian monk in particular to offer? As Leclercq says, in the Christian monastic way all motivation is fundamentally Christian and works within the framework of a personal relationship with Christ. Furthermore,

> Christian monks make a deliberate free choice to serve Christ, to work for the spreading of his kingdom and to become united with him – hence the marriage symbolism – sharing his passion and his glorification, already in this present life and eternally in the life to come.[8]

So the Christian monk brings the perspective of Christ to the dialogue, the Word of the Father, through whom all are called to God.

Seminal figures of the twentieth century

To what point have the great figures reviewed in other chapters brought us? Recalling the salient contributions of those twentieth-century monastic figures, their contributions to the advance of interfaith dialogue in the monastic world may be briefly summarized.

Jules Monchanin is remembered as a scholar, dedicated to the understanding of Hindu texts and rituals, with a deeply trained theological mind, but with a personal modesty too. Formed in the years before Vatican II he had an innate cautiousness which prevented him from making as much personal use of the symbols of Hindu spirituality and practice as those who followed. He was a compassionate apostle and pastor of the poor, who 'listened, looked, and spoke,' it was said, 'from the centre of a perfect silence'.[9]

Abhishiktananda (Henri Le Saux) dared to enter with total dedication into the experiential realms of Hinduism, in particular into the *advaitic* experience of Vedanta and the tradition of *sannyasa*. As a Christian monk he sought to embody the Indian way of renunciation and agonized at the very interface of Christianity and Hinduism, in the end surrendering the very possibility of any tangible bridge-building between the mystical depths of each. For him there was ultimately only the mystical plunge beyond all thought.[10]

Bede Griffiths continued the exploration which Monchanin and Abhishiktananda had begun. Through his warm hospitality to seekers of all religions and of none Bede Griffiths was able to bring together in a practical way the extraordinary confluence of religions which are, as he said, meeting today as never before. He continued to extend his boundaries to the end of his life, yet was careful not to lose his religious and intellectual bearings,[11] and thereby offered to innumerable seekers hope of a new and universal vision of reality born of the synthesis of the wisdom of all ages and all traditions.[12] Referring to Monchanin, Abhishiktananda and Bede Griffiths, Judson Trapnell has well observed elsewhere that

> the three represent a range of options for balancing the radical and conservative exigencies that are both required for any project of theological reform to remain intelligible to the community of faith.[13]

Christian de Chergé was a martyr, a monk and a mystic who dedicated his life to dialogue with Islam and to his own search and opening up to the divine mystery, and who entered deeply into these within himself. It might be said that his desire was for transformation and for slow patient divinization. He saw the reality as it was in Algeria, and in himself ('I could not *desire* martyrdom,' he declared), and he could grasp the evil forces opposed to his monastic community's presence in that country while holding on to his own innocence. His life and death were clearly marked by hope, by joy in everything, and by gratitude – the final word of his testimony was *A-dieu!* He was aware of God's love for his Muslim neighbours and for those who attacked him. He was at pains to declare that his life was given, and requested that they remember 'that my life was *given* to God and to this country – that God may be glorified'.[14]

Louis Massignon, not formally a monk, was yet drawn towards the monastic quest at the same time as being closely drawn towards Islam. He felt that Islam, up to then deeply suspicious of monasticism, would one day be able, in reaching out to a new mystical reality, to discover its need for full integration and completion in precisely that forbidden (and even celibate) monastic ideal. For its part, Christianity would perhaps one day also come to understand how the ascetic principle of monasticism was essentially the fulfilment of its own witness, perhaps that purity of heart which Cassian so long ago identified. For the monastic ideal, shared across the boundaries of religion and of lifestyles within the various religious traditions themselves, pertains and points in some way indeed to the end time, to the fulfilment of all things.

Thomas Merton was a pioneer in interfaith relations from another perspective, moving out towards Buddhism, Zen Buddhism and Tibetan Buddhism in particular. He identified detachment, inner experience and personal transformation as the heart of the monastic calling. The monastic archetype, to be found in all sorts and conditions of men and women is, he said, marked by a special contemplative dedication which includes detachment from 'ordinary' and 'secular' concerns, i.e. a monastic solitude whether partial or total, temporary or permanent; then by a preoccupation with the radical, inner depth of one's religious and philosophical beliefs, the inner and experiential ground of those beliefs, and their implications; and a special concern for inner personal transformation. This transformation is a deepening of one's awareness which eventually breaks through to a transcendental dimension of life beyond the ordinary empirical self and ethical or pious observance.[15] Transformation is a 'work', a discipline, and is both personal and communal. Merton continues

> Communication on this deep level must also be a communion beyond the level of words, a communion in shared authentic experience ... This demands a freedom from automatisms and routines ... monastic training must liberate [monks] from habitual and routine mechanisms. The monk who is to communicate on that deep level ... must be a living example of traditional and interior realization, wide open to life and new experience because he has fully utilized his own tradition and gone beyond it.[16]

Development of Monastic Dialogue

Despite certain groundbreaking events such as the Assisi meeting of 1986, and in the monastic world the Bangkok meeting in 1968 and the Gethsemani encounter of Buddhist and Christians monks with the Dalai Lama in 1996, and in Britain the Faith in Awakening intermonastic conference at Amaravati in 1993, monastic interfaith dialogue for the most part unglamorously remains on the level of the hidden and the ordinary, of daily personal dedication to the movement of the Spirit in prayer, *lectio* and hospitality.

It must also be said that, with notable exceptions, the need for interfaith dialogue is not generally well appreciated nor supported on the ground by church members, though it is moderately well supported by those more on the fringes of the Church and by genuine seekers. In the monastic world, where there is unequivocal encouragement from the Abbot Primate and from the organization of MID-DIM, it remains nevertheless in individual monasteries and congregations, as it must, dependent upon the particular awareness and enlightenment of superior and community, and on the opportunities afforded by the local context. But the presence of Buddhist and Hindu monks and nuns alone in Britain and their visits to monasteries has meant that the practice of simple hospitality has opened up a growing awareness among the Christian monks and nuns.

From the church leadership there are ambivalent messages. Pope John Paul II clearly believed in making striking gestures of rapprochement and reconciliation with other religions – e.g. his historic visit to the Omayyad Great Mosque in Damascus, and his invitation to a second interfaith gathering at Assisi in January 2002. But many of his curial officials had less enthusiasm, as witness the absenteeism at that latter meeting.

Nor had John Paul's approach to Buddhism, for instance, been consistent. It changed markedly from a very irenic stance in the first years of his pontificate to a new polemical defensiveness in the 1990s in his *Crossing the Threshold of Hope,* where he even showed an apparent annoyance at Buddhism's successful incursion into the once-Christian West. He was, of course, conscious of needing to preserve the uniqueness of Christianity. Perhaps it would be true to say that all faiths now find themselves being pulled in two opposed directions by competing forces: conservative tradition, on the one hand, asserting the independence and uniqueness of the religion, and, on the other, irenic solidarity urging greater mutual respect and cooperation between members of the one human family.[17]

In Britain the Catholic bishops have declared themselves for interfaith dialogue and set up an energetic organization to animate it in the dioceses. Yet preoccupation with more immediate issues pushes it down the agenda and financial backing remains limited. In other Churches the situation remains similar. Beyond the Churches awareness of the interfaith issue is expanding as, for instance, the work of the Interfaith Network and the Jubilee gathering at Buckingham Palace in 2002 attest.

So, spurred on by growing religious openness in many quarters and by political and social developments across the world, we find ourselves living in an era of growing movement towards interfaith dialogue. In the Church, however, a certain hesitancy hangs in the air, even a defensiveness, for not only is so much in faith and theology and practice under attack in this secular age, but also many have not yet understood interfaith relationships as being a source of nourishment and enrichment for their life of faith in which they come before God.

Mapping the way forward

Shared Personal Experience
In looking for the way ahead it will be helpful to bear in mind what interfaith engagement will involve in practice. First of all, fruitful and sincere dialogue will only flourish in the ground of shared personal experience. Religious faith always stands or falls on the experience of the individual practitioner; at the heart of each one there will be some form of experience of, or at least some desire for the Divine. Of course each religion explains this experience differently, but all believers are in agreement that without an encounter with the One, the Absolute, religious commitment has no meaning. Furthermore, for all monastic traditions religious experience is the experience of some form of personal transformation. Transformation, and indeed paradox too, are always the hallmarks of the monastic search. On a practical note it has been argued that the time is perhaps ripe for some bold sharing of monastic personal experience in the form of 'coinherent' meditation, that is for Christian and Buddhist monastics to enter into each other's experience of reality. Monks and nuns might sit with each other and simply watch what happens.

> The Buddhist can, leaving aside Buddhist denials of an Uncaused Cause, be alive to the possibility of experiencing a God such as one who loves and rejoices in the Christian; and the Christian can, leaving aside the Christian horror of atheism, be alive to the possibility of experiencing an open, non-theistic reality of joy, love and wisdom such as the Buddhist knows.[18]

One might ask whether perhaps this kind of experience is somewhat if remotely akin to the contemplative spirit and purpose of the silent Asian Mass described by Aloysius Pieris, whose intention is to create an ethos in which the participants might be deeply aware of and make their own the eucharistic transformation not only of the bread and wine but also of themselves.[19]

So, religious experience is a precious and a hidden treasure, and it takes time for monks, as for every sincere religious believer, to build up enough trust to share it. It takes patience and willingness to be able to share an experience of transformation, and to suspend judgement enough (if that is what has to be done) to really listen to and hear the other believer. But the rewards of being able to articulate the deeper aspects of personal faith and the discovery of comparable honesty and openness on the part of another believer can make the sharing of religious experience one of the richest forms of interfaith dialogue.[20]

Process of Liberation
For those from the monastic tradition it will be natural to try to share why they have embarked upon this unusual way of life in the first place. Fundamentally all monastic people – as many others too – are focused on conversion, the great surrender of self together with openness to the gift or grace of liberation, through a way of obedience, of celibacy for the sake of 'the Kingdom', of simplicity and stability. Spiritual freedom is not just the endpoint of the spiritual search but is the very condition for the journey in the first place. Such freedom will be an impetus towards even greater deepening which must be fed and nourished. So in sharing with someone from another faith tradition it will be important to start from the deepest, the most alive and most liberated part of oneself.[21]

Fragmented Experience of God
As faith grows the Christian believer comes to realize that all experience of God is but fragmentary, partial. So in dialogue a Christian will need to remember that God is a fragmented God, mostly hidden, revealed essentially in the woundedness and brokenness of the Cross, as Luther declared, and in the woundedness and brokenness of human life. It will be seen too that God is also fragmentarily, partially disclosed in other religions, for other religions

are not mere human creations but part of God's way with
the world. It is too soon to expect a full vision of God, which
can only come later, in life beyond. The self-disclosure of
God in Jesus Christ is also not a complete self-disclosure in
so far as the humanity of Christ is itself fragmentary and
incomplete. So here and now God can be found fragmentarily in other religions, as in our own, as too in those
suffering violence, injustice and poverty.[22]

Suspension of Judgement
It has been pointed out that dialogue must make room for
mutual testimony of one's faith, a two-way exchange, if it is
not to be mere monologue. Respect for the dialogue
partner must not prevent this kind of testimony. While
attempts to convert the other to one's own tradition will be
out of order, a neutral stance will be no help either.[23] So
some have suggested that in sharing with those of other
faiths we have to allow a certain suspension of judgement,
epoché.[24] This has been defined by the philosopher Husserl
as 'a certain suspension of judgement, combined with a
conviction of the truth which remains unshaken', so it is
argued that to listen fully to another's beliefs one has to
stand back temporarily from one's own, not surrendering
them but leaving them, as it were, aside. Abhishiktananda,
searching in an agony of conflicting loyalties within himself
for a reconciliation between Hindu *advaita* and Christian
trinitarian faith, invoked this *epoché*. Does interfaith
dialogue need to employ such *epoché*, allowing paradoxically a temporary suspension of the judgements of faith
while the roots of this same faith remain?

Others argue it is impossible do this, and one does not in
fact do it. Faith commitments cannot just be surrendered,
indeed the ability to listen and to react to other faith posi-
tions arises out of them. As Dupuis insists,

> the authenticity of dialogue requires that partners,
> Christian or otherwise, enter into it with the integrity of
> their faith. There is no interreligious dialogue in a vacuum
> of religious persuasion.[25]

However, while there is of course no suspension of religious persuasion, there may be nevertheless for the time being a suspension of judgement in order to hear the other. As a Christian I suspend my judgement when I listen to my friends witnessing to their belief in, for instance, the divinely dictated truth of the Quran, or the doctrine of *advaita*, or the teaching on rebirth, or Buddhist agnosticism. But then I also have to ask, will my friends be happy likewise to suspend the judgement of their own faith in order to hear and engage with my fundamental stance, that Jesus is the only one who, by dying on the Cross and rising from the dead, has opened the Kingdom of God to humankind?

Indeed how far can each go with this temporary suspension? Is suspension of belief perhaps in the end not really possible, too negative a notion to entertain, a non-rational method of proceeding, out of joint with the nature of the human mind whose instinct is ever to search out the truth?

Criteria for Dialogue
One of the issues about dialogue is what criteria should govern its practice. In 1993 a document was published by the Vatican entitled *Contemplation and Interfaith Dialogue – the Monastic Context* which outlined various criteria for monks and nuns engaged in dialogue.[26] A brief mention should be made of such criteria. One important criterion was thought to be discernment, or *diacrisis* for the Desert Fathers, for it was held that discernment is the very work of monks. It will be vital to discern how authentic the dialogue partner is and what authority he or she has, viz. how well trained, how unattached, how regarded in the specific tradition. The competence of the other to speak for his faith will also need to be clear, his balance and his moderation. And there will need to be on both sides humility and respect for the mystery of what they are both engaged in, and a certain simplicity.[27]

Unobtrusive Dialogue

Today it is being realized that dialogue is fostered only unobtrusively, and quick or impressive results cannot be expected. The Benedictine Abbot Primate, Notker Wolf, has pointed out that

> It is important in dialogue not to succumb to the temptation always to look for something new. Rather it is important to persist and to deepen relations, between monks and with members of other traditions, which may then expand into strong friendships, and to remain in contact – these are in themselves the strengths which allow growth in a climate of real, firm trust. It is not a matter of MID-DIM becoming a large organization which hands down initiatives from on high, but of nurturing both strong and weak elements in what is already in place in order to set things in motion, to set the fire burning. This is true both for individuals and for communities. The fire will depend on the depth of a faith nourished by study of the Scriptures, by familiarity with thinkers and theologians of various traditions – a faith articulated and arising from a broad understanding, which allows new meetings and partnership with other organizations engaged in dialogue to take place.[28]

More Robust Engagement

On the other hand, some will say that there needs to be a more robust engagement in dialogue. Customary monastic courtesy may make for confusion. More clarity is needed about where a Christian stands, more care to guard against one's convictions disintegrating while one tries to be sensitive in exchange. It will be important to admit the shortcomings of one's own faith position and to be ready for sharp doctrinal debate. For example, in dialogue with Buddhists Christians will come to see how limited is the concept of *caritas* which, unlike Buddhist *compassion*, is not required to embrace all sentient beings but is reserved solely for fellow humans.[29] It will be necessary to iron out confusions about meditation and be clear about Christian meditation techniques, perhaps matching them with Buddhist ones where possible and being open about differences which will emerge.³⁰ Perhaps it is even time to take a bold step forward and establish a joint Christian-Buddhist monastery, where day-to-day practice of the two traditions in each other's observant and respectful presence and the sharing of combined experience and accumulated wisdom may nurture dialogue at a more real and profound level than is possible with mere infrequent exchanges.³¹ Such an experiment might initially be made on a temporary basis only.

Conclusion

Merton went to the East in order to drink from ancient sources of monastic vision and experience. He declared in 1968

> Communication in depth, across the lines which have traditionally divided religious and monastic traditions is ... most important for the destinies of twentieth-century man ...³²

Have these hopes been fulfilled? It seems fairly clear that the interfaith agenda is in fact the agenda for the present new century. It would perhaps be true to say that the ecumenical task, that of repairing and fostering the unity of the Church, was the task for the Church in the twentieth century; this task is sadly still incomplete and must be worked on further. But the task and challenge of the twenty-first century, when men and women are increasingly conscious of their common humanity and increasing globalization, is the interfaith task. The Church, and especially the monastic tradition in the Church, has to learn to look outwards and focus on deepening relationships with the other world faiths, sharing what the Spirit is saying to mankind today and hearing where he blows in the various faith traditions themselves. These words of an American Catholic theologian, David Burrell are apt:

> We are invited in our time on a voyage of discovery stripped of colonizing pretensions: an invitation to explore the other on the way to discovering ourselves. The world into which

we have been thrust asks nothing less of us; those of us intent on discovering our individual vocations cannot proceed except as partners in such a variegated community. And as that journey enters the domain of faith, our community must needs assume interfaith dimension. What once were boundaries have become frontiers, which beckon to be broached, as we seek to understand where we stand by expanding our minds and hearts to embrace the other. Put in this fashion, our inner journey can neither be syncretic nor procrustean: assimilating or appropriating. What is rather called for is mutuality of understanding and of appreciation, a critical perception which is already incipiently self-critical. Rather than reach for commonality, we are invited to expand our horizons in the face of diversity. The goal is not an expanded scheme, but an enriched enquirer: discovery of one's own faith in encountering the faith of another.[33]

Our pioneers point us to the task and encourage us in the commitment.

Notes

 1 Cf. R. Panikkar, *Blessed Simplicity – Quest for the Monastic Archetype*, Seabury Press, 1970.
 2 J. Leclercq, 'Christian Monasticism and its Present Encounter with Other Religious Traditions', in *Monastic Studies* vol. 18 (1988) pp. 64–78.
 3 Ibid., p. 65.
 4 Ibid., p. 68.
 5 P. de Béthune, 'Monks in Dialogue with Believers from Other Religions', in *Studies in Formative Spirituality*, vol. 14, no. 1 (1993), pp. 129–138.
 6 R. Panikkar, *The Unknown Christ of Hinduism*, London, Darton Longman & Todd, 1964, p. 25.
 7 P. de Béthune, ibid., pp. 136–37.
 8 J. Leclercq, p. 70.
 9 *Jules Monchanin (1895–1957) as seen from East and West*, Acts of the Colloquium held in Lyon-Fleurie, France and in Shantivanam-Tannirpalli, India, Shantivanam/ISPCK, Delhi, 2001, vol. I, p. 29.
10 J. B. Trapnell, 'Catholic Contemplative Engagement with India and its Theological Implications: Jules Monchanin, SAM, Henri Le Saux, OSB, and Bede Griffiths, OSB Cam', in *World*

Christianity: Theology, Politics, Dialogues, A. O'Mahony and Michael Kirwan SJ (eds), London, Melisnde, 2003, pp. 257–84.
11 Ibid.
12 Bede Griffiths, OSB, *Universal Wisdom – A Journey through the Sacred Wisdom of the World*, London, HarperCollins, 1994.
13 J. B.Trapnell, 'Catholic Contemplative Engagement with India and its Theological Implications', pp. 257–84.
14 Bernardo Olivera, OCSO, 'Christian de Chergé – Monk, Martyr and Mystic', in *Cistercian Studies Quarterly*, vol. 34, no. 3 (1999), pp. 321–38.
15 Thomas Merton, OCSO, 'Monastic experience and East-West Dialogue', in *Bulletin: Secretarius pro non Christianis*, vol. 4, no.1 (1969), pp. 39–44.
16 Ibid., p. 43.
17 J. Cabezón, 'A Buddhist Response to John Paul II', in *John Paul II and Interreligious Dialogue*, (eds), B. L. Sherwin and H. Kasimov New York, Orbis Press, 1999, pp. 113–24.
18 R. Corless, 'Sense and Nonsense in Christian-Buddhist Intermonastic Dialogue', in *Monastic Studies*, vol. 19 (1991), p. 18.
19 A. Pieris, SJ, 'What Kind of Church do we wish to be?', in *The Month*, November 2002 (33/11), pp. 428–35.
20 Thomas Michel, SJ in *Pro Dialogo* (Bulletin of the Pontifical Council for Interreligious Dialogue of the Vatican) no. 108, 2001/3, pp. 349–50.
21 P. de Béthune, OSB, 'Christian Attitudes in this Period of Religious Pluralism', *DIM-MID International Bulletin*, 2002/1 (Edition 13), pp. 20–21.
22 C. Schwöbel, 'Interreligious Encounter and the Fragmentary Experience of God', *Concilium* 2001/1, pp. 107–19.
23 K. Åmell, OP, 'Monastic Interreligious Dialogue outside the Monastery', in *Swedish Missiological Themes*, vol. 87, no. 2 (1999), p. 245.
24 J. Dupuis, SJ, *Towards a Christian Theology of Religious Pluralism*, Maryknoll, New York, Orbis, 2001, p. 293. See also Dupuis, *Jesus at the Encounter of World Religions*, Maryknoll, New York, Orbis 1991, pp. 231–34, and R. Panikkar, *The Intrareligious Dialogue*, New York, Paulist Press, 1978. Note that P. Knitter, *No Other Name*, Maryknoll, New York, Orbis, 1985 argues the opposite position.
25 Ibid., p. 293.
26 Cf. French version in *Pro Dialogo*, 1993. English translation published by Monastic Interfaith Dialogue (UK), 1995, also another translation in AIM Bulletin 1994 (56). This document was based on replies to a questionnaire sent to Christian monas-

teries of North America and Europe, in response to *Various Aspects of Meditation* of the Congregation for the Doctrine of the Faith, 1990.
27 Cf. Åmell, ibid, pp. 246–48.
28 Abbot Primate at DIM meeting, St-Benôit-s-Loire, June 2002 (see *DIM-MID International Bulletin* 2002/1 (E13) p. 4).
29 R. Corless, 'The Christian Exploration of Non-Christian Religions: Merton's Example and where it might lead us', in *The Merton Annual* no. 13 (2000), p. 116.
30 Ibid. p. 117.
31 Ibid., p. 118.
32 Merton, ibid., p. 42.
33 Preface to R. Arnaldez, *Three Messengers for One God*, Notre Dame, Indiana, University of Notre Dame Press, 1994 (quoted in A. O'Mahony, 'Reflections on the Encounter Between Christianity and Islam', in *The Merton Journal*, vol. 9, no. 2, 2002, pp. 4–16).

Chapter 3

Thomas Merton's Dialogue: The Quest for a Normative Christianity

Eoin de Bhaldraithe, OCSO

Plato, Cicero, Jesus; St Augustine was a disciple of all three. Thomas Merton's legacy to the Christian Church was to show that discipleship of Jesus must come first. His teaching on peace was the most concrete result of his dialogue with other Christians. Augustine's doctrine on war was really from Cicero and was followed by most churches in the West. Merton espoused an earlier doctrine, which he saw exemplified especially in Origen.

Our brief in this chapter is to examine Merton's dialogue with non-Christians. We believe that this will be better understood if we look first at his Christian ecumenism. His encounter with Hinduism and Buddhism is perhaps the best known. We shall see that the strong platonic element of patristic and medieval Christianity gave legitimacy to this dialogue.

When Merton seeks to learn from Islam he is led in a different direction again. Because of the very strong Christian element present in the religion of Islam, it becomes a way of discerning the genuine Christian norm. In particular it leads us back to a primitive Christology.

Merton: The Peacemaker

Thomas Merton kept journals from the time he was only sixteen to the end of his life. These were published in seven volumes. Recently they were condensed into a single volume of seven chapters.[1] While writing a review of this volume, it was surprising to see how conservative he was. One is surprised in particular at his unawareness of liturgical development. As late as 1963 he is writing of the joy of his private Mass, completely unaware that two years later concelebration would virtually oust the practice.[2] In 1964 he records his surprise at 'a way-out Mass' celebrated by Dan Berrigan which was 'extreme' not only in giving communion from the chalice but even giving communion to Protestants.[3] His interest in inter-Christian ecumenism lay in another direction.

Merton's major achievement was to change the teaching on peace in the Roman Catholic Church. This has also affected the other mainline churches and must be attributed to the influence of the radical peace churches.

His mother was a Quaker who told his father it would be murder to take part in the First World War. In the early stages of his diary, anti-war sentiments already appear. In those early days, however, he espoused what he saw as the Catholic position. He believed 'that the Church can call upon the armies of Christian nations to defend the order established by God. This is a principle which every Catholic will accept.'[4] To us now this is rather a strong statement yet it was surely this attitude that inspired Cardinals Spellman and Cushing to urge their government to get involved in Vietnam.

Merton read Roland Bainton on the history of Christian attitudes to war, when it was published in 1960.[5] This book presents the just war theory as formulated by Plato, Aristotle and Cicero. The Early Church was against war but Augustine took in the theories of Cicero. It was this realization that gave Merton the strong basis for his convictions on peace. If he had not come to see that Augustine had departed from the tradition and that the Catholic position was basically Augustinian, Merton could never have proclaimed his own doctrine with such conviction.[6] It was

Bainton who had the decisive influence in creating Merton the peacemaker.

In 1962 Merton wanted to publish an essay which would apply his newly adjusted faith to the contemporary world crisis. The following are the main points.[7] Stating his principles, he says that 'Whoever believes that Christ is the Word made flesh believes that every man must in some sense be regarded as Christ.' This is very close to the Quaker belief that the light of Christ is in every person (and not just in Christians). We must struggle against the Communists and also against our own violence even though this may end by 'diluting the strong conviction that our side is fully right and the other side is fully wrong'.

If we are obsessed with power we will be blind to some realities. We will not see that love might be better than force. Disarmament is not enough; mutual trust is needed. To be a 'peacemaker' is more than being a 'pacifist'. At the end of this section he deals briefly with the Christian repugnance to war in the early centuries. Then he comes to 'War in Origen and Augustine'. Merton quotes Bainton later in his section on the Crusades but the contrast of the two Fathers and his insistence that Augustine has 'drawn to a considerable extent from Cicero', show his dependence on Bainton for the earlier period also. Evidently then Merton was very impressed by the change of direction occasioned by Augustine's theology. He regarded the teaching of the New Testament and the Early Fathers, especially Origen, as the genuine Christian position. He says that this was not actually pacifism, but he gives such a narrow definition of the position that hardly anybody would hold it. He claimed that he was a peacemaker rather than a pacifist.[8] He had to be very careful as pacifism was officially a heresy for Catholics at the time.[9]

Needless to say Merton's novel views did not have an easy passage. John Courtney Murray and John Ford were leading thinkers who described themselves as 'relative pacifists' but they thought that Merton had gone beyond the official Catholic position. In 1962 the Abbot General, Gabriel Sortais, forbade him to write on peace. Merton argued that his thought was already reflected in the speeches of Cardinal Albert Meyer of Chicago. But Sortais said it was for bishops to teach and monks to pray.

Ironically at this time he was helping Pope John XXIII to write *Pacem in Terris*. In thanks for his help, the Pope gave him a gift of the stole he wore at his coronation. The encyclical does not deal much with war but rather with the conditions necessary for peace. When it appeared in 1963, Merton believed that it vindicated him against Ford. He wrote to ask the Abbot General to allow publication now of the article on peace but Sortais said there was no change as the Pope was condemning only aggressive and not defensive wars. Merton was quite angry at the reply as we see from his cynical remark that Sortais really believed 'that France should have the bomb and use it if necessary'.

Sortais died in late 1963 and the new General, Ignace Gillet, told Merton he was still forbidden to write on war but could now write on peace. This probably contained a deliberate element of ambiguity. In any case his essay was passed by the censors of the Order and published a year later. It is the principal item in *Seeds of Destruction*, a rather disparate collection of essays. The essay on war is the only one dated. The others were put together hastily, it seems, from already published writings. That is probably why it was never published on this side of the Atlantic.[10]

In 1967 Cardinal Franz König of Vienna, a close collaborator of Pope Paul VI, went to the USA. König asked James Fox, Abbot of Gethsemani, to allow Merton to speak along with him. There was great pressure on Fox to allow Merton to go, but the Abbot 'won the battle against considerable odds'.[11] Fox's main argument was that Merton was a hermit but it is highly likely that there were deeper forces at play. König would never have asked for Merton without the Pope's approval. Fox may have suspected that it was the Pope himself who wanted Merton but home politics would have weighed very heavily. Cardinal Francis Spellman was all in favour of the Vietnam war. He visited the battlefield and gave a speech as Ordinary of the forces saying that anything other than total American victory was unthinkable. The speech looked like a flat contradiction of the attitude of Paul VI. Fox would have largely shared the

Cardinal's viewpoint, so it is quite likely that he felt that to let Merton speak publicly would have been a challenge to Spellman.

It is amazing to see Merton as a pawn in the conflict between Montini and Spellman. Perhaps that is why the bishops of the United States were to take Merton's teaching so seriously at a later stage. It is enshrined in their pastoral letter, *The Challenge of Peace*. This is a major teaching document of our time. While it was being composed the bishops experienced considerable difficulty with the Vatican.[12] The pacifist position is now legitimate in the Roman Catholic Church as a direct result of Merton and this pastoral. The mainline churches now take the just war doctrine much less seriously. If church leaders of many denominations opposed the Gulf War twelve years ago and do so again today, they are following Merton's example.

'An Asian Journey'

Merton's Asian Journal is a landmark of spirituality and literature. Yet some people insist that he was only forty days in Asia and made very little effort to increase his knowledge.[13] So perhaps I could give some account of my own passage to India.

I was reared in a totally Catholic society, not meeting a Protestant socially till I was twenty-seven. By this time I was back from Rome where the inspired teaching of Magnus Löhrer in the Benedictine University of Sant'Anselmo gave us an enthusiasm for the new Catholic discipline called ecumenism. I decided to study the question of mixed marriages as it was causing a lot of tension between church leaders. Unexpectedly my fate was rather similar to that of Merton in his efforts to teach peace to the American Church.

A journey to India in 1990 awakened me to another dimension, however. A visit to the mosque in Bhopal, during my first week, was an unsettling experience. When I entered with bare feet the disturbing question came to mind, could I and should I pray here? With great liberality, as I felt, I decided that here I should even invoke Allah as

God. It was a matter of retarded development, however, as Vatican II had already said of the Muslims, 'along with us they worship the one merciful God who will judge humanity on the last day'.[14]

As I was leaving, one of the nuns said to me, 'Look at this boy coming in.' He went over to the pool and washed his arms up to the elbow, just as was mentioned in the Gospel. True, Jesus seemed to abolish the practice, but there it was before my eyes. Then he walked around to stand in front of the three arches. 'Watch him,' the nuns said, 'he is now saying a prayer similar to the Jesus prayer.' One could see his lips moving as he said, 'Allah is great; Allah is good' etc. Then he made the profound bow before the arches. This was exactly the bow we learnt when we joined the monastery. We did not genuflect as the seculars did, we bowed. Then after a further period of prayer he made the characteristic Muslim gesture of touching his head to the ground. Later when I saw the monks in Kurisumala doing the same, they told me that it was originally a Christian gesture but taken over and retained by the Muslims. There was something in this mosque very close to home.

Later in the Benedictine monastery of Makkiyiad, Fr Anthony told me that in the Persian empire of the first Christian centuries, dissidents were expelled. This applied to both Jews and Christians. So it happened that in the area about Mecca, which was just outside the empire boundary, there were many unhappy and even heretical Jews and Christians. It was among those that Muhammad received his religious inspiration.

Later I was introduced to the Hindu temple. At first I saw an elderly woman lighting a little lamp before a statue of a bull. It reminded me very clearly of my mother lighting the Sacred Heart lamp. The Catholic priest who accompanied me asked me to accept a blessing from the holy elephant but I did not feel able to do so. As we left, I said there was something rather sexy about Hindu worship. The priest said that was so but he was too shy to show me the lingam of Shiva.

Later in Shantivanam I was to meet Bede Griffiths. Like the sister monastery, Kurisumala, there was a reading from the Hindu writings at vespers each evening. The monks wore the saffron robe of the Indian holy persons. At the end of vespers the tabernacle was incensed in Hindu fashion. Then all touched the holy light. Next sandalwood was blessed and placed on the forehead as a *tilak*. Finally all made the Muslim gesture of touching the forehead to the ground.

For me the most memorable encounter was with Br John Martin, Griffiths' disciple. While I was emphasizing my credo of the importance of relationships with the Protestants, Martin told me that he felt they had a very low concept of God while the Hindu concept was very high. He showed me his thesis on Shankara and Eckhart.[15]

Shankara lived about the end of the eighth century AD. It seems that he opposed the asceticism of Buddhism and the devotionalism of theism and wanted to make spirit the basis of all religious practices. Even though Buddha was born in India, it is due largely to the influence of Shankara that Hinduism rather than Buddhism prevails in India today.

Eckhart lived from 1260 to 1328. In this time he was accused of pantheistic tendencies and was condemned after his death. He was strongly influenced by neo-Platonism. At the end of his first chapter Martin writes, 'When we observe the conception of the godhead or the absolute reality according to both our mystic philosophers, we are wonder struck at the similarities of their understanding.'

On the notion of a personal God he says that 'it is very clear to us how our two authors are faced with the same problem'. Eckhart distinguished between the God-head and the Trinitarian God in a way that Martin finds unacceptable to Christians. Unlike Shankara, Eckhart maintains that God creates the soul. Christians easily accept that God created everything out of nothing because the Bible says so. Shankara seems to think creatures are both created and eternal. Eckhart says that God does not create outside himself. Many think this is not acceptable to Christians but Martin thinks it is orthodox. When he comes to the mystery of salvation, Martin believes that Shankara's 'realization of the Brahman' and Eckhart's 'birth of Christ in the soul' are essentially identical though expressed according to their different cultural backgrounds. Finally for both, life on earth is life in a foreign land. Work does not matter, only arriving at mystical consciousness.

This gives us some realization of the similarities and differences between Christian and Hindu thought. One suspects that the Greek philosophy which was so eagerly embraced by many early Christians was in fact very close to Indian thought. Some go further and say that Indian monks are the paradigm for the Christian variety. One wonders about this as Jesus and his personal celibacy come out of the Jewish tradition, emerging from it and transcending it. The same is true of the early ascetics of the New Testament and elsewhere, committed to the celibate life. There was abundant influence from outside in later periods, as we shall see shortly.

Later in Sri Lanka I was introduced to Buddhist culture. The exemplary role of the monks received strong emphasis. Their celibacy was apparently considered as an encouragement to marital fidelity. Surprisingly they had no ideal of separation from the world or from those around them. The people supported and admired them and generally tried to protect their celibacy. Abstinence from sexual intercourse for Hindu monks was frequently temporary but Buddhists monks generally aimed at lifelong celibacy. Furthermore nowadays many of them receive higher education, often in the West.

Issues in Dialogue

If Origen passed on Christian pacifism undiluted, he was instrumental in bringing neo-Platonism into our theology. The mysticism, which developed after Origen, makes dialogue with Hindus and Buddhists possible and fruitful.

Anne Carr sees the problem as follows. Some are worried that today Christianity might be seen as just one other religion among many. Some even worry about Merton having become a Buddhist at the end of his life. Yet for all his interest, he affirmed the differences strongly. The different religions do not even meet at the top, as some claim. After serious dialogue, Zen and Catholicism would be 'utterly alien to one another'.[16] While doctrine will not converge, there can be quite a rapprochement on the level of experience. Merton was able to use his acquaintance with the 'apophatic mystical way' as an instrument of dialogue. He tried to recover 'the wisdom of Christianity and of the religions of the East'. He began with Cassian's 'purity of heart' and went on to John of the Cross's night of the spirit. Then he mentions Eckhart's 'poverty' – the Christian who is truly poor shares the same relationship to God as does Christ. Such a radical union was possible because of 'Eckhart's neo-platonic ontology that maintained the virtual existence of all created things in the Godhead'.

Merton thought that the Christian tradition of 'divinization' was especially valuable for interreligious dialogue. It is something that happens already on earth and so resembles the Buddhist enlightenment that can occur in the present. Buddhism ends there and has no parallel to resurrection. Carr concludes by saying that 'just as Christianity absorbed neo-Platonism in expression of its mystical doctrines' so we need the wisdom of the Asian traditions today. We could ask her, however, if in absorbing this Greek mysticism, it had not already got much of the Asian tradition in its system.

Perhaps the proper question to ask about Merton is not, did he become a Buddhist, but was he both Buddhist and Catholic. It seems that the concept of 'double belonging' was first widely used by George Kilcourse as a strategy for the children of interchurch marriages.[17] The concept does not necessarily mean being a full member of both Churches. Yet the belonging would be pretty thorough. It should be possible nowadays to be both an Anglican and a Roman Catholic, especially after all the agreed statements. To be a Catholic and a Buddhist is more problematic. James Corless suggests that this is where Merton's example is leading us.[18] It may be acceptable if we understand it as Carr does: Buddhism goes so far but Christianity goes further by accepting resurrection.

Whatever the answer to this but we may get some light from Clement of Alexandria. In the *Stromata* (2:21) he discusses the 'opinions of various philosophies on the chief good'.[19] He examines the epicureans, the Aristotelians and the stoics but finds them generally defective. He mentions briefly Anaxagoras who held 'contemplation and the freedom flowing from it to be the end of life'. The title of the next chapter is 'Plato's opinion, that the chief good consists in assimilation to God and its agreement with scripture'. For Plato the highest perfection is knowledge of the Good and likeness to God, which is justice and holiness with wisdom. This Clement discusses at length, comparing many biblical texts. He concludes that this likeness or assimilation is the aim of faith and is equivalent to the ideals of scripture. For Clement it seems that the platonic ideal is equal to that of the Scriptures. No doubt he believed that Christ was his saviour, unlike Plato. It is then rather like Christianity going beyond Buddhism. Many will recognize the themes of image and likeness which will permeate the mystical writing of the future. It appears that later centuries would not be able to distinguish between what comes from Christ and what from Plato.

Clement himself would surely claim to be a Platonist as well as a Christian. With some later writers one wonders if we had platonic substance with just a Christian veneer. For Christians, in any case, we believe that the presence of the Holy Spirit can sanctify anybody no matter how mistaken their theology may seem to be. It is also important that the evangelical spirit should be able to penetrate all cultures. The Early Church probably needed some kind of an inculturation like this if it was to win the stoics and Platonists. What is not good is that people would no longer be able to distinguish what comes from Christ and what from other philosophies. As Christians we are committed to preaching the Gospel. Our commitment to any other philosophy can only be on a much lower level.

The Platonism of Clement prepared his disciple Origen for the neo-platonic writings. The Enneads of Plotinus were not Christian but they quickly influenced Christianity. While Origen does not seem to have known this work, he and Plotinus had a common teacher in Ammonius Saccas. This teaching had a strong influence on desert monasticism, as it was to develop a century later. Above all the last sentence of the Enneads, 'alone with the Alone', seems to have provided the foundation principle for the hermit life. It is from here that the concept of 'flight from the world' and 'withdrawal to the desert' comes. Arsenius witnesses to this ideal when he says 'I cannot live with God, if I live with people'.[20] Merton was also in continuity with this when he said that he had become a stranger to his brethren in the community.

Origen wrote the first commentary on the Song of Songs. The theory of mystical union he advocated there continued through Gregory of Nyssa, Bernard, and John of the Cross. While one must admit that the doctrine is thoroughly Christianized, it is still an importation from the Greek tradition. When someone in this tradition gets into dialogue with Buddhism, it is most likely that both are coming from the same source. This is strongly confirmed by Martin's comparison of Shankara and Eckhart. That is why there can be such a fruitful meeting of minds.

There were many people in Egypt at the time living the celibate life, usually in a family context. *The Life of Anthony* by Athanasius became a model, however. Henceforth, true monasticism required withdrawal to the desert. A 'theological construct' was generated by which the earlier type of celibate was removed from history. The Pachomians were really 'village monastics' but the later history claimed they were desert monks.[21] A similar transition took place in Syria in the sixth century, also inspired by the 'official' Egyptian literature.[22]

The influence of Greek philosophy is more obvious to us today than to our ancestors. In order to inculturate Christianity in a world of stoicism and Platonism it was necessary to adapt many positive aspects from their philosophy, just as today we need to get involved with other philosophies. It seems imperative, however, to be able always to recognize the original Christian message and to see its normative value.

Islam

Merton's involvement with Islam was less prominent but probably more profound than his encounter with Buddhism. For more than a year he preached to the novices on the mysticism of the Sufis.[23] The first westerner to analyze the Quran logically was Nicholas of Cusa. He said it consisted of a basic strand of Nestorian Christianity. Inserted into this were the anti-Christian sentiments of Muhammad's Jewish adviser. Finally Jewish 'correctors' worked on the text after Muhammad's death.[24] Today we would be hesitant about the word 'Nestorian'.[25] A better designation is Antiochene, as distinct from Alexandrian, theology. The Jewish corrections would most obviously be circumcision, kosher meat and divorce.

The common features are more striking. There was a famous dialogue session in the sixteenth century between some Jesuits, Muslims, Hindus and Buddhists on the nature of God. At the crucial point the Muslims said that they held whatever the Christians held.[26] It is surprising to find Jesus and Mary treated with honour. The tradition of prayer at certain hours is very closely related to the Christian performance of the Divine Office. Clergy may be less fervent nowadays about fulfilling their office in private. But with the Muslims we see the old tradition of observing the hour whether in private or public. The Irish round tower, used to call people to prayer, closely parallels the Muslim minaret.[27] It seems that the original common tradition was to use a hand bell and the voice, as is still done in many Benedictine monasteries as a signal to rise from bed. The traditions grew apart, the Muslims retaining the voice and the Christians developing the bell.

The encounter with Islam is in a different league from dialogue with Buddhism. Muslim doctrine is actually a source for us. In Christianity we need to go back to the sources continually to recover anew the original vision. If Islam carries with it genuine elements of Antiochene Christianity, then it is immensely valuable for us. Nowadays we strive to rediscover a pre-Originean spirituality.[28] Here then is a source with no influence from Alexandria.

Islam rejects Christianity and claims that it has been

abrogated. Only the Quran is the genuine word of God. According to Anthony O'Mahony the conflict between us centres on three issues: 'the reality of Jesus' crucifixion and death, the doctrine of the Incarnation, and the Christian understanding of God as Trinity'.[29] The Docetists questioned the reality of Jesus's death. It seems then that some of this teaching has survived in Islam.[30] We offer here some thoughts on a Christology that could learn from Islam. This peace offering may help to neutralize the current wave of anti-Muslim feeling, which could be described as sectarianism. This is being defined nowadays as emphasizing the differences and seeking to strengthen the boundaries.[31]

Christology

Today we accept that much of the New Testament shows us Jesus becoming divine when he rose from the dead. The resurrection itself is realized eschatology. Christ is the first fruits of the general resurrection. The end-time gift of the Spirit is now given, first to Jesus and then to his disciples. 'You are my Son. It is I who have begotten you this day', was understood of the Messiah and is now realized in the risen Lord. The Johannine Martha says: 'I know he will rise on the last day.' The reply is, 'I am the resurrection' now. 'The hour is coming, indeed it is already here', is a virtual refrain in this Gospel. For the Greek mind this is an utter contradiction. If the hour is here it cannot be coming; if it is coming it cannot he here! Yet it seems that the Jewish mind had little problem with this.[32]

According to Peter's first speech in Acts, the gift of the Spirit shows that the 'last days' are already here. So when Mark writes his Gospel he can bring the end a little further forward and interpret the baptism of Jesus as also realized eschatology. The conferring of the Spirit and Sonship takes place here. In the same way Luke brings this on to the Annunciation by adapting a 'kerygma' statement (as found in Romans 1:3) to the conception of Jesus. The Spirit and the Sonship are already anticipated here. It is significant that Luke should feel free to do this as his theology in Acts preserves the resurrection Christology for us. For Luke then Jesus becomes divine at his conception and at his baptism. But those are only anticipations of the resurrection which itself anticipates the end.

Many see the Prologue of John's Gospel as extending Jesus' divinity and sonship back to the beginning with the Word.[33] But is it not possible that 'the Word became flesh' at the resurrection of Jesus? It was then he came to dwell 'within us'. This is how the Syriac translation of c. AD 200 renders the ambiguous Greek. The disciples saw his glory at the resurrection. It was only then that we could receive from his fullness (for there was no Spirit till then). The scene of Jesus breathing on the disciples has its closest parallel in 1 Cor 15 where Jesus becomes a life-giving Spirit.

Ignatius of Antioch is very close to the Johannine school. For him Jesus is Spirit after the resurrection but he is also flesh. This is polemics against those who said he was flesh and became Spirit.[34] Justin is the next in line and he emphasizes that Jesus was Spirit and flesh already in his earthly life. Justin is Greek and so, for him, Jesus either was or was not divine. That the future could be anticipated and coincide with the present is beyond possibility for his Greek mind.

We get a more thorough hellenization in Alexandria. In platonic terms Jesus had a soul (more real than the body), which was an idea in God. So Origen postulated that this soul was co-eternal with the Word of God. He was also the first to ascribe eternal generation to the Word. The conflict with Antioch arose because they did not insist on the divinity of the earthly Jesus with the same emphasis as at Alexandria. Ignatius, Theophilus and Paul of Samosata, all bishops of Antioch, held that Jesus became divine at the resurrection.[35]

When we are aware of this background some of the well-known Islamic texts take on a new meaning. The Quran denies that Jesus is God or the Son of God; he is simply the servant or prophet of God. In other parts, however, he is called the Messiah. He is the Word of God and the Spirit of God. He has a place of preeminence and proximity to God in this world and the next.[36]

We recognize here two of the strands identified by Nicholas of Cusa. The denial of divinity is to be understood in the context of the Christological disputes and what looked like victory for Alexandria. The second group of texts is not fully consonant with the first. They must have come down traditionally. Apparently one strain of Christianity survived in the East which was hesitant about calling Jesus God, but regarded him as Messiah and further as the Word of God and the Spirit of God.

For us those are two distinct persons of the Trinity, but we are aware that the distinction is not so clear in the new testament. 'The Lord is the Spirit', according to St Paul (2 Cor 3:17). In the Old Testament Word and Spirit of God are usually identified, certainly set in frequent parallel.[37] Is this also the case in John's Gospel? If it were, it would shed a new light on the Prologue and on the most famous Christological text of them all, 'the Word became flesh'.

In any case the tradition remains strong in Islam. There is a story that Muhammad was taught by a Christian monk. His name is normally given as Sergius (Bahira in Syriac) but many Christians called him Nestorius in order to discredit his teaching. The story survives both in Islam and among the Christians. Sidney Griffith says that in the Islamic account the monk, who lives by a well, singles out the teenage Muhammad and foretells his prophetic career. On this story the Christian writers build an apologetic. Their version accounts for the rise of Islam and suggests that it is actually a form of Christianity. Griffith claims that the Christian version is a total construct. However the reality to which it witnesses, that is, the Christian element in Islam, is so striking that there must be more to it than that. It is 'not lacking in verisimilitude', says Griffith, but surely there is more than similitude here.[38]

One version has the monk declare that he is a Christian. When Muhammad asks what is Christianity, the monk replies that it is being anointed and this is further explained by a quotation from the Quran, 'The Messiah is the Word of God and his Spirit' (*an-Nis~'* 4:171). When Muhammad asks how this could happen, we find the reply in two versions. The Jacobite or Monophysite version emphasizes incarnation at the moment of Jesus' conception while the Nestorian version is much less specific.

Perhaps this is enough to show where we really stand in relation to the Muslims. The Second Vatican Council said that they share the faith of Abraham.[39] But if they regard Jesus as Messiah, as Word of God and believe that 'the Lord is the Spirit' (we cannot deny the text) then they are really our brothers and sisters in Christ. For a very different view, let us recall what Thomas Merton wrote in 1954:

> We may perhaps be inclined to think that he (Bernard) ought to have read the translation of the *Koran* which Peter the Venerable sent him, from Cluny, to study and to refute. Bernard seems to have felt no need to know or to understand anything about Islam: as if knowing the Muhammadans to be 'pagans' was to know quite enough.[40]

The Middle Ages needed to define the Muslims as 'infidels' to justify the Crusades. It was amazing to hear President Saddam Hussein use the very same language when exhorting his soldiers during the Gulf War of 1990.[41] Whatever the past, we must regard today's Muslims as brothers and sisters in Christ, separated from us, unfortunately. So we must at least return to the attitude of St John Damascene who regarded them as Christian heretics.[42] We must strive to break down the barriers our ancestors built in the Middle Ages. But more than that we must recognize that nobody can say 'Jesus is Lord' except in the Holy Spirit. They say that God has punished us Christians with division among ourselves (*Surah* 5:14). Today we are painfully conscious of this. All Churches are now deeply involved in ecumenism in an effort to overcome our Christian division. As we progress, we may hope that Muslims will be inspired to accept us as friends.

Conclusion

As we conclude this chapter we are surprised at how many times we encountered Origen. It was from him Merton learnt the pacifism of the Early Church. It was his acceptance of philosophy into the Christian system that enabled Merton to enter into fruitful dialogue with the eastern religions. It was

Origen too who launched the Hellenization of Christology. To our surprise, and perhaps our discomfort, we find in Islam a more original way of looking at Jesus. As the Churches strive to overcome the divisions for which Islam chides us, the quest for a normative Christianity takes on a certain urgency. Most Western Churches have, for example, recovered and revitalized the use of the Eucharistic prayer. All of us are fully aware now of the Christian teaching on peace. We still find it hard to distinguish what comes from Christ and what from philosophy. We realize that Chalcedon or even Nicea cannot be the ultimate norm. There is still a long way to go in seeking for this pearl of great price.

Notes

1 Patrick Hart, Jonathan Montaldo (eds), *The Intimate Merton: His Life from His Journals*, Oxford, Lion, 2000; our review in *Studies* 89 (2000), pp. 189–90.
2 Ibid., pp. 257–58.
3 Ibid., p. 279.
4 T. Merton, *The Last of the Fathers*, London, Hollis, 1954, 40.
5 R. H. Bainton, *Christian Attitudes Toward War and Peace. A Historical Survey and Critical Re-evaluation*, London, Hodder & Stoughton, 1961. Bainton (1894–1984) was a Congregational minister, born in England and taken to Canada by his father in 1898. He taught church history at Yale Divinity School 1920–64.
6 G. Zahn mentions Merton's apparent departure from the traditional teachings on the morality of war as set forth originally by Saint Augustine, confirmed by Saint Thomas Aquinas, and then expanded and elaborated upon by the neo-scholastics. Zahn believes that this was a grossly unjust misunderstanding of his position. *The Nonviolent Alternative: revised edition of Thomas Merton on Peace*, New York, Farrar, 1980, p. xvii. It seems to us that his departure was not apparent but real.
7 'The Christian in World Crisis: reflections on the moral climate of the 1960s', T. Merton, *Seeds of Destruction*, New York, Farrar, 1964, pp. 93–183. This essay is dated June 1964.
8 'The Christian as Peacemaker', ibid., pp. 116–34.
9 Suarez, *De Bello* (Section X of *De Legibus ac Deo Legislatore*) 1. At the beginning of his great treatise on the just war, Suarez has to deal, very briefly, with the pacifist heresy. S. Windass, *Christianity Versus Violence*, London, Sheed and Ward, 1964, p. 84.

10 The essay was later published by G. Zahn in *Thomas Merton on Peace*, New York, Farrar, 1971.
11 M. Mott, *The Seven Mountains of Thomas Merton*, Boston, Houghton-Mifflin, 1984, p. 495.
12 E. de Bhaldraithe, 'St Bernard, Thomas Merton and Catholic Teaching on Peace', *Word and Spirit: a monastic review*, 12 (1990), pp. 72–74.
13 G. Woodcock, *Thomas Merton: Monk and Poet: A Critical Study*, Edinburgh, Canongate, 1978, p. 168.
14 *Lumen Gentium* 16.
15 K. John Martin, *A brief comparative study of Shankara and Master Eckhart*, Bangalore, St Peter's Institute, 1963.
16 T. Merton, *Zen and the Birds of Appetite*, New York, New Directions, 1968, p. 3.
17 G. Kilcourse, *Double Belonging: Interchurch families and Christian Unity*, New York, Paulist Press, 1992.
18 J. Corless, 'Fire on the Seven Storey Mountain: Why Catholics are looking East', in M. B. Pennington, *Towards an Integrated Humanity: Thomas Merton's Journey*, Kalamazoo, Cistercian, 1988, 204–21; idem, 'The Christian Exploration of Non-Christian Religions', *The Merton Annual* 13, (2000), 105–22.
19 M. Wilson (tr.), *The Ante-Nicene Fathers* II, Grand Rapids, reprint 1979, pp. 374–77.
20 B. Ward, *The Sayings of the Desert Fathers*, Kalamazoo, Cistercian, 1975, 9.
21 J. Goehring, *Ascetics, Society and the Desert: Studies in early Egyptian Monasticism*, Harrisburg, PA, Trinity 1999; review by M. Neuman, *American Benedictine Review* 52, (2001), 351–55.
22 S. Brock, 'The Ascetic Ideal: St Ephrem and proto-monasticism', *The Luminous Eye*, Kalamazoo, Cistercian, 1992, pp. 131–41.
23 B. Dieker, 'Merton's Sufi Lectures to Cistercian Novices, 1966–68' in R. Baker, G. Henry, *Merton and Sufism*, Louisville, Fons Vitae, 1999, pp. 130–62.
24 R. W. Southern, *Western Views of Islam in the Middle Ages*, Cambridge, Mass., Havard, 1962, p. 93.
25 There is now a 'Common Christological Declaration between the Catholic Church and the Assyrian Church of the East'. See text in *L'Osservatore Romano* (English) 16 November 1994 and the remark that this Church 'has often been called *Nestorian*'.
26 Southern, *Western Views*, 48.
27 G. Carville, 'From Camus to Moone', *Monastic Studies* 14 (1983)161–78 (171).
28 A. Veilleux presents his work on Pachomian cenobitism as such a recovery.

29 A. O'Mahony, 'Islam *face-a-face* Christianity' *The Way Supplement* 104 (2002) 75–85.
30 K. Triger, 'Jesus, the Koran and Nag Hammadi', *Theology Digest* 38 (1991) 213–18.
31 J. Liechty, C. Clegg, *Moving Beyond Sectarianism: Religion, Conflict and Reconciliation in Northern Ireland*, Dublin, Columba, 2001, 'What is Sectarianism', pp. 102–47; on the Pope urging the Irish to fight the English heretics as the Crusaders fought the Muslims, p. 75.
32 O. Cullmann, *Christ and Time: The Primitive Christian Conception of Time and History*, London, SCM, 1951; J. P. Sampley, *Walking Between the Times: Paul's Moral Reasoning*, Minneapolis, Fortress, 1991.
33 'an explicit statement of incarnation, the first, and indeed the only such statement in the new testament', J. Dunn, *Christology in the Making*, London, SCM, 1989, p. 241.
34 E. de Bhaldraithe, 'The Christology of Ignatius of Antioch', *Studia Patristica* 36 (2001) 200–6.
35 For a different view, see R. Williams, *Arius: Heresy and Tradition*, London, DLT, 1987, 158.
36 For a convenient summary, see 'Quran', *New Catholic Encyclopedia*, 2nd edn., 2003, 11: 879–80.
37 'Wisdom, Word and Spirit are near alternatives as ways of describing the active, immanent power of God.' Dunn, *The Making*, 196; cf. 219.
38 S. Griffith, 'Muhammad and the Monk Bahir', *Oriens Christianus* 79 (1995), 145– 74.
39 *Lumen Gentium* 16; A. O'Mahony, 'Christians and Muslim-Christian Relations: Theological Reflections', in A. O'Mahony, A. Siddiqui, *Christians and Muslims in the Commonwealth*, London, Al-Tajir World of Islam Trust, 2001, pp. 90–128 (108).
40 *Last of the Fathers*, 41–42. Peter had employed an English scholar to translate the Qur'an. Southern, *Western Views*, 37.
41 E. de Bhaldraithe, 'Jean Leclercq's Attitude Toward War' in E. R. Elder, *The Joy of Learning and the Love of God: Essays in Honor of Jean Leclercq*, Kalamazoo, Cistercian, 1995, pp. 217–37.
42 Ibid., p. 233.

Part Two

Catholic Encounters with Islam

Chapter 4

Charles de Foucauld (1858–1916): Silent witness for Jesus 'in the face of Islam'

Ian Latham

'His vocation has always drawn him towards the Muslim world.'[1] So wrote Charles de Foucauld's spiritual director and friend, the Abbé Huvelin.[2] His scholarly 'successor', Louis Massignon, went further: 'I feel that he was predestined for Islam, that his death was for it [Islam].[3] This attraction towards Islam and the 'Muslim world' undoubtedly begins early in Foucauld's life, from his experience as a young lieutenant of the French army in Algeria and clearly dominates his last fifteen years in that country. It is perhaps more extensive still. Can we add that this relationship was Foucauld's 'destiny', as Massignon[4] implies and certainly thought? And what form did this relationship take? We need to look more closely at Foucauld's life to form a judgement.

* * *

At the age of fifteen, Charles lost all faith. Why? Remaining on the intellectual level (of course his emotions were deeply involved), it was certainly due to the natural questioning of an intelligent adolescent in a sceptical and relativistic age (Charles was an ardent reader), but it was also due, most probably, to something more specific. To quote a letter of Charles to an officer acquaintance whose faith was 'shaken':

Your faith has only been shaken, mine was completely dead for years: for twelve years I lived without any faith: nothing seemed to me to be sufficiently proven; the equal faith with which people follow such different religions seemed to me the condemnation of them all; less than any, the religion of my childhood seemed to me admissible, with its 1=3, that I couldn't bring myself to consider; Islam pleased me a lot, with its simplicity, simplicity of dogma, simplicity of hierarchy, simplicity of morality, but I saw clearly that it was without divine foundation and that the truth was not there; the philosophers are all in disagreement: I remained twelve years without denying anything, without believing anything, in despair of the truth, not even believing in God, as no proof seemed to me evident enough.[5]

It is important to see the whole of this key text. Charles suggests that his loss of faith in the Christian revelation of God, while based upon a general rational doubt, was due specifically to the 'challenge' of Islam: if there was a God, God should be 'simple', and not 'Trinitarian'.

Given the context of this letter, Charles is most probably 'foreshortening' the history of his period of non-belief: he is attributing the explicit admiration for Islam of his later years to the time of his adolescent doubting. But Islam was almost certainly one of the several religions to which he refers, and most probably the religion most present to his mind. For the French colonial presence in Algeria since 1830, and more particularly the well-publicised activities of Cardinal Lavigerie and the newly-founded 'White Fathers' and 'White Sisters' in the early 1870s,[6] had brought the 'challenge' of Islam to the fore among the French intelligentsia, whether 'religious' or 'lay' (meaning, then, 'believing' or 'agnostic'). If this 'reading' of Charles' loss of faith experience is correct, it is of considerable significance: it is a sign of the presence of Islam in his life, precisely as *challenge*.

When Charles recovered his 'childhood faith' (an undeveloped faith, hidden in the womb of his family 'piety'), it was, as he explicitly and repeatedly affirms, through Islam.

Yes, you are right, Islam produced in me a profound 'overturning' ('un profond bouleversement') – the sight of this faith, of these souls living in the continual presence of God, made me catch a glimpse of something greater and more true [more real] than earthly occupations: 'ad majora nati sumus' ...[7]

This clearly refers to the two years he spent in Algeria as an army officer and particularly to the eighteen months of his exploration of Morocco. In the following letter to the same correspondent, Charles goes further, affirming: 'Islam is extremely seductive: it seduced me to excess.'[8]

Did Charles 'wish to become a Muslim', as his friend Laperrine wrote in a letter to a fellow officer? He was undoubtedly 'seduced' by the beauty of certain quranic prayers with their classical Arabic cadences and traditional melodies, using them himself both before, and at times after, his conversion. Was this attraction due primarily to that sense of beauty dear to the aesthete, as Hugues Didier,[9] the historian, supposes? To my mind, it almost certainly went well beyond this aesthetic attraction, as we can judge by its consequences. But, as Jean-François Six[10] carefully argues, it implied no real voluntary wish to convert to Islam, let alone the wish to make the act of pronouncing the 'Shahada', the act of witness in which Islamic conversion consists. As Charles' lengthy correspondence with Henry de Castries makes clear, when taken as a whole, the key concept for Charles is that of 'adoration':[11] adoration as the human response to that 'something greater', a reference to the famous *Allah akbar* of the *asser* ritual prayer.

For Charles de Foucauld, like his friend Henry de Castries, had been impressed – marked for life we can say – by the Muslim adoration of God's greatness. 'I saw the ample burnous (hooded cloaks) of my troops bend down together in a superb gesture of ritual prostration, and I heard the repeated invocation, with increasing intensity: *Allah akbar!*'[12] So wrote Henry de Castries at the beginning of a then famous book entitled simply *Islam*. He was struck by the 'majestic beauty' of this act of homage, with the 'grandiose immensity' of its Saharan background, and by the fact that it was an act of 'men' in the open air (in contrast to the muttered prayer, mainly of women, inside the walls of Christian temples!). Charles had been struck by the same ritual act of homage: an act seen and heard, an act impressing the imagination and stirring the emotions, an act of public witness to 'something greater' than the purely human, for it involved the immediate cessation of all ordinary human activities in order to witness to the 'beyondness' of God: *God is great*, or, to be more exact, *God is greater.*

But while de Castries remains with the visible beauty of the human act of homage, with its appeal to the imagination, and seems unable to get beyond this, Charles is seized, 'seduced', by the beauty of the One to whom the homage is addressed. Hence his constant reference to 'adoration', seen as the 'loss of self', in 'love', in the immensity of the Other. 'Adoration, my dear friend, which is the most complete expression of perfect love, is pre-eminently the human act! Yes, it's our habitual activity as human beings if we act according to our nature and reason!'[13]

Reflecting on his experiences in Morocco, as the writing of his book *Reconnaissance au Maroc* obliged him to do, and in the context of renewed contact with the family of his discreet but deeply believing cousins in Paris, Charles almost 'naturally' put to himself the question of the 'truth' of that 'something greater' to which the Muslims had alerted him and attracted him. 'I began to pray this strange prayer, "My God, if You exist, make me know You."...' While reticent to the point of silence on the nature of his sudden conversion in the confessional of the Abbé Huvelin, Charles will constantly recommend this prayer to those of his family and friends who found themselves in his position of doubt. For his prayer is answered, and he discovers the reality of God, a reality so strong that 'immediately I knew there was a God, I realized that I could live only for God'.[14] The story is well known, but the key point, hidden by Charles' discretion, is usually missed. Charles discovers the living God not in the silent immensity and solitude of the desert, but in the living presence of the man Jesus, who enlightens his doubts, heals his past and feeds him with the living Bread of Life. For Charles' conversion occurs through his participation in the sacraments of confession and communion, offered, even pressed upon him, to his own surprise (he had only come to ask for information!) – and that by an old and sick minister of the Church, in a dark and stuffy church building! His friend Henry de Castries, from a similar starting point, the 'seduction' of Islam, never, it seems, discovered this living 'presence' of Jesus, which became the bedrock foundation of Charles' spirituality.

Did, we may ask, Charles compromise the absolute 'transcendence' of God that he had glimpsed in Islam, and which, as he increasingly discovered, was the one foundation, the one uncompromising and uncompromisable foundation, of Islam? On the contrary, Charles feels called, we can say, to accentuate in his words and life the 'All' of the 'One' God, that Absolute in face of whom the whole creation is as 'nothing'. Nor does he diminish the real humanity of Jesus; on the contrary he sees Jesus as primarily the 'workman of Nazareth': the 'divine workman', yes, but one who is fully human, 'like us', 'one of us'.[15]

Charles, therefore, is, as it were, 'caught'. He will never deny the truth and grandeur of the basic Muslim affirmation, 'God is great', and the corresponding natural obligation of all humans to 'adore'. On the contrary, he will declare that the Muslims fail to go far enough: 'Islam has not enough contempt for creatures to be capable of teaching a love of God worthy of God: without chastity and poverty, love and adoration remain very imperfect'.[16] But he is internally obliged, by the inner logic of the faith of his conversion experience, to affirm by his life that this transcendent God is the 'God-with-us', who is in person this man Jesus of Nazareth.

This lived faith-experience of the essential relationship between Islam and Christianity, as Charles came to reflect on it and formulate it, underlies his existential relationships with his Muslim neighbours after his return to North Africa as a 'monk'.

Following his conversion (in Paris, 1886, aged twenty-eight), Charles, after three years of search for his personal vocation, became a Trappist monk, going at his own request, a few months after his entry, to a poor and distant foundation in Syria. After seven years he left the Trappists. He felt called to a literal 'imitation' of Jesus' Nazareth life, and spent three years as a 'domestic' with the Poor Clares in Nazareth itself. In both cases he was in close touch with Muslims, a fact of which he was conscious (he regretted, for example, not to have suffered at the hand of the Muslim Turks, in one of the Armenian massacres',[17] along with many of his neighbouring co-religionists), but for the whole of this period the basic thrust of his life was away from human contacts, in the whole-hearted search for God as the one and all-absorbing absolute. Charles, however, was persuaded to accept ordination, which he had long resisted, and his pre-ordination retreats (he was again, for nearly a year, with the Trappists) gave him the urge to return to Algeria with the intention of founding a 'fraternity', as a 'presence' among the local Muslims. This overall intention covers the remaining fifteen years of his life, from 1902 until 1916. It was a complete reversal: the original search for God continues unabated, but Charles now feels called to live this basic thrust in contact, in an increasingly close and consciously chosen contact, with his Muslim neighbours: neighbours to whom he 'went', to whom he felt himself 'sent'.

During this period, Charles normally refers to himself simply as a 'monk'.[18] Occasionally he will use the expression 'missionary-monk', meaning 'monk in a missionary situation', but always with the proviso that the role and work of a 'missionary' is not his. Obviously he was an unusual monk, as he humorously remarks! He was alone, he had only his own self-made rule, he was constantly drawn away from any sort of stability or regularity, he spent less and less time in formal prayer, being absorbed in linguistic studies and human contacts... But, as an agnostic visitor who knew him well, remarked, he was 'in no way the ex-soldier (as many then, and later, imagined), but every inch the monk!' And – a small but significant fact – he absolutely refused to have his linguistic works published under his name: was he not called to be 'a monk, dead to the world'?[19]

Charles, then, came to Beni Abbes, an Algerian oasis just south of the Atlas mountains and close to the frontier with Morocco. There were gardens, worked by slaves from central Africa, local nomads with property in the oasis and many visiting nomads from further afield, travelling merchants both Muslim and Jewish, and a French military force representing the occupying power. The French soldiers built a small 'hermitage' for Charles (rebuilt, it is still there), near, but deliberately separate from, the main settlement. It was poor and rough, built of mud bricks and palm branches, with a chapel, a small courtyard and six tiny cells.

Did Charles intend to found a poor but basically traditional Christian monastery, a 'Trappe' in miniature, as some have said? True, there are elements of this; but – as Charles makes clear – the basic inspiration was Islamic! As Charles told his friend, Henry de Castries, it was intended to be a 'a *zaouïa* of prayer and hospitality'.[20] Charles had been received in such Muslim *zaouïas* while exploring Morocco, especially by a certain Sidi ben Edris, the grandson of the local 'marabout', Sidi ben Daoud, to whom he had revealed, at the risk of his life, his 'Christian' and 'French' identity, a confidence reciprocated by the handing over to Charles of a secret letter to the 'Ambassador of the French Government'.

A *zaouïa* was a Muslim confraternity for ritual worship and hospitality, often at the centre of the religious and socio-political life of the area.[21] Drawing on this Moroccan experience, Charles, now again in an Islamic context with the same cultural background, chose to found a similar *zaouïa*: 'a *zaouïa* of prayer and hospitality, from which will radiate such a "piety" as to spread light and warmth to all the country around'. The finality and the form are clearly the same. But there is an essential difference. For inside the chapel, above the tabernacle with the sacramental 'presence', is a life-size outline drawing of Jesus with outstretched arms and a symbolic heart, done by Charles himself. The living Jesus, hidden in the tabernacle but forcefully expressed to the view of all in the painted drawing, is put at the 'centre' of this 'Christian' *zaouïa*. And the love that Jesus lived is to be the living motivation of its members' relationships with all who come. Charles' dress and title express this same intention. He wears the Muslim *gandourah*, but with a red heart-and-cross roughly stitched on it. And he was called, with his approval, the 'Christian marabout', *marabout*[22] being the normal title of the head of a *zaouïa*.

Is this a case of religious 'inculturation'? Although the concept did not then exist, it could legitimately be seen as an example of unconscious inculturation, inspired by Charles' basic desire of 'imitating' Jesus in his 'Nazareth' life as 'one of us'. This motivation is undoubtedly there; Charles refers to it frequently. But the key point is that the mental movement is the exact opposite of that normally invoked for practising inculturation. Charles does not start from his Christian belief and practice, moving towards an appropriate Muslim adaptation; rather, he begins by reflecting on the truth and value of his Muslim experience (that profound experience which was at the origin of his discovery of an adult faith), and 'completes' that experience with the explicit content and centre of that faith: the living person of Jesus with his radiating Love, a content given in a still more profound experience. In other words, Islam is for him the way to Christ, who becomes its subjective 'fulfilment'. Charles does not consciously reflect on the meaning of this 'movement' in his life (unlike his disciple and successor Louis Massignon), but it seems to penetrate his 'spiritual unconscious' and so to influence all his concrete decisions and actions.

Charles' time in Beni Abbes, between two and three years, is usually seen as marked by his expressed desire to be, and to be seen as, the 'universal brother': 'I want to accustom everyone here, Christian, Muslim, Jew or pagan, to look on me as their brother, as the "universal brother"' (a brother to every one of them); and, 'The building is known as the *Khaoua*, the "fraternity"'.[23] Charles has in mind two quite disparate sources: the French Republic, with its slogan 'Liberty, Equality, Fraternity', and the Gospel words, 'You are all brothers' (in his letters, he frequently quotes both 'texts', often in the same passage).

The intention, clearly, is to make an initial contact with a person, whoever they be, by respecting that person as an 'other' of 'equal' worth to one's own. As Charles found out, the practice of this 'brother to brother' approach was difficult! – all the more difficult in the colonial context in which both 'sides', the colonized and the colonizers, had strong hierarchical structures. But the interest for us is that this approach provides the 'secular' basis for any form of 'interfaith' dialogue, while being open to the religious dimension (the notion of 'brotherhood' being common to Islam and Christianity, as indeed to most religions). Charles did not use the vocabulary of secularity (the term then had a connotation of 'a-religious', tending towards the 'ir-religious'), but talked simply of 'meeting' people – and later of 'living with' people – in the context of their everyday life and concerns. The word 'brother' is for him a summons to welcome the other who comes in their 'otherness' and concrete difference, while acknowledging what is 'common'; their humanity. It was, clearly, a solid 'foundation' on which to build a dialogue of minds and spirits: not a dialogue about one's faith (though this was not excluded), but a *dialogue of life*, starting from the 'bottom up', from the ordinary little things of a shared life.

After two years in Beni Abbes and a year largely of travelling in the southern Sahara, Charles settled in the central Saharan 'hamlet' of Tamanrasset. He was to remain there, except for three visits to France, for the next, and last, eleven years of his life (1905–1916).

Tamanrasset, now a town of some thirty thousand or more inhabitants, was then a scattered collection of 'twenty hearths, in the heart of the Hoggar mountains', the centre for the Dag-Rali, the principal Touareg tribe, and of their chief, Moussa agg Amastan. The Touareg,[24] who had recently accepted the French presence, were nomadic warriors, with flocks of sheep, goats and camels, the women having a distinctive but equal role. The noble warriors were followed by three 'lesser' classes, and a group of captured Negro slaves. Their faith was Islam, but their language and culture was Berber, anterior to and quite distinct from the Arabic culture of the north. Charles considered that they were 'less Islamic' (the outward expression of their Islam was certainly much different), and might even have derived from the North African Christians of St Augustine's time!

To be with them, Charles no longer built a 'hermitage' as at Beni Abbes, but a simple wattle hut, long and narrow, with just enough room for himself. And, significantly, it was a part of the village: on the edge, but fairly close to the neighbouring dwellings. In fact, in contrast to his previous desire to be 'separate', he now wished to be near, in 'proximity'. Did not Jesus choose to live 'with us', as 'one of us'? That was, as always, his underlying motive.

He was no longer satisfied with being the 'universal brother' (with its rather cover-all approach), wishing rather to become a particular 'friend'. Of course he remained the Christian monk, the Christian 'marabout': he continued to hold to an imaginary '100 metre enclosure'! To quote a 'text' that Charles had written before returning to North Africa; 'Like our Lord Jesus ... we should be universal friends, universal brothers, and as far as possible universal saviours.'[25] This highly idealistic programme (designed for Charles' future 'Petits Frères') remained to the end Charles' intention and aim. The considerable evolution was in the day-to-day living which Charles wisely adapted to circumstances, more exactly to concrete people and his relationships with them.

Charles was little given to theoretical analysis. But it is worth noting that, for him, the term 'brother' expressed the intention to be, and to be seen, in a relation of basic equality with the other, whoever that 'other' might be. The term 'friend', while presupposing this recognition of the equal worth of the other in their difference, adds the desire to be, as far as possible, 'one' with that other: to be united with that other in the 'sharing' of common interests and concerns. And, of course, genuine friendship, as he came to understand, is not only lasting, but also reciprocal and gratuitous. It is not 'for' some ulterior purpose.

A lasting friendship has, obviously, to be patiently constructed and to grow of itself. In Beni Abbes, and while travelling in convoy, Charles had been a 'benefactor', giving what he had (and he had 'more' for this purpose), to help the needy, certainly, but also to 'win over' the other who was, not unnaturally, mistrustful in the face of the unknown and conquering stranger. Now, alone as a European (and therefore at risk), with no extra means of support (above his own strictly limited means), Charles was, simply, a neighbour: a special and peculiar neighbour, yes, but one with no other resources than his capacity to relate and to be accepted in relation. The small 'gifts' that he continued to give to this or that person, on special occasions, were a part of the local culture determining the proper way to relate.

After some two years of limited links, during a winter of famine, Charles noted: 'Am sick. Obliged to stop all work. Jesus, Mary, Joseph, I give you my soul, my spirit and my life.'[26] Charles was not a person to exaggerate his sickness. And he was desperate to continue his linguistic work. He thought he was dying: alone, useless, with nothing accomplished. Having given away the little that he had, he was growing weaker and weaker. But local people managed to find some goats' milk, and saved his life. Without his awareness of the reason for it, his relationship with the people changed: 'I see quite a few people, they come to see me ...' After visiting him, his officer-friend Laperrine wrote: 'He came into my camp on horseback, amid a group of Touareg horsemen – he is more popular than ever among them, and they appreciate his presence more and more.' Instead of being self-sufficient, he becomes, of necessity, the one who receives. The friendship is growing because it has become reciprocal.

This reciprocity is particularly evident on the level of cultural exchange. Charles begins to realize that the common way of looking at the Touaregs in his milieu – a view that he himself had shared – was inexact. To the French colonizers, the Touaregs were 'infidels and barbarians'. Had not Charles seen them as 'the furthest off' and 'the most abandoned', far from 'the faith' and with no 'civilization'! He was most surprised to discover that the Touaregs saw the French conquerors in exactly the same light! 'You possess the earth, but we possess the heavens!'[27] Charles heard these things, and he came to see that they were true. But Charles went further. He spent many hours with an interpreter, Ba-Hammou, to study in detail and in depth the Touareg language and, through the language, the Touareg culture. For ten years Charles patiently continued this work, often working, as he notes with precision, ten hours forty-five minutes a day!

Why did Charles devote so much of his time and energy to this intensive linguistic study? At first his motif is clear and simple. 'My intention,' he writes to his 'bishop', 'is to begin evangelizing the Touareg by settling among them, learning their language, translating the Holy Gospels, becoming friends with them as best I can.' So he translates the four Gospels, and produces a 'little dictionary and an elementary grammar'[28] and he affirms: 'The Touareg language is very easy, a hundred times easier than Arabic.' With his usual 'fougue', he works in haste! But he soon realizes that a proper knowledge of the language is more complex! With this in mind, he calls on an experienced linguist, Motylinski, who comes to spend some months with him. Apart from the learning of the required technical skills for studying an oral language, Charles learns from him to change his perspective and method: instead of 'translating what he wished to communicate to the Touareg, he should rather listen to them and to their spoken language, both prose and poetry'. But at first he remains convinced that a 'scientific study of the language is outside my vocation'. However, after his physical and psychological crisis of January 1908, he writes: 'So much linguistic work remains to be done: it will take thirty years', and a little later he adds: 'My life is mainly taken up with the study of the Touareg language ... I had thought that it was poor and simple; on the contrary, it's rich and complex.' There is little doubt that Charles' motivation changes. He studies the language and culture not just as a means but as an end in itself, and as an essential component of a genuinely reciprocal friendship. And his steadfast refusal to allow his linguistic works to be published under his own name is a sign that this work, with all the human relationships that it involved (hours of participating in gatherings of men and of women recounting their stories and their poems), was genuinely gratuitous.

But can Charles' approach to evangelization be reconciled with his desire for a genuine friendship that is both reciprocal and gratuitous? When coming to Tamanrasset, Charles clearly intended to propose the Gospel to the people when appropriate; was it not his initial reason for learning the language? But soon after his near-death crisis, he writes: 'There may well be centuries between the first digging of the earth and the harvest.'[29] A month later he adds: 'To preach Jesus to the Touaregs is not, I believe, something that Jesus wishes, neither from me nor from anybody. It would be the way of retarding, not advancing, their conversion. The need is to get to know them, with great prudence and gentleness.' This long-term perspective leaves the present free: free to 'get to know' the other as the other is and wishes to be. The penetration of another culture, and the cultivation of patient personal contacts, are sure ways to come to know these persons and their communities. And such a search for 'scientific' knowledge is the gateway to friendship, already in fact a key constituent of it.

We need to look more closely at Charles' conception of evangelization, to examine its compatibility with genuine friendship and dialogue. In a long correspondence with a certain Joseph Hours,[30] a merchant of Lyon, Charles, in answer to a question on evangelization among the Muslims, gives a more or less systematic account of his own approach. The first step, he points out, is to establish an 'intimate contact', followed by an effort 'to make oneself known and to get to know them', and by the expression of a 'whole-hearted love'. Only then will it be a matter of speaking, and only 'in particular', according to the dispositions of each. We find here, duly adapted, the exact attitude and procedure of Charles' cousin, Marie de Bondy, towards Charles himself on his return from Morocco. In face of his absence of faith, his cousin, 'by her silence, her gentleness, her goodness', profoundly influenced him. And 'since she was so intelligent', he was led to think that 'her religious beliefs might not be pure folly', as he had supposed. As he later said, he recognized the presence of Jesus in her person and conduct.[31]

In a similar way, Charles wished to make Jesus 'present', through the sacramental presence of the Eucharist, and, as a 'radiance' of that, through the presence of Jesus' love and goodness in his own life. It was his long-held idea: not to preach in words, but 'to proclaim the Gospel through one's life'. He had in mind the daily contact of neighbour with neighbour, and he insisted on the necessity to 'banish the militant spirit', and the need to see the other 'not as an enemy to be conquered, but as a brother, for "you are all brothers"'. In the Gospel text, this word of Jesus applies to relations within the Christian community; Charles, typically, gives it a universal extension: the Muslim is 'my brother' in the same identical sense as a fellow Christian.

The only proper motive for evangelization, as Charles sees it, is the love of the other; for that other is a 'person whom Jesus loves, and whom we ought to love as we love ourselves, and for whose salvation in consequence we ought to work'. In other words, it is an act of friendship: 'I must offer my friend my dearest treasure'. But the 'offer' is to be made with discretion, in no way forcing the other. Charles frequently refers to the 'model' of Mary carrying Jesus, hidden in her womb, to her cousin Elizabeth. Mary's act is a simple neighbourly act: she comes to live with her cousin in her pregnancy, but Jesus is 'present' in their relationship, though in a hidden and unobtrusive way.

Charles personal understanding of the 'Visitation'[32] (on which he frequently meditated), and his concrete practice in Tamanrasset (more simple and spontaneous than his theoretical reflections would suggest!), indicate clearly how he *lived* that delicate combination of being both friend and, in his way, evangelist. For to evangelize, for him, was essentially to 'make Jesus present'; not in word but 'in person'; not in an open way (that would be the way of the 'militant spirit'), but hidden, 'incognito' we might say, in the human actions of the human person who is there simply as a 'friend'; not as an 'interested' friend, with some concealed ulterior aim, but with the gratuity of true friendship. For the living of friendship is itself the evangelization, the 'making present of Jesus', and any 'conversion', if and when it happens, is God's work alone.

How, in Charles' view, could his neighbours, as Muslims, receive his presence? In this correspondence with Joseph Hours, which dates from the central years of his time in Tamanrasset, he insists that 'all the Muslims whom I have known are of good faith', and that 'they are intellectually our equals':[33] two simple but vital essentials of any form of authentic dialogue.

Considering, however, that 'all religious discussion is impossible', Charles, without using the word, proposes another way of 'dialogue'. It is an inter-personal religious exchange not in the field of knowledge and verbal communication, but in the activity and relationship of love and friendship. So he is constantly both reminding himself and recommending to his Muslim visitors the twin commandment of: 'Love God with all your heart and your neighbour as yourself'. He calls this 'natural religion'.[34] The implication is clear: this command of 'double love' is present, explicitly or at least implicitly, in the teaching of all religions, and its role is to clarify and stimulate the fundamental orientation of the human 'heart', which is basically the same whatever the cultural and religious history of the people concerned. Jesus comes to 'fulfil' this 'law' of the human heart, in his own life, and then in the life of his followers. But the 'law' itself is the same for all, Christian or Muslim. In this perspective, which Charles does not explicate but which he seems to imply, the call to 'conversion' of the other is fundamentally the same as the call to the 'conversion' of oneself: a call Charles constantly recalls, 'Lord, convert me!'

We have here a genuine 'reciprocity': the reciprocity of 'brothers' recognizing the worth and equality of each other, the reciprocity of 'friends' in their mutual exchanges, and the reciprocity of 'fellow pilgrims' ('saviours of each other' to adapt Charles' phrase) on the same path to the same end: together on their pilgrimage way to the one God.

Charles records:

> The Touareg community are a great consolation to me; I can't say how good they are to me, how many upright people

there are among them; a few are real friends, something so rare and precious everywhere. I have at least four 'friends' on whom I can count entirely... We relate together..., and they have came to know that they have a friend in me, that I am devoted to them, that they can have confidence in me – and they have reciprocated what I am for them.[35]

Charles' death, long prepared, can be seen as the final act of friendship. He chose to remain with his neighbours and friends in spite of the obvious danger. The war of 1914–1918 between the European colonizing powers had profound repercussions in the central Sahara: it was for some an opportunity for a 'just struggle' to expel the 'foreign unbelievers' and to restore the true Islamic religion, a struggle which involved inter-tribal conflict and instability. In this confused situation, Charles was shot and killed (in a moment of panic by a young member of a raiding band who intended, most probably, to take him as a hostage).[36]

He had long expressed the wish, in prayer, to 'die a martyr', adding in a meditation that his death might well appear otherwise. In fact his death was an 'accident', but his desired intention remains. His motive was, simply, to 'imitate' Jesus: to die like Jesus, and so to 'give his life' with Jesus 'for the salvation of all'. Who were these 'all'? In the first place the Touareg neighbours, the Muslim people who had become 'his people'. Certainly also for 'all without exception', a constant intention of Charles. Did Charles also offer his life for Islam, as Louis Massignon, his 'successor', claims?[37]

Given his particular intention for the Touaregs, and clearly for the Touaregs as Muslims, and given Charles' constant inclination to 'universalize' his prayer intentions and self-offering (did not Jesus, his 'one Model', while living with only a few, offer his life for all?), we can say that he probably, implicitly at least, included in his self-offering 'the whole house of Islam'. In any case, his death was seen as 'the death of our friend' by Moussa agg Amastan. He wrote to Charles' sister, Madame de Blic:

When I heard of the death of our friend, your brother
Charles, my eyes closed. There was darkness all about me. I
wept and shed tears ... Charles the Marabout has died not
only for all of you, he has died for us too. May God have
mercy on him, and may we meet in Paradise.[38]

The friendship was not limited to Tamanrasset: it was for
ever ...

Were all the Muslim appreciations of Charles' presence
as positive? Ali Merad, an Algerian Muslim scholar and
university professor, has given us a personal 'testimony' on
the 'significance, in the eyes of Islam, of this Christian life
planted right in the land of Islam'. His conclusion is simple:
'Charles de Foucauld seems to have been called by his
destiny to be a mystical witness for Jesus, **in the face of**
Islam.'[39] The key word is 'in the face of' (**'devant'** in the
French original, in bold characters). It expresses, essentially, a 'challenge': not a hostile or aggressive challenge,
but the firm and uncompromising challenge of the
Christian brother and friend in relation to his Muslim
brother and friend. For, as Merad insists, Charles' one aim
was 'the imitation of Jesus': he 'conceived the imitation of
Jesus as his greatest happiness, and, even more, as the true
reason for his existence'.[40] More particularly, he witnessed
to the 'poverty and humility of Jesus, to the Jesus who *took
the last place*'. As such, he is the 'witness': a 'mystical' witness
'for' Jesus ('mystical', meaning here 'totally committed to
God'), 'in the face of' the community of Islam as a 'fraternal challenge'. In spite of emphasizing Charles'
participation in the 'colonial mentality' of the time, with its
secular depreciation of Islamic culture and its religious
triumphalism towards the Muslim religion, Merad
concludes by saying: 'this exceptional human adventure
will continue to challenge the Muslim conscience just as
much as the Christian conscience', and he adds, 'This
fragile light (like the 'monk's lamp' dear to the ancient
Arab poets) is like the joyful sign of a *fraternal presence*.'[41]

A challenge supposes something held in common and
something on which one differs. Between Charles as the
God-seeking monk, the 'Christian marabout', and his

Muslim neighbours, what is common is clearly the adoration of God's greatness – *Allah akbar*. What differs is the mediation: the prophetic word and example of Muhammad, or the self-revealing and salvific word and example of Jesus.

A small, apparently insignificant, incident encapsulates Charles' approach. Charles is writing to his 'apostolic prefect', Mgr Guérin:

> Yesterday, long visit from two men from Tafilalet, two marabouts. They had heard about you, and asked if you had been to Tafilalet – No, he will go another time – [...] Does he travel on foot? – No, by camel ... This question, put by some marabouts, has made me reflect ... They travel on foot, leading their donkeys... We are disciples of JESUS, we want JESUS to live in us ('the Christian is another Christ'), we are always speaking of poverty. They are disciples of Muhammad: their question really makes me reflect.[42]

We can see here, in life, Charles' attitude of accepting, and desiring to make, a fraternal challenge, a mutual challenge!

In what sense, then, can Charles' approach to Islam be said to be that of dialogue? 'He was in no way a pioneer of Islamic-Christian dialogue',[43] declares Hugues Didier. In the sense of a dialogue seeking to know and to appreciate the faith of the other, this is most certainly true. Following his conversion, Charles made no further study of Islam as a religion (ceasing, for example, to read the Koran, and neglecting the study of classical Arabic, a necessary concomitant).

He did, however, seek to know and appreciate the culture of the Touaregs, devoting up to ten hours a day for ten years of his life to this end, and this culture, as Ali Merad has pointed out in detail, was impregnated with Islamic themes. Maurice Serpette,[44] in a work which highlights Charles' 'scientific' research, especially in the linguistic field, sums up by saying: 'For Charles, the "universal brother", knowledge of the other was an obsessional duty of charity'. And Jean-François Six,[45] the first to undertake a serious study of Charles de Foucauld's spiritual journey, adds in an 'afterward' to Serpette's book:

'The secret of this extraordinary labour ... should be seen in that ... ardent and exact 'recognition' of the other ..., the fruit of his fraternal love.' It was, then, a dialogue of fraternal presence, motivated by faith, but whose starting point was not the differences of faith but rather the unity of (native or adopted) language and culture. This language and culture, certainly, were 'carriers' of faith (permeated with references to the 'Most High' and his 'angels', to 'the prophet' and the 'holy city of Mecca'), but they had their roots in the everyday life of the people (their tents and camels, their wars and loves), a life that Charles came to share, and which he did share, indirectly but with empathy, through the fraternal relationships involved in listening to their stories and poems, as they recounted them together.

The dialogue, then, was a dialogue of 'presence', a dialogue between 'brothers', a dialogue of 'friends', a dialogue of 'fellow pilgrims', a dialogue where each 'challenged' the other on their pilgrim way, not by their words but by their actions, a dialogue where all 'hoped' to enjoy God's presence, in the here-and-now, and in the final Paradise, where all would be filled to overflowing in God's glory, not alone but all together ...

Perhaps these terms need some explication, some contextualization. Charles came to the Sahara to be with the Muslims (not to be a 'hermit'!), as a Christian monk (not as a kind of missionary!). His motive was solely the 'imitation' of Jesus: not of his 'public' life, with its public 'proclamation', but of his Nazareth life, with its 'hiddenness' and kind of 'incognito'. It was simply, no more no less, a 'being with', a 'presence'.

Having this 'presence' as a concrete base, Charles was able to 'relate' both as a brother, recognizing the dignity of the other as equal in value precisely in their otherness, and as a friend, uniting with the other in common interests and concerns.

Further, Charles felt called to be, as far as possible, a saviour – as and with Jesus – of those who were becoming brothers and friends. His intention was to push friendship to its ultimate limits: a true friend is one who 'gives his life for his friends'. For Charles this covers both the domain of our so-called earthly concerns, both personal and communal, and the field of our eternal destiny. And he implicitly admits the reciprocity of this 'saving' role, as the following event illustrates: Charles is informed of the 'very beautiful attitude' of a noble Touareg woman who refused to allow her husband to kill some wounded French prisoners, helped to heal their wounds, and saw to their repatriation. He notes: 'Should we not write and tell her that the charity with which she has gathered, cared for, defended and sent home our wounded soldiers, is known to us and fills us with joy and thanks towards God';[46] he even wants to ask the Holy Father to write to her in person!

This presence as brother, friend and saviour is conceived and lived as a challenge. The story of the visit of the two marabouts travelling 'on foot' leaves one in no doubt about the truth of Ali Merad's definition of Charles as the 'mystical witness for Jesus in the face of Islam'. In fact, Merad contrasts Charles de Foucauld with Louis Massignon, whom he describes as 'the tireless Christian witness for Islam'.[47]

More exactly, Charles' relationship is not with Islam as such, but with the concrete Muslim people he is in contact with. He both affirms his Christian identity, and recognizes their Muslim identity. Admittedly his total conviction of the absolute truth of his Christian faith, basically a personal faith-experience in the person of Jesus, leads him to deny the truth of Islam, and to hope for a final acceptance of Jesus. But this 'final acceptance' is more and more seen as 'far ahead'.[48] In the meantime, he fully accepts Islam's positive, indeed providential, role in his own faith-journey, and also accepts much that is true and beneficial, and equally providential, in its practice by his Muslim neighbours. His presence remains a 'challenge', both concerning the 'way' to God, and in matters of everyday honesty and goodness. And he is, increasingly, open to accept the 'challenge' from his neighbours: when sick and near to death, he learnt that some Muslim women were praying for his 'conversion' to Islam before it was too late![49] And he frequently expresses admiration for the good acts and attitudes of many of his newly-found friends: they 'challenge' him, as he does them.

Ali Merad confesses that he was repeatedly 'confronted' by the 'message' of Charles, and he, in his turn, writes to 'confront' his Christian colleagues (one of whom, a French priest, writes the preface to his book).[50]

Charles' approach, therefore, is not, as I would see it, a faith dialogue with Islam, but rather a dialogue of life with living Muslims, in a stance of mutual challenge. It supposes a common 'end', and a common 'providence' leading to that end, but differs in the concrete 'way': Jesus, or Muhammad. But this challenge, though painful, is not negative: each is called to summon the other to what is better, so that together they may attain the 'goal'. 'May we all meet in Paradise!', as Moussa had said to Charles' sister on hearing of his death.

Notes

1 Jean-François Six, *Itinéraire spirituel de Charles de Foucauld*, Paris, Seuil, 1958, p. 267. This is the first (and remains the principal) serious study of Foucauld's spiritual journey.
2 The Abbé Huvelin (1838–1910) was the spiritual director of Foucauld from the latter's conversion in 1886 until his own death in 1910. A remarkable man, he had a profound influence on many, including Maurice Blondel and Friedrich von Hugel. See Lucienne Portier, *Un précurseur: l'abbé Huvelin*, Paris, Cerf, 1979. See pp. 93–107 for his relationship with Foucauld.
3 From an article by Hughes Didier, 'Louis Massignon and Charles de Foucauld' Jacques Keryell (ed.), *Louis Massignon et ses contemporains*, Paris, Karthala, 1998. Cf. revue *Jesus Caritas*, 1951, no. 84. pp. 17–20.
4 Louis Massignon, Foucauld's friend and 'testamentary successor', was responsible for causing his first biography to be written, and so making him known: René Bazin, *Charles de Foucauld, Explorateur au Maroc, Ermite au Sahara*, Paris, Plan, 1921. This was soon translated into English: R. Bazin, *Charles de Foucauld Hermit and Explorer*, London, Burn Oates & Washbourne, 1923.
5 *Charles de Foucauld: Lettres à Henry de Castries*: introduction by Jacques de Dampierre, Paris, Grasset, 1938, p. 94. This correspondence is a key source for Foucauld's connections with Islam.
6 Joseph Cuoq, *Lavigerie, les Pères Blancs et les musulmans maghrébins*, Rome, Societé des missionaires d'Afriques, 1986.
7 Correspondence Ch. de F./ H. de Castries, op. cit., p. 86.
8 Ibid., p. 90.

9 Hugues Didier, *Petite vie de Charles de Foucauld*, Paris, Desclée de Brouwer, 1993, pp. 56–57. This 'Life', though short, is excellent for situating Foucauld in his historical context.
10 J-F. Six, *Itinéraire*, op. cit., p. 44 (see also pp. 45–47).
11 Correspondence Ch. de F./ H. de Castries, op. cit., p. 89.
12 Ibid., p. 33.
13 Ibid., p. 89.
14 J-F. Six, *Vie de Charles de Foucauld*, Paris, Seuil, 1962, pp. 31–34.
15 Didier, *Petite vie*, op. cit., p. 72.
16. Correspondence Ch. de F./H. de Castries, op. cit., p. 91.
17 The Armenian massacres, often forgotten, left a deep mark on the conscience of Charles de F. See Bazin (English) pp. 97–98; Six, *Vie*, pp. 61–62; Didier, *Petite vie*, pp. 86–89.
18 Antoine Chatelard, *Le chemin vers Tamanrasset*, Paris, Karthala, 2002, p. 268 (and the whole chapter, pp. 265–282).
19 Ibid., pp. 284, 274.
20 Correspondence Ch. de F./H. de Castries, op. cit., pp. 87, 123, 167 (cf. p. 118). For Charles' experience of the *zaouïas* in Morocco see his *Reconnaissance au Maroc*, Paris, Challamel, 1888 passim (an experience recalled in Correspondence Ch. de F./H. de C., pp. 162–163). Cf. also Six, *Vie*, pp. 21–24, 84–86.
21 Charles, receiving a letter from the important 'marabout' *Sidi ben Daoud* twenty-one years later, replies, addressing him as 'my brother in God' and adding 'I pray God to accord you his favours in this world and heaven in the next' (letter written both in French and Arabic by Charles in March 1905, quoted in Correspondence with H. de Castries, pp. 170–71).
22 Ali Merad, *Charles de Foucauld au regard de l'Islam*, Paris, Chalet, 1975, translated into English, with a Foreword and Afterword by Zoë Hersov, as *Christian Hermit in an Islamic World*, New York, Paulist Press, 1999, but lacking the valuable annexe *L'Islamisme des Touaregs*. This work, by an Algerian Muslim, a professor of Arabic literature and civilization in Lyons (France), is, in his own words, 'a [personal] testimony motivated by the desire to make a contribution ..., to the Muslim-Christian dialogue' (p. 14. French; same page in English). Well-written and well-argued, it is the 'key' work on Charles de Foucauld's relationship with Islam from the Muslim side. For Charles as 'the Christian Marabout', see pp. 39–51 in French (chapter II in English).
23 For Charles' role as 'universal brother' and his conception of 'Fraternity', see, Six, *Itinéraire*, pp. 275–76, 331; Six, *Vie*, pp. 91–94, 98; Chatelard, *Chemin*, pp. 143–62.
24 For Charles' settling in Tamanrasset and for a description of the

local Touareg society, see Elizabeth Hamilton, *The Desert my Dwelling Place*, Hodder and Stoughton, London, 1968, pp.153–59; see also Chatelard, *Chemin*, op. cit., pp. 231–34.
25 Chatelard, *Chemin*, op. cit., pp. 147–62.
26 Ibid., pp. 247, 258–59.
27 Six, *Vie*, op. cit., p. 218; cf. Hamilton, op. cit., pp. 171, 173.
28 Maurice Serpette, *Foucauld au Désert*, Paris, Desclée de Brouwer, 1997, ch. VII: L'oeuvre linguistique de Ch. de F.; see also the 'Postface' de J-F. Six, pp. 247–50.
29 Six, *Vie*, op. cit, pp. 184–85 (On the invitation of Moussa, Charles assists at the death of his aunt, Tihit, exhorting her to 'Ouksed Massinin'– 'Fear God'; while known and accepted as the 'Christian marabout', he is ready to use the appropriate Islamic formula).
30 Correspondence inédite [unpublished] du Père de Foucauld à M. Joseph Hours, letters of 25 Nov. 1911, 3 May 1912, 12 Oct. 1912.
31 Six, *Vie*, op. cit., pp. 29–31.
32 Oeuvres Spirituelles, *Anthologie*, Paris, Seuil, 1958, pp. 313–15. Charles frequently returns, in his meditations, to the 'model' of the Visitation: Jesus is seen as present and active in the interpersonal life of the Christian who is united with Him (and, as Jacques Maritain has added, the more effectively so, paradoxically, when the person acting is unconscious of this hidden presence: see *Approches sans entraves*, Paris, Seuil, 1975, p. 82–85.
33 Correspondence Ch. de F/J. Hours, letter of 12 October 1912.
34 Ibid., letter of 25 November 1912.
35 Chatelard, *Chemin*, op. cit., p. 150.
36 A. Chatelard, *La Mort de Charles de Foucauld*, Paris, Karthala, 2000, passim.
37 Hughes Didier, *Louis Massignon et Charles de Foucauld*, op. cit., pp. 93–98. To my mind, the 'spiritual intuition' of Massigon that Foucauld 'offered his life for Islam' is correct (against Didier), the difference being that Charles saw his self-offering in terms of 'solidarity', while Massignon spoke of 'substitution', pp. 96–97.
38 Hamilton, *The Desert my Dwelling Place* op. cit., p. 207.
39 Ali Merad, op. cit., p.75 (French). The English translation, p. 44, while materially correct, fails to bring out the implied sense of 'challenge': Charles witnessed for Jesus in the face of Islam, in the sense that his life 'remains a challenge to the Muslim conscience' (p. 129), just as much, the author adds, 'as to the Christian conscience'! This challenge is not that of an 'outsider', but of one 'who chose to live and die in a Muslim land', choosing 'to rest there until the Resurrection', p. 128.

40 Ibid., p. 28; pp. 45–48 French (English pp. 21; 29–31).
41 Ibid., p.129 French (English p. 74: the French 'interpeller' is better translated as 'challenged', rather than as 'summoned').
42 Chatelard, *Chemin*, op. cit., p. 200.
43 Didier, *Petite vie*, op. cit., p. 152; cf. Didier's article, *Louis Massignon* ..., op. cit., pp. 104–108.
44 Maurice Serpette, *Foucauld au Désert*, op. cit., p. 243.
45 Ibid., Postface de J-F. Six, p. 255. This remarkable 'postface' brings out the significance of Foucauld's intellectual studies, as seen by Louis Massignan and Emile Gautier: they show at once 'the secular fury to understand', typical of the modem 'scientific' mindset, and the 'experimental discovery of the sacred' in the gratuitous search to know the other in their alterity.
46 Chatelard, *Chemin*, op. cit., pp. 165–66.
47 Merad, op. cit., p. 75 French (English p. 44).
48 Six, *Vie*, op. cit., p. 184.
49 Ibid., p. 186.
50 Merad, op. cit., p. 14 French (English p. 14) and pp. 7–9 ('Préface' of Michel Lelong; replaced in the English translation by a new preface by the translator, Zoë Hersov).

Chapter 5

Between Christendom and Islam: The Martyr Mystic Christian de Chergé and the Atlas Cistercians in Algeria

Jean Olwen Maynard

On 15 January 1971, a prospective new monk arrived at the tiny Cistercian Abbey of Our Lady of Atlas, Tibhirine, Algeria. Fr Christian de Chergé had never before seen the house and community to which he was determined to commit himself for the rest of his life. Some aspects disappointed him. The premises were grander than he'd expected – ridiculously large for the handful of monks rattling around inside – and although they weren't luxurious their size seemed to evoke the painful inequalities of the colonial past. Although this bothered him, it didn't seem to bother the Muslim villagers whom he described admiringly as: 'poor but smiling, proud and without resentment, believers, and respectful towards a monk whoever he may be – so long as what's in the back of the shop matches the window display'.[1]

Christian had already completed a period of novitiate at Atlas' mother-house, Aiguebelle Abbey in France, a large, prestigious and secure institution. Atlas, located not only in a poor rural area of a developing country but also one that was overwhelmingly Muslim, was a stark contrast. It had been founded with great confidence back in 1934, when Algeria was supposed to be an integral part of France – 'a land French forever'. Virtually all the original monks had left when Algeria gained its independence, and too few were now living there for it to be properly viable. Unable to run its own noviciate, it was under constant threat of closure. The community was a complete ragbag of men who had come to Algeria for all sorts of reasons: some of them were oddballs by any standard, and Christian made yet another oddball to add to the collection. A firm but discerning superior should have been able to bind them together with a sense of common purpose, but none of them were leadership material, and there weren't enough stabilized monks to hold a valid election. A series of *ad nutum* superiors had been appointed by Aiguebelle, seconded from other monasteries and coming and going in rapid succession, each one taking a different line from his predecessor. Christian's arrival brought the number of monks up to eleven, but only four were stabilized in Atlas. The rest were on loan from other monasteries: there was always a question mark about how long they would stay – and there was also a question mark about whether they should even be permitted to take vows of stability in Atlas, should they decide they wanted to, for common sense demanded that it be given the coup de grace. The life of the monastery preserved a certain outward serenity thanks to the constant daily round of prayer and manual labour, and the persistent Trappist habit of eschewing unnecessary chatter. Underneath, the situation was a mess.

From the start there was friction between the new recruit and the rest. As a group the others were quite elderly – not a single one under forty-five, whereas Christian had celebrated his thirty-fourth birthday just a few days after his arrival. But it wasn't just a question of age. Between him and them loomed the massive watershed of the 1960s. For the Catholic Church there had been Vatican II, and for France and Algeria there had been Algerian independence – a deeply traumatic experience for both peoples. The older monks deserved every credit for the immense effort they had made to adjust to all the change, but it hadn't been easy for them, whereas Christian had, as it were, grown up with it.

Like most of the other brothers, he had some previous

experience of Algeria – coloured initially by the warm nostalgic glow of childhood, since his father was an army general, and had been posted there for three years during the Second World War when Christian was a small boy just beginning to take notice of the world around him. Later, in 1959, his seminary education in Paris had been interrupted so he could do his military service – fighting the insurgency in Algeria. However he had not been assigned to the combat forces but to a Specialized Administration Unit, a sort of peace corps with responsibility for promoting rural development. Despite his aristocratic military background, his sympathies had essentially lain with the Muslim Algerians; what he experienced during that time would change his life for ever. Back in the seminary during the early 1960s, Christian greeted with excitement the upheavals of Vatican II. He also began spending his summer holidays at Toumliline, a large Benedictine monastery in Morocco, which was hosting international Muslim-Christian youth gatherings. Unfortunately the high profile of these gatherings, which were patronized by the Moroccan royal family, gave rise to problems; they had to be discontinued, and soon afterwards Toumliline closed down and the Benedictines abandoned Morocco. Although by 1964 Christian was sure that his vocation was to the monastic life – albeit with an unusual twist – he was persuaded to be ordained for the Archdiocese of Paris and give five years' service there. He spent those five years working at the Basilica of the Sacré Coeur in Montmartre, but once they were up he cleared out his office, gave away most of his books, and announced, 'I'm going to become a Trappist monk so I can go to Algeria to pray with the Muslims.'

Eager to prepare himself for a future in which he was sure that, under God's leading, his destiny would be linked to that of the Muslim believers among whom he had come to live, Brother Christian threw himself into learning Arabic. His studies had to be fitted in as and when, however, for the monastery was not an academic ivory tower. The community gathered at frequent intervals in the chapel to pray the seven Hours of the Divine Office, and in between times there was plenty of hard manual labour to be got through on the farm and in the oil press. Christian didn't resent these demands, which he saw as part of what seemed to be God's plan for his life; however it wasn't easy to shoulder his full community responsibilities *and* find time for the other pursuits which were also so necessary for him. The fact that intellectually, he had the edge on everyone else in Tibhirine didn't make him any more popular, and nor did the pig-headedness with which he sometimes insisted on defending his point of view. The older monks did their best to swallow their irritation while they waited patiently for him to realize that he'd mistaken his vocation. If he was so keen to work with the Muslims he'd do better to transfer as a secular priest to the Diocese of Algiers, or perhaps join the Little Brothers. Nevertheless, towards the end of his first year in Tibhirine Christian made his first, temporary vows. He chose to make them on 1 October, the feast day of St Thérèse of Lisieux, the Carmelite whose hidden life turned out to have such an important message for today's world.

In August 1972 Jean de la Croix, Abbot of Aiguebelle, intervened to give both sides a break: he sent Christian off to do a two-year course in Arabic and Islamology at the Pontifical Institute of Arab Studies in Rome. Following his return to Atlas, in October 1975 the monks suddenly received an order from the government giving them a week to leave the country. They were already hard at work packing up the library when another order arrived, cancelling the first. Despite this incident, which underlined the extreme precariousness of the community's existence, Christian's conviction of being called to spend his life 'praying with the Muslims' grew ever deeper. For several years in succession he renewed his vows, though still on a temporary basis, and meanwhile, in the eyes of his confrères, the eccentricity of his behaviour increased. He fasted throughout Ramadan, slipped off his sandals before entering the chapel, and took to greeting everyone in Arab fashion. He also quite often took short breaks away from the monastery, in response to invitations from the Archdiocese of Algiers, or other religious communities, to give talks or retreats; these absences provided a safety valve, but also underlined the distance between Christian and the rest of the community.

Abbot Jean de la Croix knew that that Our Lady of Atlas played a crucial role in the life of the tiny Church in Algeria. Of the small number of priests and sisters who had chosen to go on living and working there, many would have said that their visits to the monastery and occasional retreats there were the only thing that kept them going. He was personally committed to do whatever he could to help this struggling daughter house survive and flourish. It was precisely because of this commitment that he had been willing to foster Christian's vocation – for this man *might* be able in time to provide it with leadership and with a new vision. During a visit in autumn 1976, the abbot spoke to each of the monks individually, and arranged for Christian to be given the opportunity to explain before all the brothers how he understood his own calling to Atlas. This involved telling them a story about himself which he hadn't told anyone before.

> During his military service Christian had been based in Tiaret, a small market town in the Atlas Mountains 300 km west of Algiers, and the first month was spent learning at first-hand about rural development in a village to the north of the town named Aïn Said. A friendship developed between him and a village policeman named Muhammad, despite their being widely apart in age and experience. Muhammad was an older married man with ten children and no formal schooling, who had known poverty all his life. Christian's upbringing had been very sheltered and quite privileged, and at twenty-two he still had several years of full-time education ahead of him. What attracted him to Muhammad was his deep spirituality born out of a life of faithful prayer. He didn't talk much, but what he said made sense, and he was a good listener. Here was someone Christian could talk to about his own life with God, and be understood. Muhammad also responded with ready understanding to Christian's ambivalence about the war and its politics; it struck a chord in the ambivalence of his own position, as an Algerian Muslim working for the French state. To the insurgents he was a collaborator and a traitor. He knew

that, and yet he didn't hate the insurgents; he understood their point of view, too ...

Aïn Said was normally very peaceful, but this was a guerrilla war, and armed men could suddenly appear anywhere, any time. One day when Christian and Muhammad happened to be taking a walk together, they ran into trouble. Christian was very struck by the way Muhammad handled the incident: intervening first to protect Christian, then to defuse the situation and discourage reprisals against the 'enemy'. Once all was quiet again, Christian did what he could – which wasn't much – to organize some additional protection for Muhammad over the next few days: they both knew that his actions had made him a target for assassination. Before they parted Christian added, 'I'll pray for you.'

'I know you'll pray for me,' quietly replied Muhammad. 'But you see, Christians don't know how to pray!' A few days later he was found dead near one of the village wells, his throat cut.

Eighteen years later, Christian at last found words to explain to the brothers in Atlas how the self-sacrificing death of this Muslim friend had led him to the conviction that God was calling him to live a life of prayer in Algeria. This life, he understood, must be led not alone, but in a community, 'in order to be truly a witness of the Church'. He had reflected deeply on his vocation, looked at the situation from every possible angle, and Our Lady of Atlas was his 'chosen fiancée'. Like any other fiancée this community wasn't perfect in the way he'd imagined, but in its unique reality he would encounter God in encountering the other. What ensued seemed to Christian like a miracle of communion: it was agreed that he should make his solemn profession, and at the same time four other brothers decided to be stabilized at Atlas. He chose once again the date of 1 October. After the ceremony he asked forgiveness of the community for the many times he had behaved insensitively.

In 1978 Jean de la Croix, having stood down as Abbot of Aiguebelle, became the next *ad nutum* superior of Atlas. The following year, a handful of Catholics in Algeria formed a discussion group to explore the spiritual world of

Islam. They named it 'Ribat-es-Salam', which meant literally 'Bond of Peace' and was partly an allusion to Ephesians 4:3; 'ribat' in Arabic also meant a fortified monastery, and they hoped to become a 'stronghold of prayer'. Jean de la Croix encouraged the Ribat to meet at Tibhirine, in order to root its explorations in the monastic tradition, and Christian immediately became involved. No one else in the community did. Some of the other monks, although they got on amazingly well with Muslims as people, felt distinctly uncomfortable about this attempt to engage so directly with Islam as a religion. But mostly they just weren't interested in all the talk, talk, talk – which in any case they couldn't follow. Nobody except Christian had ever had the chance to undertake serious studies in both Arabic and Islamology.

Towards the end of 1979 Christian went through such a serious crisis that he was given permission to go off and make a retreat at Assekrem, a high plateau in the Sahara where Charles de Foucauld had built a small hut for the times he needed to be completely alone. Christian spent weeks anguishing over whether perhaps he had made a big mistake: were the interminable tensions with the community a sign that he wasn't meant to be a Trappist after all? He returned to Tibhirine in January, a lot thinner and with an untended growth of beard, but smiling and at peace once more. While he had been away a Sufi brotherhood from Médéa, the nearest town, had becanme involved in the Ribat. From then on, about a dozen of them participated regularly in the three-day residential meetings which took place in spring and autumn each year. The Christian Ribat members, well aware of the traditional tension between Sufism and mainstream Islam, welcomed their participation while at the same time making special efforts also to involve a few 'normal' Muslims for the sake of balance.

In 1984, with the next General Chapter of the Cistercian Order approaching, Jean de la Croix was worried that if Atlas did not regularize its situation there would be renewed talk of closure. By now nine monks were stabilized, with the right to vote – though unfortunately three were absent. Agreeing that the urgency of the situation demanded it, the remaining six came together to hold the necessary deliberations and vote on the future of the community. Christian's proposal that the house adopt the status of autonomous priory, rather than that of abbey, was accepted. The monks then proceeded to hold an election for prior, and the choice fell on Christian.

The prior-elect had to set off fairly soon afterwards for Holyoke in the USA, to take his place at the General Chapter. The gathering seemed to him to be dominated by the abbots of all those large and important monasteries from the rich, developed world – a whole monastic scene, complete with grandiose ceremonial, which he saw as of the past rather than of the future. Himself he saw as representing the voices of Vatican II and of the Third World. The older abbots were perhaps somewhat surprised when he read out a fraternal message from the Sufis of Médéa, but they happily gave him one to take back. A key point on his personal agenda was to obtain a small but significant amendment in the Order's constitution. Trappists were officially supposed to offer monastic hospitality to 'those who share our faith'; he wanted this changed to 'people of goodwill'. While in Holyoke, Christian also issued an appeal for other monasteries to send monks to Atlas. The assembled abbots took note of this appeal, and did their best to encourage serious consideration within their home communities of the idea of transferring to Atlas.

Unfortunately, welcoming men to Algeria was only the start: the next question was how to keep them there. Living in so small a community could be quite claustrophobic – so much so that Christian introduced a policy, quite unusual in Cistercian tradition, of giving each monk two days off each month during which he was free to go anywhere he liked to get away from the monastery. Even so, the brothers got on each other's nerves. One of the principle irritants remained Christian himself: patience was not his strongest point, and in his early years as prior his handling of personal relations could be quite insensitive. A number of brothers left because of him. Another serious obstacle was the poverty of the house. Since Vatican II monastic life wasn't usually as austere as it had been in the past, but at

Atlas it was austere out of sheer necessity – and some prospective recruits couldn't take it. Only a tiny handful liked what they found in Tibhirine, managed to adjust, and stayed. As time went on a further cause of tension arose, again centring on Christian. This was the growing importance of his role vis-à-vis the wider Christian community in Algeria: he was constantly in demand as a speaker, retreat-giver and spiritual director. The monks often felt that all their prior's concern and attention – his love, if you like – were lavished on the Muslims, the secular clergy and nuns, and the people staying in the guesthouse, leaving nothing over for them. When the circumstances of a community give rise to such a perception, the question of whether or not it is valid is perhaps beside the point: valid or not, it hurts.

The enthusiasm with which the Pope was received when he addressed a gathering of 80,000 young Muslims in Casablanca, Morocco, in 1985, set Bishop Hubert Michon of Rabat to wondering if a monastic presence in Morocco might once again be envisaged. The following year he happened to make a trip to Algiers, during which it was only natural to pay a call on his old friend from seminary – Christian de Chergé. He was deeply impressed by what he saw at Tibhirine – particularly the relations between the monks and the villagers: Our Lady of Atlas was integrated into the surrounding society in a way that Toumliline had never been. After careful reflection, he put forward a proposal. Christian freely admitted it was crazy to agree – but he did. In 1988 Tibhirine opened an annexe in Fez – an embryonic daughter house across the border in neighbouring Morocco. The tiny community was sorely stretched to spare even a few monks for a second house. However the Algerian government wanted Tibhirine limited to a maximum of thirteen monks; assuming it ever reached that figure, a linked house in a neighbouring country would offer the only potential for accommodating any further increase. It also meant that potential recruits denied visas by the Algerian government did not have to be turned away, because it was a lot easier to get into Morocco. Christian organized a rotation schedule between Tibhirine and Fez, to give the brothers in each house a change of scenery and companionship from time to time.

Tibhirine's village school, which had been started and run for many years by the monks, had been taken over by the government, and in 1988 a mother-and-child clinic which had been run on monastery premises also closed. Christian wasn't worried: social services did tremendous good, but he had never seen them as the raison d'être for the Christian presence in Algeria. The clinic had been held in a room adjoining the enclosure wall, with its own door, and he offered the village the use of this room as a mosque and Qur'an school. Soon the muezzin's call to prayer could be heard mingling with the sound of the monastery bell.

Every two years a gathering is organized in Rome, by the Pontifical Institute of Arabic and Islamic Studies, for Christians who are working in the Muslim World. This has become a regular event in the life of the Church under the title 'Journées Romaines' ('Roman Days'). During the seventeenth Journées Romaines, in 1989, Christian was asked to make a presentation. He began by explaining that the monks of Tibhirine saw themselves simply as 'People who pray, in the midst of others who pray. This was the self-definition which our little monastic community – a piece of Cistercian "flotsam" in an ocean of Islam – arrived at in an independent Algeria in 1975, when it seemed we had just one week to leave that place ... where we still are today.' Christian went on to suggest that in that self-definition lay the seeds of an answer to the question being considering in that summer's Journées Romaines: how Christians and Muslims could work together for a common vision of society.

> The few reflections which I will stammeringly express here can have no meaning unless they arise from that place where we have been endeavouring day by day, since 1934, to live in community. I will speak therefore as a witness, but the witness who is speaking is actually a community – even if my brothers have given me the task, among various others, of being their spokesperson for purposes of encounter and sharing. It's impossible to explain anything except in the context of a constant communitarian presence, and of the faithfulness of each one to the humble

everyday reality of the doorkeeping and the garden, the kitchen and the 'lectio' and the Office of the Hours.

The dialogue which we have established has its own pattern, characterized essentially by the fact that we never take the initiative in it. I would freely describe it as existential. It is the fruit of a prolonged 'living together', and of shared concerns, sometimes very concrete. In other words it is rarely of a strictly theological order. We would rather avoid debates of that sort. I regard them as narrow-minded.

So then, we have an existential dialogue, one that is both manual and spiritual, both of the everyday and of eternity – because we cannot welcome the men and women who approach us in any way other than in their concrete and mysterious reality as children of God, 'created in Christ Jesus from the beginning' (Eph 2:10). We would cease to be Christians – to be human beings even – if we should venture to amputate other people's hidden dimension, in order to encounter them merely – as some would put it – 'person to person'; that is, on a human plane sanitized of all reference to God, of all their personal and therefore unique relationship with the Wholly-Other, of all opening onto an unknown beyond.

So conceived, the vocational life of the monk surely becomes more directly part of the prophetic mission of the Church, a mission assumed here but 'destined to throw out bridges elsewhere', as John Paul II emphasized in addressing the Christians of Morocco. Together with many other Christians who also live embedded in the 'House of Islam', I would like to witness that in Islam, as in Christianity, prophecy is not dead.[2]

Christian went on to consider the image of the monastic life as a ladder – the ladder of Jacob – evoked by so many traditional spiritual writers from John Climacus to Ghazzali.

> Between the pillars of Islam and the essential observances of all consecrated life, there are obvious connections which make them like successive rungs for a common ascent. The whole purpose of a rung is to be deeply inserted on either side in the two uprights of the ladder – preferably at the same level! It's when we try to define these 'levels' of authentic spiritual progress that we are suddenly astonished

to find ourselves so close. We need to list them: the gift of the self to the Absoluteness of God, regular prayer, fasting, giving of alms, conversion of heart, the memorial or dhikr, trust in Providence, the imperative of boundless hospitality, the call to spiritual combat, to pilgrimage (which is also something inside ourselves) ... in all this, how could we fail to recognize the Spirit of holiness of whom you cannot tell where he comes from or where he is going (Jn 3, 8) ...[3]

Ora et labora (prayer and work), the two traditional well-springs of Benedictine spirituality, were also the sources of the existential dialogue which Christian saw as having sprung up in Tibhirine. Quoting a verse from the Qur'an – 'Oh you who believe! Bow down, prostrate yourselves, adore your Lord, do good. Perhaps you will be blessed.' – he sought to explore the potential for communion through the 'double prostration' of prayer and deeds of mercy.

> A small point: the meeting in Assisi took place on a Monday. The day before, Sunday, the Church gave us the Gospel of the Pharisee and the Publican (Luke 18:9–14–30th Sunday, Year C). In commenting on it, I noted that the pilgrims the following day, in Assisi, should be able to join each other in the prayer of the publican: 'Have pity on me, a sinner!' When we met again on the Monday evening – about thirty of us – the Muslim friend who began the prayer started precisely with that: 'Rabbi, irhamna!' There was no longer a question of whether we should pray together, or come together to pray: we were a single community prostrated in the attitude of the publican ... A hadith says, 'All human beings are the family of God, and among them the one God loves most is the one who renders most service to his family.' We must learn, therefore, to practise more and more together this other prostration which has become for us almost sacramental ever since Jesus, rising from table, that last evening, practised it with the gesture of washing the feet of each disciple in turn, Judas included: 'Do this in memory of me! ... I have given you an example so that you may copy what I have done to you' (Jn 13:1 ff).[4]

In 1990 Christian was re-elected as prior of Atlas. His first term might well have been a trial to the community, but monks have their feet firmly on the ground: they know that nobody is perfect. The brothers appreciated that Christian had tremendously positive qualities – however much these positive qualities contributed to making him difficult to live with at close quarters! They also appreciated that it was only his vision, and his clarity about his calling to Atlas, which had kept their community in being. Finally, Christian was still the only realistic candidate for prior: if they were unable to accept him as he was, the house would probably have to close. Nevertheless, in confirming his mandate, the brothers asked him to pay more attention to them in future – and also to pay more attention to his own needs, and not work himself quite so hard.

Meanwhile the political situation in Algeria was deteriorating badly. Independence had failed to work the socio-economic miracles which had been hoped for. Seeing the country as being run for the sake of a privileged minority, and offering them no future, more and more young people turned to armed violence. A number of guerrilla movements formed, but the GIA (Groupe Islamique Armée) was the most savage and dangerous. It wasn't a unified organization, but a network of small quasi-autonomous units scattered across the country: the local GIA *emirs* were in constant rivalry, occasionally even fighting each other. The area around Tibhirine became a battleground between the guerrillas and the army. To stress his community's absolute non-violence and neutrality, Christian encouraged the monks to call the guerrillas 'brothers of the mountains' and the army 'brothers of the plain'. The 'brothers of the mountains' were quite often to be seen praying in the Tibhirine mosque, or queueing up to see Luc – an elderly lay brother who was a qualified doctor. The monks schooled themselves not to react. All of them, including Luc, knew that a group of Algerian army doctors had been executed in Médéa for providing medical treatment to guerrillas.

In October 1993 the GIA issued an ultimatum, ordering all foreigners to leave Algeria before the end of the following month. Some did get out, but the majority just took extra precautions. The local authorities tried to persuade

Christian to accept an armed garrison for the monastery's protection. He refused, partly on principle, but also because a military presence would make the house a target. He agreed only to instruct Muhammad, the gatekeeper, not to open the gate to anyone after 7.30 p.m. – though there was no way to stop anyone climbing over the wall. That autumn's Ribat meeting had to be held without the Sufis: for security reasons they were forbidden to come any more.

The killings of foreigners began early in December: one here, one there. The biggest shock for the monks at Tibhirine came on 15 December, when they heard on the radio the news of a massacre only a few kilometres away. The twelve victims were their friends the 'Yugos', a group of Croats contracted by the state hydroelectric company to build a reservoir. For several years running they had come to the monastery at Christmas and Easter for midnight Mass, but were shortly due to be repatriated. They were watching television in their common room when a horde of guerrillas arrived, marched them outside and cut their throats. Once again the local authorities pleaded with Christian to accept a garrison. Again he refused, agreeing only to tell Muhammad not to allow anyone in after 5.30 p.m. As calmly as possible the monks discussed the situation, going over their reasons for staying. They agreed that, in the event of an attack on the monastery, there should be no pointless heroics: each brother should do his best to flee or hide.

On Christmas Eve just after supper an armed man suddenly entered the building and shouted in Arabic for everyone to kneel down against the wall. Others followed, one of whom was introduced as Sayah Attiyah, the local GIA *emir*. The brothers were quickly rounded up, except for two who ran down into the cellar and hid in empty wine barrels. Attiyah next sent for 'the Pope of this place'. As Christian walked the short distance from his office, outwardly calm but inwardly sure that the moment of death was at hand, he repeated softly the meditation phrase which the Ribat had agreed to adopt at its latest meeting. It was the opening phrase of each of the Hours of the Divine Office: 'O God come to my aid. O Lord make haste to help me'.

Attiyah wasn't much more than twenty, but Christian

knew he was a hardened killer, responsible for the massacre of the Croats. Nevertheless, at the prior's insistence, he agreed to step outside before presenting his demands. He wanted money, medical supplies, and a doctor to come and serve his fighters in the mountains. Christian refused on all counts. Firstly, the monks lived in poverty and had no money over and above their essential needs. Secondly, any medical supplies they had were only sufficient to maintain Luc's clinic, where they were given out as needed. Thirdly, the only doctor was Luc, and he was far too old to go and live in the mountains (he was nearly eighty). The GIA knew very well that if they needed treatment, they could come to the monastery for it: Luc had always treated anyone who came for help, without distinction and without asking awkward questions. The two continued to talk for about fifteen minutes. Then the emir agreed to go away and come back another time – though when he did, he would expect from the monastery a definite agreement to assist the GIA. The three men shook hands with everyone and quickly left. A shiver went down the spines of some of the monks when they thought that these hands might be the same ones which cut the throats of the Croats only ten days before.

On 26 December the community met to discuss what to do. What would happen when Attiyah returned and met with a flat refusal? They had no desire to commit collective suicide, nor did they want to risk the lives of the Muslims who worked with them in the monastery. Presumably, therefore, they would have to leave. So they had better start planning how best to do it without attracting undue attention, and where to go – since they were determined to keep the community together. News of their decision spread quickly through the village grapevine, and one of the monks reported a comment he'd heard from a neighbour: 'You still have a little escape door by which you can leave. We don't. No way out, no escape door.' Mgr Henri Teissier, Archbishop of Algiers, arrived to express his concern about the impact their departure would have on Christian morale in Algeria. Christian was also concerned about that, and he arranged to speak with each brother individually: each one admitted he was not at peace with the decision to leave. A second chapter meeting resulted in a unanimous reversal of the previous decision: the community would stay.

On 1 January Christian completed a letter to his family which he had begun on 1 December. It was the fruit of serious reflection over the past month, as he struggled to express his understanding of the context in which he was living from day to day. He sent it in a sealed envelope to his youngest brother Gérard, who was also his godson; it was only to be opened should anything happen to him. Attiyah was killed the following month. Badly wounded after his unit was ambushed by the army, he had hidden up for nine days not far from Tibhirine before dying of his injuries.

The monastery, despite its isolation and apparent vulnerability, was as safe if not safer than the country's capital city. Attiyah was believed to have extended his *aman* (promise of protection) to the monks, and after his death the local GIA continued to respect it. When, for the first time, a priest and a sister were assassinated, it was in Algiers in broad daylight. Their deaths hit the international headlines. Fr Henri Vergès, one of the Ribat's founder members, was particularly well-known to the Atlas community, but the grieving monks urged the importance of getting the killings into perspective: thousands of ordinary Algerians had been slain, as had at least fifty imams who refused to give their moral support to the extremists' 'religious war'. One of the brothers commented:

> 'Martyr' – that's a rather ambiguous word around here ... If anything should happen to us, though I hope nothing does, we want to live here, in solidarity with all the Algerian men and women who have already paid with their lives. We just want to stand side by side with all the unknown victims.

Christian, thinking of the army doctors in Médéa, insisted: 'Christians are not the only martyrs of charity. Muslims are, too.' After two Augustinian Sisters were killed in Algiers in October, a number of religious congregations decided to pull out. The White Fathers chose to remain, and on 27 December four of them were killed in Tizi-Ouzou.

Every six months the brothers of Atlas met together to

review their decision to remain, and each time it was unanimously reaffirmed. No rational calculations were involved, only the conviction that – for the time being at least – this was where God wanted them to be. The chapter room where the community meetings were held was very simply furnished: a square table covered with a handwoven Berber cloth, and on the wall a reproduction of Roublev's Trinity – an evocative reminder that God himself is community. The eight brothers – Christian, Luc, Célestin, Christophe, Michel, Paul, Jean-Pièrre and Amédée – usually gathered there each morning for Terce, and again each evening between dinner and Compline, shelling peas or filling lavender sachets while Christian gave them a digest of the day's news which he had heard on the radio. As their beloved Algeria dissolved into anarchy, they came to depend more and more on the support of their life as a community: the daily round of work and prayer and mutual forbearance through which God was present to them.

In a circular letter of April 1995,[5] sent out to all their friends and well-wishers, Christian spoke of their ongoing discussions as to whether to go or stay. The question had been particularly acute during the closing months of the previous year, when more and more congregations were leaving, and when nevertheless they couldn't help asking themselves – as he put it: 'How can we deprive our Church, at a time when she is only the shadow of herself, of the monastic charism – that essential aspect of her face, insofar as that face can be shown within the Muslim world?' In December Mgr Teissier had come to facilitate the process of discernment, speaking with each brother individually and also with the community as a whole, and at the end left a written record summing up what had been said:

> You emphasize first of all the meaning of your Eucharistic celebration and your common prayer lived in the midst of this crisis, in communion with the people who are suffering ... You are aware also that the hardships caused by the situation are focusing your religious life on what is essential ... You recognize the new depth of the ties established with your Algerian environment in this situation of great tension. This village has not, up to now, been subjected to

the same troubles and attacks as families in the neighbouring villages. There is every reason to think that this is due to your presence, which appears to have spared your neighbours the excesses of the two sides ... You remain aware of the precariousness of your presence which can obviously, at any moment, be called into question by a decision from the security forces, or a change in attitude by the guerillas, or because of new demands which could be made on you. But having taken all this into account, it seems that you accept this situation with serenity, judging that you are able to hang on provided nothing serious happens to change the circumstances.

Following this process, Christian wrote:

At the beginning of Lent we set aside time for a long sharing on the theme: 'During the past eighteen months, what changes have there been within us and between us?' On the face of it nothing had changed: same places, same people! And yet ... although our characters remained the same – our nice side and our rough edges – there was among us a new quality of harmony and mutual acceptance. We'd achieved a greater capacity to listen, thanks to the overwhelming need to work out decisions, and the obvious fact that we had to go forward step by step, in faith. Afterwards, we had a strong feeling of having been inspired and, as it were, accompanied. The danger is there every day, everywhere. Each one knows this, feels this, for himself and for the whole environment in which we are living. The action of grace is also there every day ...

On 8 March 1996 Christian was in Algiers to give a short retreat to a small group of laypeople – students, teachers and civil servants, and some pensioners. Most of them had been born in Algeria, or elsewhere in Africa. Yet the big question for all of them, as much as for any of the European religious, was whether to go or stay. 'Normally,' Christian began, 'a monk can only help his brothers and sisters on their path towards God in his own place, with his community. But it's true that our place is a bit difficult to get to at the moment. Our bishop told me, "It's easier to move the piano-stool than the piano!"' Speaking of how each one of us has a calling from God, he recalled the funeral Mass of Sisters Bibiane and Angèle, murdered the previous September in Belcourt, the working-class district of Algiers where they worked and lived. After Communion the legate specially sent by the Pope had read from the constitutions of the Congregation of Our Lady of the Apostles, to which the two women belonged:

> Article 7: We are ready to risk everything for the Lord. Article 11: In accepting the hardships and difficulties of each day, we will enter into the paschal mystery of death and resurrection inseparable from all apostolic life. Article 13: The ideal of the congregation is to become a seed of hope, of salvation, especially among the poorest of the poor.
>
> I thank you, in the name of the Church, because you have truly lived what is written here. It was not a lifeless document. What the Holy Spirit put in your hearts, as a calling, he also gave you the strength to fulfil, as a call of the Gospel. In fact, it was fulfilled not only in their brutal end. Thirty years living in the Belcourt district, day after day, signified to us and to everyone else thirty years of precisely that faithfulness. Afterwards, the legate wanted to meet the superiors of the religious congregations. He told us: 'The Church ought to be present in all situations without exception, and therefore also in Algeria at the present time. She can be present only through you. Yet she cannot lay any obligation on anyone, other than pointing out to you the consistency between the vows you have taken ... and what you have to live through in these days.[6]

Christian next moved into his main theme of the Church being the continuation of Christ's Incarnation: 'The mystery of the Incarnation remains that which we have to live, and there it seems to me are rooted most deeply our reasons for staying, our reasons for being where we are.' What had he and his brothers done on Christmas Eve 1993, after Sayah Attiyah left? They celebrated the birth of the Prince of Peace, the Christmas Vigils and midnight Mass.

> It was what we had to do, and we did it. Our salvation lay in having to get on with all those everyday realities: the cooking, the gardening, the Office, the bell ... day after day

... We got on with it, saying to ourselves: we are still holding fast today, and then tomorrow, and then the day after tomorrow ... Our bishop helped us. We had to let ourselves be disarmed, renounce that attitude of violence which would have led us to react to the provocation by growing hard.

In a telephone conversation the Cistercian Abbot General Bernardo Olivera (who, Christian stressed, was the guardian of the charism, not the sort of superior who handed down orders) had told him half-jokingly, 'The Order needs monks, not martyrs.' So, 'Was that supposed to mean, "don't put yourselves in a situation of danger"?' If the Order needs monks, surely the real question was, "Does the Order need us to be monks in this reality which we are in? Does the Church need monks in every reality in which she finds herself?" Even, "Does this country need monks? Does this country need us?' ... Well to that, our answer was, "Yes."'[7]

If murder is forbidden, it's because when you kill someone, you kill the image of God. In everyone there is something of the eternal, something which goes beyond homicide, which is why I cannot take revenge ... When, for a quarter of an hour, I had a private conversation with the murderer of the twelve Croats, Sayah Attiyah, who was the big chief of the GIA in our parts, he presented himself as such. He had come to demand certain things. He was armed, a dagger and an automatic pistol. There were six of them altogether, and this was during the night. He began by agreeing to step outside the house, because I didn't want to speak with an armed man in a house dedicated to peace. Once we got outside ... as far as I could see he was no longer carrying the weapons. We stood face to face. He presented three demands and three times I told him no, or 'not like that'. He said: 'You have no choice'; I said: 'Oh but I do have a choice.' Not only because I was the guardian of my brothers, but also because I was also the guardian of this brother who was facing me and who needed to discover within himself something other than what he had become.[8]

Christian explained to the little group how, after the news

broke of Sayah Attiyah's death, when everyone was talking about the guerrillas as 'worthless animals, not human beings' he had tried to imagine what it was like for someone with so much innocent blood on his hands (he was believed to have murdered 145 people) to appear before the face of God. And so he had continued to pray for this man who had threatened his community, pleading with God for Attiyah's soul, making excuses for him. Firstly, the *emir* had held back from killing the monks. Secondly, he had agreed to step out of the house at Christian's request and, although he must have been in agony all those days when he lay wounded and dying, he had not compromised the monastery by sending for help. And thirdly:

> After our conversation in the night, I told him, 'We're getting ready to celebrate Christmas, which for us is the birth of the Prince of Peace – and you come in like this, with weapons!' He replied: 'I'm sorry, I didn't know ...' I'm not trying to do a whitewash ... It's not for me to pass judgement, every one of his crimes is horrendous, but he's not a worthless animal. It's now up to God to exercise his mercy.[9]

Concluding his talk on a very simple note, Christian suggested 'five pillars of peace', all beginning with 'p' to make them easy to remember! They were:

> Patience – Poverty – Presence – Prayer – Pardon. As it happens pardon – forgiveness – is the first name of God in the Litany of the 99 Names, Ar Rahman, Ar Rahma. And patience is the last of the 99, Es Sabour. But God himself is poor, God himself is present, God himself is prayer.[10]

Christian's second six-year term in office was due to end in 1996. Bruno Lemarchand, the superior of the Fez annexe, arrived on 18 March to be present for the election which was scheduled for Palm Sunday. Christian was hoping to step down, but the other brothers thought no one else was ready yet to take over, and he would probably be re-elected. No Ribat meeting had been held for two years, but despite the ongoing insecurity one had been arranged for this spring: the group needed it so much. Three priests and nine women religious arrived on the Feast of the

Annunciation, Monday 25 March, and spent the following day in discussion and reflection. The members present numbered a healthy fifteen since, besides Christian, two of the more recently arrived monks were now regular participants. The other brothers still usually avoided the discussion sessions, but joined in the prayer times. Christian was very late getting to bed that night: the light in his office remained on for some time as he prepared material for the following day. Since Christmas 1993 he had taken to sleeping in his office, on the ground floor, to be on hand if anything happened.

About 1.15 a.m. a monk who slept on the ground floor was wakened by sound of voices in the corridor. Peering round the edge of a curtain he saw a man wearing a turban and carrying a gun, and heard Christian ask, 'Which of you is in charge?' Next he saw Luc come out with his medical bag. He remained in his room, praying quietly, and did not see the raiders go up to the first floor and bring down five more of the brothers. After quickly pillaging some of the rooms they disappeared, and silence fell again on the monastery.

A quick search showed that seven monks were missing – Christian, Luc, Bruno, Michel, Célestin, Paul and Christophe – and the telephone wires were cut. The two remaining brothers, with some of their priest-guests, prayed the rosary together, went back to bed to snatch a few hours' sleep, rose again for Vigils at 5.15 a.m., then sat waiting for dawn. They expected to hear the call to prayer, but it didn't come: the villagers already knew what had happened, and they were too frightened to come to the mosque. Once it was fully light a car set off for Médéa, to report the abduction to the police and phone Mgr Teissier.

For almost a month nothing was heard, but on 18 April a message appeared fly-posted on walls around Tibhirine. The full text of the GIA's 'Communiqué 43' was published a week later in London. A lengthy document, much of it was taken up with attempts to justify the abduction of the Trappists against widespread moral indignation within the Islamic world, and even within other GIA factions. The communiqué ended with an offer to return the monks safe and sound in return for the liberation of imprisoned GIA leaders: 'The choice is yours – release for release. If you refuse, we will cut their throats.'

In mosques throughout Algeria, prayers were offered for the monks' safety. The Pope remembered them during an Eastertide Mass celebrated in Tunis: 'May the risen Christ grant them to see their trial end with their release! May God sustain the Church's hope in this country and guide the Algerian people on the path of peace and reconciliation!' At the Cathedral of Notre Dame in Paris, Cardinal Lustiger presided at a gathering of 2,500, including representatives of the Muslim, Jewish and Protestant communities in France. During this service, which was televised, seven candles brought from Atlas were solemnly lit, to remain burning until the monks were set free. Similar prayer vigils took place all over France. On 7 May Muslim leaders in Paris issued a *fatwa* condemning the indiscriminate violence of the GIA, and the abduction of the monks.

> Dragging them into this political business shows the incapacity and weakness of their abductors, because they have picked on unarmed men without any means of protection ... God says: 'Whoever kills a man who himself has neither killed, nor committed violence upon the earth, will be considered as one who has killed all men; and whoever saves a single man will be considered as having saved all men.'
>
> (Qur'an, sura V, verse 32)

Communiqué 44, issued 21 May, stated that negotiations with the authorities had broken down, and therefore: 'We have cut the throats of the seven monks'. A week later the Algerian police announced that the monks' remains had been found. In Paris, Cardinal Lustiger solemnly extinguished the seven candles: 'We pray for all those who have died in these massacres, for all those whom the monks did not wish to abandon. I am sure that at the last moment, they forgave. Their death must be a sign of hope: love is stronger than hatred. All those who can, I ask to go on praying for peace in Algeria.'

Unsealing the letter which Christian had sent him for safekeeping two years before, Gérard called his mother and the rest of the family together, and read it out to them. They agreed unanimously that they should not keep it for themselves alone, but share it with the whole world.

When an 'A-Dieu' takes on a face
If it should happen one day – and it could be today – that I become a victim of the terrorism which now seems ready to engulf all the foreigners living in Algeria, I would like my community, my Church, my family, to remember that my life was given to God and to this country. I ask them to accept that the Sole Master of all life was not a stranger to this brutal departure. I ask them to pray for me – for how could I be found worthy of such an offering? I ask them to be able to link this death with the many other deaths which were just as violent, but forgotten through indifference and anonymity. My life has no more value than any other. Nor any less value. In any case it has not the innocence of childhood. I have lived long enough to know that I am an accomplice in the evil which seems, alas, to prevail in the world, even in that which would strike me blindly. I should like, when the time comes, to have the moment of lucidity which would allow me to beg forgiveness of God and of my fellow human beings, and at the same time to forgive with all my heart the one who would strike me down.

I could not desire such a death. It seems to me important to state this. I do not see, in fact, how I could rejoice if the people I love were to be accused indiscriminately of my murder. To owe it to an Algerian, whoever he may be, would be too high a price to pay for what will, perhaps, be called the 'grace of martyrdom', especially if he says he is acting in fidelity to what he believes to be Islam. I am aware of the scorn which can be heaped on Algerians indiscriminately. I am also aware of the caricatures of Islam which a certain Islamism encourages. It is too easy to salve one's conscience by identifying this religious way with the fundamentalist ideologies of the extremists. For me, Algeria and Islam are something different: they are a body and a soul. I have proclaimed this often enough, I believe, in the sure knowledge of what I have received from it, finding there so often that true strand of the Gospel, learnt at my mother's knee, my very first Church, already in Algeria itself, in the respect of believing Muslims. My death, clearly, will appear to justify those who hastily judged me naive, or idealistic: 'Let him tell us now what he thinks of it!' But these people must realize that my avid curiosity will then be satisfied. This is what I shall be able to do, if God wills – immerse my gaze in that of the Father, and contemplate with him his children of Islam just as he sees them, all shining with the glory of Christ, the fruit of His Passion, filled with the Gift of the Spirit, whose secret joy will always be to establish communion, and to refashion the likeness, playfully delighting in the differences.

For this life lost, totally mine and totally theirs, I thank God who seems to have willed it entirely for the sake of that joy in everything and in spite of everything. In this thank you, which sums up everything in my life to this moment, I certainly include you, friends of yesterday and today, and you, my friends of this place, along with my mother and father, my sisters and brothers and their families, the hundredfold granted as was promised! And also you, the friend of my final moment, who would not be aware of what you were doing. Yes, I also say this Thank You and this A-Dieu to you, in whom I see the face of God. And may we find each other, happy good thieves, in Paradise, if it pleases God, the Father of us both. Amen! (In sha'Allah)

Algiers, December 1, 1993 – Tibhirine, January 1, 1994
Christian[11]

Notes

1 I have used the following books and articles in compiling my study: Mireille Duteil, *Les martyrs de Tibhirine,* Éditions Brepols, 1996; Robert Masson, *Tibhirine – les veilleurs de l'Atlas,* Paris, Cerf/Saint-Augustin, 1997; Marie-Christine Ray, *Christian de Chergé: Prieur de Tibhirine,* Paris, Bayard Éditions/Centurion, 1999; René Guitton, *Si nous nous taisons ... Le martyre des moines de Tibhirin,* Paris, Calmann-Lévy, 2001; John W Kiser, *The Monks of Tibhirine – Faith, Love and Terror in Algeria,* London/New York, St Martin's Press, 2002. Two important studies by Bernard Olivera, OCSO, the Abbot-General of the Cistercian order – *How Far to Follow?* Petersham, Massachusetts, St Bede's Publications, 1997; 'Monk, Martyr and Mystic: Christian de Chergé (1937–1996)', *Cistercian Studies Quarterly,* vol. 34, no. 3, 1999, pp. 321–38; and the collection by the former abbot of Nunraw Abbey, Scotland Donald

McGlynn, OCSO, *A Heritage Too Big for Us*, Nunraw Abbey, 1997; and 'Atlas Martyrs', *Cistercian Studies Quarterly*, vol. 32. no. 2, 1997, pp. 149–94; and Julian Doherty, OCSO, 'The Wider Horizon of the Algeria of the Heart', *Cistercian Studies Quarterly*, vol. 32, no. 2, 1997, pp. 195–222.
2 Quotations from Christian's writings in *Sept vies pour Dieu et l'Algérie*, Bruno Chenu (ed.), Bayard Éditions/ Centurion, 1996 and *L'invincible espérance Christian de Chergé*, Bayard Éditions/ Centurion, 1997, my translation. Here *L'invincible espérance*, pp. 168–69.
3 Ibid., p. 179.
4 Ibid., pp. 191–93.
5 *Sept vies pour Dieu et l'Algérie*, pp. 166–71.
6 *L'invincible espérance*, pp. 291–92.
7 Ibid., pp. 294–99.
8 Ibid., pp. 308–09.
9 Ibid., pp. 309–10.
10 Ibid., p. 318.
11 *Osservatore Romano* (English edition), April 1996.

Chapter 6

Thomas Merton and Islam

Agnes Wilkins, OSB

Thomas Merton is well known for his pioneering work in the dialogue with Buddhism, but his deep involvement with Islam has gone for the most part unremarked. It has been suggested that the reason for this is the general reluctance of Americans, and Christians in general, to explore the rich religious and cultural heritage of the youngest of the three great monotheistic religions.[1] Why should this be, one wonders? Possibly it is that we can easily understand how other religions would appear *before* Jesus Christ, but the most solemn documents of the Catholic Church tell us that Jesus Christ is the fullness of revelation, and therefore we do not expect another major religion to appear *after* him. And so we are baffled and challenged by Islam, not only by the fact of its appearance at all, but by our profound doctrinal differences. We would much rather avoid confrontation and stay within the confines and safety of the well-worn Christian path. Thomas Merton, however, had no such inhibitions. Indeed he wrote, forty years ago, to a Pakistani Sufi, Abdul Aziz, 'It seems to me that mutual comprehension between Christians and Moslems is something of very vital importance today, and unfortunately it is rare and uncertain ...' [2] Despite some progress, this is still largely true today. There would seem to be an added difficulty for monastics in the wake of Muhammad's declaration that 'there is no monasticism in Islam'. Yet it has been said of Merton that his knowledge of Sufism had reached a point beyond which a non-Muslim could not go.³ This raises the question whether Sufism might not be the Islamic equivalent of monasticism, thus accounting for Merton's ability to relate to it so easily. Could it be that, for Christians, it has the potential to be a very valuable means of penetrating and understanding the spirit of what seems initially to be the very alien world of Islam? We hope to shed some light on this question as we explore Thomas Merton's involvement with Islam, especially as encountered through his relationship with the renowned French Orientalist Louis Massignon.

Thomas Merton and Louis Massignon

Merton's monastic life was sometimes a turbulent affair. Most of it was lived in the period leading up to Vatican II and he saw with piercing clarity the need for reform. Moreover there was the additional complication of his yearning for the hermit life for which he needed the permission of his superiors, a permission they were reluctant to give. It is not surprising therefore, that at the time of his correspondence with Louis Massignon he was on the verge of leaving the monastery. Their relationship began almost by chance through the mediation of Herbert Mason, a young American convert to Catholicism who was in correspondence with Merton, and happened also to be a friend of Louis Massignon. He would write to him enthusiastically about his frequent meetings with Massignon in Paris where they both lived, and Merton was filled with a desire to be in direct contact with this apparently remarkable man. Soon afterwards they were exchanging letters. Massignon sent to Merton his work on the ninth-century Sufi martyr/mystic al-Hallâj by which, according to Mason, he was *bouleversé*.⁴ Later he told Mason that he considered Massignon to be 'the witness of our time', and became convinced that he was a 'prophet-saint'.⁵ Writing to Massignon in March 1960 Merton said, 'How can I begin to write you a letter about the amazing book of the prayers and exhortations of Hallâj? I think it is tremendous ... there is depth and the fire of knowledge of the one God. There is an inexorable force of sanctity. The sense of the Holy that lays one low ... To read Hallâj makes one lament and beat his breast.' and a little later, 'I like al-Hallâj more and more each day.'[6] The two men never actually met in person, and their correspondence spanned a mere two years until the death of Massignon in 1962, but Merton continued to build on all he had learned from the French scholar until his own untimely death in 1968. To put this brief but highly significant correspondence into perspective, we must now outline Massignon's own life and achievements, alas too little known in the English-speaking world even though a recent French publication has described him as a man 'at the heart of our times'[7] and Michael Fitzgerald has called him a 'prophet of dialogue' with Islam.[8]

Just as in the Old Testament a prophet's whole life and ministry was often foreshadowed in his call, (we only have to think of Jeremiah or Isaiah), so Massignon's whole life and destiny were forged in the furnace of his conversion experience. Born in 1883 in Paris, the son of an agnostic father and a Catholic mother, he was baptized against his father's wishes. His mother reared him in the pious style of nineteenth-century France, but by the time he was a teenager he had abandoned his faith and was living a dissolute life, albeit while developing his considerable intellectual gifts. (He eventually became a professor of the Collège de France from 1926 until 1954, and his scholarly output was enormous.) As a young man, before his conversion, his work on one occasion took him to North Africa. He did not know Arabic and was betrayed by an interpreter who grossly misrepresented him. He learnt the language for himself and applied himself with all the ardour of his twenty-one years.[9] He decided to continue his studies in Cairo where he came across some writings of al-Hallâj, the ninth-century Persian mystic. Feeling drawn to him, he made a special study of his life for his doctoral thesis, which obliged him to try and understand Islam from the inside. Soon afterwards, in 1907, there occurred an experience which he attributed to Hallâj's advocacy, together with the prayers of his mother and Charles de Foucauld who had befriended him in North Africa. He was engaged on an archaeological expedition to Mesopotamia which necessitated a boat trip on the River Tigris. It was a Turkish boat and he was the only European on board. Taken for a spy, he was afraid he would be killed and tried to flee, but was caught and taken prisoner. He then feared for his life and was tempted to commit suicide. In addition he was taken ill with a high fever, probably malaria. It was at this point that he had a mysterious encounter with One whom he later called 'the Stranger', because it reminded him of the biblical story of Abraham receiving the three 'strangers', who were angels, at Mamre (Gen. ch. 18). He sensed a presence: 'God loving him and desiring to be loved for himself alone, and for ever'.[10] He wrote later of this experience, 'How I suffered when God converted me! Because I felt that it was my whole life he wanted for himself, and that none of my actions henceforth would escape the notice of his visible Order, the Church.'[11] It would seem that his captors took pity on him for he soon found himself in Baghdad – the place of Hallâj's martyrdom – and was cared for in hospital by a Muslim family; it was an experience of Arab hospitality which moved him profoundly and coloured all his later thought on Muslim/Christian relations. A little later he was reconciled with the Church, returned to France and dedicated his whole life to God.

Charles de Foucauld, who had befriended Massignon, saw him as his successor in the Sahara desert, and it has been said of Massignon that he always thought of himself as if 'entrusted with a mission by de Foucauld to continue his work', that is to say, 'the sanctification of Islam by uninterrupted intercession before God'.[12] However, although he was very much in tune with de Foucauld's spirituality and aspirations, Massignon's own path was to be, exteriorly at least, very different. His life was in fact shaped to a far greater extent by al-Hallâj, the Muslim Sufi who was persecuted and eventually put to death by crucifixion. As he said in a letter to Herbert Mason, commenting on a letter of Merton to himself, 'Tom is not wrong in believing that my thought can be defined to the extent that the "curve of my life" is influenced by the thought of Hallâj'.[13] And another said of him that his extraordinary friendship with Hallâj 'filled his heart and shaped his mind so thoroughly that he can be seen as the greatest Muslim among Christians and the greatest Christian among Muslims'.[14] Not surprisingly he entertained the idea of a religious vocation, but eventually married in 1914, and had three children. However he became a Third Order Franciscan in 1931 and took private vows the following year. In 1934 Massignon formed a religious movement in Cairo with a longtime friend, Mary Kahil; they held regular meetings called *Al-Badaliyya*, an Arabic word which denotes a kind of mystical substitution whereby one prays and fasts for the salvation of others. The group produced a magazine, *Mardis de Dar-es-Salam*, copies of which were sent to Thomas Merton. Massignon's group concentrated particularly on the Muslims under whose political control they lived. The idea of *substitution mystique* was known in nineteenth-century France, for instance in the thought of Huysmans who was personally know to Massignon, but it was, of course, from Hallâj that Massignon chiefly drew his inspiration, and it was in his writings that he found the term *badal*, meaning the acceptance and endurance of the sufferings of another, and the transfer of suffering through compassion. One of the members of this movement, perhaps significantly for the future, was Cardinal Montini of Milan, later Pope Paul VI, who became a close friend of Massignon.[15] In 1950, Massignon, although a married man, became a priest of the Greek Melkite Rite, because for him to offer the Eucharist was the perfect way to integrate his personal act of mystical substitution for others with Christ's own gratuitous act of vicarious suffering for the whole of humanity.

Al-Hallâj then, was more to Massignon than an inspirational figure of the past. He attributed his conversion to him, and considered the fact that it was a Muslim saint leading him back to his native Christianity to be highly significant. He spent the rest of his life, among his other scholarly activities, researching his life and thought, and writing about it for others to benefit.[16] Hallâj and Islam were at the core of his conversion experience, and it was the major part his life's work to make both him and Islam better known and understood. He was fond of saying that it was not he who possessed al-Hallâj but al-Hallâj who had co-opted him. The Muslim mystic captured his fancy when he was a young man living a dissolute life, and on his deathbed he was still exhorting his friends to do whatever they could to make him better known in the world.[17] His personal relationship with Hallâj took him to the very heart of the Muslim world, and arguably his scholarly work on Hallâj has been almost single-handedly responsible for changing the attitude of western scholars towards Islam. Through Hallâj he encountered Muhammad and the Quran, which in turn brought him face-to-face with Abraham, Hagar and Ishmael, recipients of God's blessing and promise. He wrote in a letter to Thomas Merton on 9 September, 1959, that he had the sense of a deep personal relationship with Abraham, whose name he took when he became a Third Order Franciscan. His insights from a Christian perspective living from inside Islam are profound and much needed in our time. As Michael Fitzgerald has said, 'prophets of dialogue' are so because their experience, studies, and teaching have helped us to understand that dialogue is *necessary* in our time, something our faith demands.[18] Massignon more than anyone prepared the way for the positive references to Islam in the Vatican II Declaration *Nostra Aetate*. He died in Paris in 1962 on the eve of the great Council, but he had always advocated a broadening of the doctrinal position of the Catholic Church with regard to Islam, and the several audiences he had with Pope Paul VI, his friend from the early days of the *Badaliyya* movement, surely contributed towards this. The Council confirmed Massignon's work in recognizing that Muslims adore the same God as we do and in recognizing the importance of Abraham as a model of faith. Massignon saw Islam as a mysterious response to the prayer of Abraham for Ishmael, 'Your wife Sarah will bear you a son whom you must name Isaac. And I shall maintain my covenant with him, a covenant in perpetuity, to be his God and the God of his descendants after him. For Ishmael too I grant your request. I hereby bless him and will make him fruitful and exceedingly numerous' (Gen.17:18–20). He pleaded for the recognition of the 'conditional authority' of the Quran and for the partial recognition of Muhammad as a prophet, despite the fact that he declared the divine essence to be absolutely inaccessible to man, thereby implying the impossibility of mystical union. And doctrines such as the Trinity and Incarnation were of course impossible for him to accept, but three centuries after Muhammad they were opened up within Islam by Hallâj. The 'fulfilment' of the work of Muhammad by Hallâj is at the core of Massignon's thought.[19] According to Massignon, 'Muhammad halted at the threshold of the divine fire, not daring "to become" the Burning Bush of Moses; Hallâj took his place out of love'.[20] He personally was convinced that Muhammad was a true prophet, albeit a negative one, summoned to challenge Christians and other religious people to the truth of the natural religion of Abraham and warn them away from their moral errors. For Massignon the Quran points to Christ. He saw it as 'an Arabic edition of the Bible with conditional authority' because in the end it excludes the full revelation of Jesus Christ in the Gospel and in the Church.[21] It poses a challenge of purity of heart for Christians, just as Sufism does for monasticism. Thus Massignon has helped us to see that Islam has a place in God's providence. Christians, including monastics, have undoubtedly fallen short of their calling. Jews can be tempted to think of themselves as especially privileged and the appearance of both Christianity and Islam must be a challenge to them. Islam, despite being the latest of the three, cannot take pride in a sense of superiority since neither Judaism nor Christianity will fit the preconceived ideas it has of them, each continuing to have its own independent spiritual reality. Since pride is the greatest hindrance to a personal relationship with God – which is at the heart of all religion, if not its primary purpose, our mutual incomprehension may well be part of God's plan to teach us humility.

Massignon died on the night of 31 October/1 November 1962. He was a man of many gifts and many faces; an intensely committed Christian, a married man, a highly rated scholar, a friend of the Pope and other prominent Christians of his age such as Teilhard de Chardin and

Jacques Maritain, a Third Order Franciscan and a priest. All his gifts and talents had been devoted unreservedly to the dialogue with Islam, which is of exceptional value because of his inside knowledge. Thomas Merton, in a letter to the Pakistani Sufi Abdul Aziz to whom Massignon had introduced him, said of him after his death,

> The departure of Louis Massignon is a great and terrible loss. He was a man of great comprehension and I was happy to have been numbered among his friends, for this meant entering into an almost prophetic world, in which he habitually moved ... I am touched at the deep respect and understanding that so many Moslems had for him; indeed they understood him perhaps better than many Christians.[22]

In common with Christians in general, however, Massignon could not accept the Quranic view of Jesus Christ. The divine sonship and saving mission of Jesus are fundamental to Christianity, but heresy to Islam. There can be no compromise; it would seem to be the rock on which all attempts at dialogue must ultimately founder. Merton and Massignon probably came as close as anybody to circumnavigating this 'rock', not by avoiding it or denying its existence – dialogue which takes that approach is superficial and basically untrue, but by entering as deeply as possible into the *spirit* of Islam. Merton found his monastic life resonated on a deep level with Sufism, which is not an unusual, esoteric offshoot of Islam, just as monasticism is not so in respect to Christianity. To show the relationship of Sufism to Islam it will be instructive to look at the life of al-Hallâj, the Persian mystic who had such a profound influence on Massignon, after which we will look at the resonances Thomas Merton found between Sufism and his own Christian monasticism.

Hallâj, Sufism and Monasticism

Abu 'Abdallah al-Husayn b. Mansur al-Hallâj, whose name means 'the wool-carder', was born in 858 in Tur, in modern-day Iran, but his father took him at an early age to Iraq where he attended a Sufi school. When he was twenty years old he went to Basra, met a famous Sufi, 'Amr al-Makki, and after a conversion experience officially became a Sufi himself. He married, had three sons and one daughter. (It is thanks to one of his sons that his teaching was put into writing.) He moved to Baghdad in 878 and became the disciple of another celebrated Sufi called Junayd. In 895 he made a pilgrimage to Mecca where he stayed for a year. He then became an itinerant preacher, earning the title – a pun on his name – 'Hallâj-al-asrar', 'the carder of consciences'; an indication of the content of his preaching. He attracted many disciples, but also, perhaps not surprisingly, enemies. He attracted the wrath of theologians, but also of his fellow Sufis, because he would make known to the people at large 'the secret of the way'. In 903 he made a second pilgrimage to Mecca with 400 disciples, after which he undertook a long preaching tour of India and Turkestan, taking his message well beyond the frontiers of the Muslim community. After this he made his third and final visit to Mecca, where he prayed that God would exalt his name through the suffering of his servant. In 909 he returned to Baghdad where he set up a replica of the Ka'aba (the great black stone of Mecca) in his house. By night he would pray there, and during the day he preached in the market place, in the streets, mosques and graveyards, reputedly working miracles of healing. In 913 he was arrested and put in prison, the victim of what was at the time a repressive regime, but also charged with heresy and charlatanism. Eight years later, in 922, he was condemned to death, tortured, crucified and beheaded. He uttered several sentences before his execution, in one of which he is reported to have asked God to be merciful and forgive his enemies. Many years before he had declared, 'I am going to die according to the religion of the Cross'.[23]

Hallâj was not of any particular philosophical bent, but appearing at the beginning of the Sufi movement he prepared the way for later Sufi systems of thought. As an itinerant preacher he emphasized moral regeneration and the life of union in love with God. Orthodox Muslims and even other Sufis, including his teacher Junayd, repudiated him, because he took the doctrine of unity with God to extremes. He said for instance that 'I am the Real' or 'the creative Truth', which understandably was considered blasphemous. The trouble is that in Islam no less than in Christianity, human language is inadequate to express what the mystic has experienced. He also said, in slightly more orthodox language, 'I have become he whom I love, and he has become myself. We are two spirits in one body. When you see me you see him.' There is still a distinction between the divine and the human, but an attempt to get beyond duality. He also said, 'When I saw the Lord with the eye of the heart and asked "Where are you?", he replied, "Yourself"'.[24] In praying for his executioners, but also in his life of poverty and purity, his biographers claimed he followed the example of Jesus, whom Sufis regarded as the 'seal of the saints'.[25]

This brief overview of the life of Hallâj gives us a glimpse into the lived reality of Sufism in one man, albeit an exceptional one. It can be seen that it is compatible with Christianity as a whole as well as certain aspects of monasticism, such as the quest for purity of heart, union with God, and uninterrupted prayer, but can the Sufi movement as a whole bear comparison with the monastic movement in Christianity? Certainly their beginnings were similar, in that they were in part a reaction to the growing success and worldliness of their respective religions. When Christianity became the established religion of the Roman Empire, the challenge of the early centuries when they were a despised minority, frequently persecuted under repressive emperors, was no longer present. Inevitably a certain laxity set in, and many fled to the desert for a more intense and demanding religious life. Similarly Sufism was a reaction to the worldliness resulting from the success of the Arab armies, and was likewise a search for a more pure and inward religion.[26] And just as monasticism can be thought of as a little odd and on the fringes of mainstream Christian life, so the same might be said about Sufism in regard to Islam, but just as monasticism is an expression of the essence of Christianity, more or less present in everybody, so Sufism, despite the fact that it borrowed from early Christian monastic and Indian yoga practices, was a natural development *within* Islam, and also of its essence. This in any case was the opinion of Louis Massignon on conclusion of his researches into the subject.[27] Some writers have denied the existence of mysticism in early Islam because of the 'great gulf' theory between God and man, but this is questionable even in the Quran.[28] Christianity is nothing if not the religion of the nearness of God, primarily in the incarnation of the Son of God, but also because of his continued presence with us through the Church and her sacraments, especially the Eucharist, and the indwelling of the Holy Spirit. In Islam it is Sufism which has the potential to draw together the two extremes of God's transcendence and majesty, the prime emphasis of Islam, and his presence among us, the focus of Christianity.

When Thomas Merton first discovered Sufism it was an almost unknown phenomenon in the West. Nowadays the name is familiar to most people, if not the reality. Scholars in the field of Islamic studies do not agree what the term means, or how the Sufi way of life originated, but in his own discovery of it there can be no doubt that Merton felt he was entering a spiritual universe parallel to his own. It was around Islam's third century (our ninth) that certain people called themselves 'Sufis' for the first time. The same people were also sometimes called 'knowers' 'ascetics', or 'renouncers'. The last two names especially were also used of early Christian monks. The reality of Sufism is too subtle and elusive to lend itself to neat delineation and classification, but William C. Chittick, Professor of Comparative Religious Studies at the State University of New York, has given a helpful analysis of how it fits into Islam as a whole.[29] Islam, he says, has three basic dimensions; practice, knowledge and interiority, which can be thought of as its body, mind and heart. The first level concerns externals such as right and wrong practice, rituals etc. It finds its chief expression in the *shariah*, a great compendium of systematic law based on the Quran. The second level is concerned with understanding, its fundamental focus being on how to understand the objects of faith such as God, angels, Scripture, the prophets etc. The third and deepest level is what happens in the heart. Here Islam teaches people to transform themselves so that they may come into harmony with all being. Neither activity (the first level) nor understanding (the second level), are sufficient of themselves. For those sensitive to the interior life, the various terms that are employed in discussing the focus of this third dimension are immediately recognizable as the *raison d'être* of religion itself. It is Sufism which corresponds to this third level, which could be roughly understood to refer to the inner life of practising Muslims, an essential part of their religious experience; 'the secret quest for God in the inner castle'.[30] This is true even though the name itself has become suspect among modern-day Muslims.

Thomas Merton's knowledge of Islam was basic, but he had no difficulty in cutting through the obfuscations of scholars to get to its heart. After the death of Massignon he continued deepening his knowledge through reading and personal contacts. Remarkable among the latter was his friendship with the Pakistani Sufi Abdul Aziz, to whom Massignon had introduced him. They continued to correspond and exchange books of mutual interest right up to the time of Merton's death in 1968.[31] Interestingly there was one book that Merton declined to share, and that was one of his very first works after entering the monastery, namely *Seeds of Contemplation*, in which he spoke of 'the sensual dreams of the Sufis as a poor substitute for the true contemplation that is found only in the Church'.[32] The brief excerpts that follow, of conferences Merton gave to the novices at Gethsemani in the last two years of his life, are a measure of how far he had travelled in his own monastic life enriched and broadened by his private reading (*lectio divina*) and the relationships he had developed, especially his friendship with Louis Massignon. The style is inimitably his own, delightfully informal, at times humorous; casual but profound. It would be surprising if the novices did not find them highly enjoyable as well as enlightening. They show that he understood the deep and significant relationships between Christianity and Islam, and especially between Sufism and his own contemplative life.

> So the basic idea of Islam is this union of God and man, God manifesting himself in the world created by him, and man in the world as the one who has the job of knowing that God is manifesting his love in him and in the world, and of responding to that knowledge. And man is granted the gifts of intelligence and freedom and speech in order to respond to Allah's love ...[33]

It is to be remembered that these are taped lectures devoid of his usual literary polish.

> You are here to seek God, and any ordinary monk can deepen his knowledge of God by living the monastic life. This is assumed in these talks, so get rid of your despair which you have been nourishing now for some time. Get rid of it and stir up your hope ... God isn't all that hidden. He didn't bring us here out of a kind of trick. He didn't lure us here to get us in this box in order to ... torture us for the rest of our lives. He brought us here for real, and He wills that we know Him.[34]

In another talk he says,

> The Muslims place an enormous amount of importance to the Names of God. See they've got the idea that these Names are in God clamouring to the invisible, unknown, absolute abyss of God for manifestation. And God breathes on them and they are manifest in creatures. All creatures are not manifestations of the Hidden Essence of God, they are manifestations of Names of God. And the Name of God which is top of the pyramid [other than Allah] and which includes every other Name is Merciful. The Mercy of God in everything. And of course one of the chief Christian Sufis of the last hundred years is Saint Thérèse. The Little Way of St Thérèse is Sufism. It's a form of Christian Sufism, and it is based on this particular attitude toward God, this idea of God.[35]

And on the same topic,

> So, a saying of the Prophet [relating to God's words]: 'I was a Hidden Treasure', he says, 'and I loved to be known, I desired to be known.' The word for 'loved to be known'/'desired to be known' here is the same kind of word that our Lord uses in the Gospel, 'with desire I have desired to eat this Pasch with you,' this sort of thing, this intense desire of God to make Himself known as He is to His creatures, as Merciful to His creatures. And the duration of Mercy is an intensely personal relationship. 'Accordingly I created the creatures, and thereby made Myself known to them, and they did come to know Me. I was a hidden treasure and I loved to be known. Accordingly I created the creatures and made Myself known to them and they did come to know Me.' That's Islam in a nutshell. God wishing to make himself known to His creatures and He makes creatures that they may know Him ... Everything that happens is love and is mercy. Not that it always appears to be that way, very often it appears to be just the opposite. But everything that happens is love. And of course the ones in Islam who emphasize this the most are the Sufis, because the great thing in Sufism is Love.[36]

And again on the monastic life,

> You come to a monastery because you are looking for something, and you stay here because you are looking for it, and the whole thing about it is that you believe that there is a point to this search and when you get away from this search ... you begin to hear the voice, 'This isn't the job you're supposed to be doing. Get back on the track of what you are looking for. Do the thing you are supposed to be doing.' ... Once a person has received from God the charge to seek what he has to seek, then he puts everything else aside and seeks it. On the basis of a truth like this you get a Sufi and you get a monk.[37]

One could go on, but the above examples are enough to demonstrate how easily Merton passed between Sufism and monasticism.

What is it about monasticism, we may ask, that enables it

to enter into the spirit of another religion in a way Christianity as a whole seemingly cannot? The answer may be its universalism, by which we mean that there is a *monastic archetype*, or what we might call a contemplative dimension, however undeveloped, in every human being. When it comes to fruition one of the ways in which it expresses itself is the institutional monasticism which varies in expression from age to age and from culture to culture. It could be identified with Karl Rahner's 'supernatural existential'. This phrase was coined by him in the theological debate about nature and grace to encapsulate his view that grace is not something 'added on', but our human nature is 'graced' simply by virtue of being human. The universal nature of monasticism is brought out by Frithjof Schuon (1907–1998) a Swiss specialist in comparative religion, in an essay which greatly appealed to Merton called *The Universality of Monasticism and its Relevance for the Modern World*.[38] In it he makes the point strongly that monasticism is not something strange and esoteric, but fundamental to human nature. The monk's mission, he says, is 'to remind men what man is'. He is not a being apart but 'a prototype, or a model, or a spiritual specification, a landmark'. For 'man is fully man only in rising above himself'. And he turns our normal perception on its head by the statement, 'It is not monasticism that is situated outside the world, it is the world that is situated outside monasticism'.[39] Thus monasticism has a universal and inter-religious character on the grounds that the 'supernatural' is in the nature of man, whether or not it finds expression in a particular form. Christian monasticism possesses this universal character but also something specifically Christian, namely, its all-absorbing Christocentrism which implies the exclusion of all 'worldly' pursuits; marriage, career, having children etc. But what about Islam? We have seen that Sufism could be described as the monasticism of Islam, but Schuon goes further. He declares that the *raison d'être* of Islam is precisely the possibility of a 'monastic society', because it aims to carry the contemplative life into the very framework of society as a whole.[40] And indeed the regular calls to prayer, the fasting, the special robes and the orderly prostrations have a real monastic 'feel' about them. It succeeds in realising the conditions of structure and behaviour that permit of a contemplative isolation in the very midst of the activities of the world. What corresponds to the monastery for the Muslim is above all 'attachment to a brotherhood, submission to a spiritual father, vigils and fasts', and the isolating element with respect to the world is observance of the *sunna*. So 'no monasticism in Islam', says Schuon, really means that the contemplative must not withdraw from the world, but on the contrary that the world must not be withdrawn from contemplatives.[41]

Monastic Bridges

Thomas Merton discovered that his contemplative life could be a 'bridge' to the heart of other religions. His particular genius was with Zen Buddhism, but we now have ample evidence that his monastic life also aided the dialogue with Islam. Here we shall look briefly at three points of contact that he discovered; the story of Hagar and Ismael, the Sufi practice of *dhikr* ('remembrance'), and *le point vierge* (the virgin point).

In a letter to Louis Massignon after receiving one of the issues of the *Mardis de Dar-es-Salam*, he said, 'I was above all deeply moved by your own short meditations on the desert and the God of Agar and Ismael'.[42] It is not difficult to imagine what ideal monastic *lectio divina* such meditations would make. A Belgian monk of Clervaux, Louis Leloir, writing almost twenty years after Merton's death, has called this story found in the book of Genesis, which is also foundational to Islam, a 'source-event' and 'the first draft of a spirituality of the desert'.[43] The Mesopotamian image of the desert was of a fearsome place, inhospitable and the abode of outlaws, but it becomes in this episode the place of divine encounter, the place where Hagar, cast out by Abraham because of the jealousy of Sarah, meets the angel of God (that is, God himself). It is the place of her humiliation which opens her to God, as the desert of the monastery is for the monk. It is the place of poverty and dependence on divine providence. Hagar, with the son whom she had been commanded to name Ishmael 'because Adonai has heard thy humiliation' (Gen.16:11) was blessed in her banishment and promised descendants too numerous to be counted. The desert of the monastery, where there is no begetting of children, should be a place of spiritual fertility for the world.

Another theme of great interest to Merton was that of remembrance of God. There is a Sufi prayer method called *dhikr* (in Arabic, 'remembrance', 'recollection' or 'invocation'), which is 'the very heart of Islamic practice'.[44] Merton spent a considerable amount of time studying *dhikr*, as is evidenced in his letters to Abdul Aziz and his talks to the novices at Gethsemani. He saw it as a parallel to the Jesus Prayer; 'Lord Jesus Christ, Son of God, have mercy on me a sinner', so characteristic of Orthodox spirituality and especially associated with Mount Athos. It is an attempt to put into practice the biblical injunction to 'pray unceasingly' (1 Thes. 5:17) and has been called the 'prayer of the heart' because as it is repeatedly recited with the lips it eventually penetrates the heart, transforms it, and continues of its own accord; a continuous plea for the mercy of God. Merton's conjunction of *dhikr* and hesychasm is a perfect example of the way he penetrated to the heart of another religious tradition.[45]

The third bridge is created by that evocative phrase of Merton's, *le point vierge*. He wrote in *Conjectures of a Guilty Bystander*,

> Again, that expression, *le point vierge* (I cannot translate it).
> At the centre of our being is a point of nothingness which is untouched by sin and by illusion, a point of pure truth, a point or spark which belongs entirely to God, which is never at our disposal, from which God disposes of our lives, which is inaccessible to the fantasies of our own mind or the brutalities of our own will. This little point of nothingness and of *absolute poverty* is the pure glory of God in us. It is so to speak His name written in us, as our poverty, as our indigence, as our dependence, as our sonship. It is like a pure diamond, blazing with the invisible light of heaven. It is in everybody, and if we could see it we would see these billions

of points of light coming together in the face and blaze of a sun that would make all the darkness and cruelty of life vanish completely ... I have no programme for this seeing. It is only given. But the gate of heaven is everywhere.

He says in the same context, 'There is no way of telling people that they are all walking around shining like the sun.' He describes his own great joy in simply being a human being because of this *point vierge* and wished that everyone could see themselves as they really are. He knows because of a mystical experience he had one day among a crowd of people in Louisville. It was as if he suddenly saw 'the secret beauty of their hearts, the depths of their hearts where neither sin nor desire nor self-knowledge can reach, the core of their reality, the person that each one is in God's eyes ...'[46] Merton first came across the phrase *point vierge* in an article by Massignon called 'Foucauld au Désert: devant le Dieu de Abraham, Agar et Ismail', published in an issue of *Les Mardis de Dar-es-Salam*.[47] He made this evocative expression inimitably his own, as for instance in another passage of *Conjectures of a Guilty Bystander*,

> The first chirps of the waking day birds mark the *point vierge* of the dawn under a sky as yet without real light, a moment of awe and inexpressible innocence, when the Father in perfect silence opens their eyes. They begin to speak to him, not with fluent song, but with an awakening question that is their dawn state, their state at the *point vierge*. Their condition asks if it is time for them to 'be'. He answers 'yes'. Then, they one by one wake up, and become birds.[48]

And in a letter to Abdul Aziz (30 January 1961) he spoke of the dawn as 'the time when the world is silent and the new light is most pure, symbolizing the dawning of divine light in the stillness of our hearts'. It was the time when he usually said Mass in a remote part of the monastery.[49]

Merton encountered the expression *le point vierge* through Louis Massignon, but to appreciate its relevance as a bridge it is important to realize that Massignon first came across it in his study of al-Hallâj, and in turn made it *his* own. Hallâj saw the spiritual path as a gradual purification of the heart through the destroying of the 'veils' surrounding it until we reach God. The final veil is the *sirr*, that is, the latent personality, implicit consciousness, the deep subconscious, the secret cell walled up and hidden to every creature, the 'inviolate virgin'. The 'virgin point' in Massignon's parlance is the last, irreducible, secret centre of the heart. He used the phrase in his own way as Merton did. For instance, the faith of Abraham was the true *point vierge*, that is, the very axis, of Islamic teaching.[50] Hallâj's teaching is grounded firmly in the Quran which says that the heart is the organ prepared by God for contemplation. It is also the place where our conscience is formed and where we experience the sacred. However, according to Massignon, Hallâj went beyond the Quran when he spoke of the latent personality ... the inviolate virgin, and of a 'secret, holy place, in each one of us, always entire and intact, whether we be rich or poor, erudite or illiterate, whether or not we deserve it. Our fears and sufferings make no difference to its presence, nor does our habit of going in the opposite direction, or even our evil desires. The *point vierge* is a call to recognize the Transcendent within us and overcome our illusions of power and authority'.[51]

When Thomas Merton first discovered Sufism he was in a state of crisis, intent on leaving the monastery at all costs. We do not know what made him change his mind, but we do know that he was on the brink of an exciting discovery. Through his correspondence with Massignon he was brought face to face with the unfamiliar world of Islam, and he found that he was at home, not in spite of his monastic way of life, but because of it. And he found what might be called the *point vierge* of his own monastic life in the hermitage which was given to him in the grounds of Gethsemani. From there he wrote to his friend Dom Jean Leclercq, 'For the first time in twenty-five years I feel I am leading a really *monastic* life. All that I had hoped to find in solitude is really here ... It is good to have this silence and peace to be able to get down to the *unum necessarium*'.[52] In his own secret cell in the woods of Kentucky, and in the *point vierge* of his heart, his life expanded to include all mankind, for he said about the same time, 'Literature,

contemplative solitude, Latin America, Asia, Zen, Islam, etc
... all these come together in my life. To me it would be
madness to live my monastic life while excluding all these.
I would be less a monk'.[52]

Notes

1 See the article by Bonnie Thurston, 'Thomas Merton's Interest in Islam', in *The American Benedictine Review*, vol. 45, no. 2 (1994), p. 131.
2 Ibid., Letter of 26 Dec., 1962.
3 Burton B. Thurston, 'Merton's Reflections on Sufism', in *The Merton Seasonal* 15, 1990, 4. Quoted on p. 132.
4 See Herbert Mason, 'Massignon and Merton', in *Louis Massignon au Coeur de Notre Temps*, Paris, Editions Karthala, 1999, pp. 247–58, here p. 248. French translation in the same volume, Massignon et Merton, pp. 351–62.
5 Ibid., p. 249 and p. 255.
6 *Witness to Freedom: The letters of Thomas Merton in Times of Crisis*, selected and edited by William H. Shannon, New York and London, Harcourt, Brace & Co., 1994, p. 276 (18 March 1960) and p. 277, 12 May 1960.
7 Herbert Mason, 'Massignon and Merton', op. cit., p. 248.
8 Archbishop, Michael L. Fitzgerald, 'Les prophètes du dialogue', in *En Hommage au Père Jacques Jomier, OP*, Etudes réunis et coordonnées par Marie-Thérèse Urvoy, Paris, Les Editions du Cerf, 2002, pp. 19–30; and in English, 'The Prophets of Dialogue: Massignon, Monchanin and Merton', *The Merton Journal*, vol. 11, no. 1, 2004, pp. 34–40.
9 Details of Massignon's life are taken from Fitzgerald, *Les prophètes du dialogue* op. cit., pp. 19–30; Anthony O'Mahony, 'Christianity and Islam in the Thought of Louis Massignon', in *The Merton Journal*, vol. 10, no. 2, 2003, pp. 4–12; and Sidney H. Griffiths, 'Merton, Massignon and the Challenge of Islam', in *Merton and Sufism: The Untold Story, A Complete Compendium*, Louisville, Kentucky, Fons Vitae, 1999, pp. 52–63. This study was originally published as S. H. Griffiths, 'Merton, Massignon and the Challenge of Islam', *The Merton Annual: Studies in Thomas Merton, Religion, Culture, Literature and Social Concerns*, vol. 3, 1990, pp. 151–72. See also the recent study by S. H. Griffiths, 'Mystics and Sufi Masters: Thomas Merton and Dialogue between Christians and Muslims', *Islam and Christian-Muslim Relations*, vol. 15, no. 3, 2004, pp. 299–316.

10 Fitzgerald, 'Les prophètes du dialogue', op. cit., p. 21.
11 J. Petit (ed.), *Claudel-Massignon* (1908–1914), in *Les Grandes Correspondances*, Desclée de Brouwer, 1973, p. 91, quoted by Dorothy C. Buck, 'Le Thème du Point Vierge dans les Ecrits de Louis Massignon', in *Louis Massignon au Coeur de Notre Temps*, Paris, Editions Karthala, 1999, p. 279–86, here p. 279.
12 Fitzgerald, 'Les prophètes du dialogue', op. cit., p. 21, quoting Abbé Guy Harpigny, *Islam et Christianisme selon Louis Massignon*, Louvain-la-Neuve, Homo Religiosus, 1981, p. 77.
13 Herbert Mason, *Memoir of a Friend: Louis Massignon*, Notre Dame, Indiana University of Notre Dame Press, 1988, p. 152. Quoted by Sydney H. Griffiths, 'Un entretien sur toutes choses humaines et divines au travers de la correspondance de Louis Massignon et de Thomas Merton', in *Louis Massignon au Coeur de Notre Temps*, Paris, Editions Karthala, 1999, pp. 259–78, here p. 265.
14 See A. O'Mahony, 'Christianity and Islam in the Thought of Louis Massignon', op. cit. p. 7.
15 See Introduction to Massignon's letters to Thomas Merton in *Witness to Freedom: The Letters of Thomas Merton in Times of Crisis*, p. 275.
16 His dissertation for the Sorbonne was published as *La Passion d'al-Hosayn-ibn Mansour al-Hallâj, martyre mystique de l'Islam*, Paris, Geuthner, 1922, first edition, 2 vols. Massignon continued to work on a new edition of this work until his death in 1962. After his death, the new edition was assembled by a group of scholars working together with the Massignon family and friends, which was published as: *La Passion de Husayn ibn Mansur Hallâj, martyre mystique de l'Islam*, Paris, Gallimard, 1975, second edition, 4 vols. The second edition was translated into English by Herbert Mason as: *The Passion of al-Hallâj: Mystic and Martyr of Islam* Bollingen Series XCVIII. Princeton University Press, 1982, 4 volumes.
17 See Sydney H. Griffiths, 'Merton, Massignon and the Challenge of Islam', in *Merton and Sufism* op. cit., p. 69.
18 Fitzgerald, *Les prophètes du dialogue* op. cit., p. 20.
19 See O'Mahony, *Christianity and Islam in the Thought of Louis Massignon*, op. cit., p. 8.
20 From *Massignon* J-F Six (ed.), Paris, L'Herne, 1970, p. 156. Quoted by S. H. Griffiths, 'Merton, Massignon and the Challenge of Islam', in *Merton and Sufism* op. cit., p. 70.
21 S. H. Griffiths, 'Merton, Massignon and the Challenge of Islam', in *Merton and Sufism*, ibid., pp. 71, 72.
22 S.H. Griffiths, 'Merton, Massignon and the Challenge of Islam', in *Merton and Sufism*, ibid., p. 63.
23 Louis Massignon, 'Hallâj: Mystic and Martyr' quoted in Chawcat

Moucarry, *Faith to Faith: Christianity and Islam in Dialogue*, Inter-Varsity Press, Leicester, 2001, p. 298.
24 Louis Massignon, 'Le Diwan d'al-Hallâj', (1955), quoted in Geoffrey Parrinder, *Mysticism in the World's Religions*, Sheldon Press, London, 1976, p. 135.
25 Parrinder, *Mysticism in the World's Religions*, op. cit., p. 135.
26 This is the opinion of Geoffrey Parrinder, *Mysticism in the World's Religions*, op. cit., 130. Ninian Smart expresses the same view in *World Philosophies*, London, Routledge, 1999, p. 161.
27 See Parrinder, *Mysticism in the World's Religions*, op. cit., p. 129. We are referred to Massignon's work, *Essai sur les Origines du Lexique Technique de la Mystique Musulmane*, 1954.
28 Parrinder, *Mysticism in the World's Religions*, p. 131.
29 William C. Chittick, 'Sufism: Name and Reality', in *Merton and Sufism*, pp. 15–31.
30 Ibid., p. 31.
31 Excerpts from this correspondence with commentary are provided by Sidney H. Griffiths, 'As One Spiritual Man to Another: The Merton-Abdul Aziz Correspondence', in *Merton and Sufism*, pp. 101–29.
32 Griffiths, 'As One Spiritual Man to Another: The Merton-Abdul Aziz Correspondence', p. 102. Thomas Merton's *Seeds of Contemplation* was published in New York by New Directions in 1949.
33 Bernadette Dieker, 'Merton's Sufi Lectures to Cistercian Novices, 1966–68', *Merton and Sufism: The Untold Story*, p. 130.
34 Ibid., p. 136.
35 Ibid., p. 138.
36 Ibid., p. 141.
37 Ibid., p. 147.
38 Frithjof Schuon, 'The Universality of Monasticism and Its Relevance in the Modern World' in *Merton and Sufism: The Untold Story*, pp. 319–34.
39 Ibid., pp. 321, 333.
40 Ibid., p. 322.
41 Ibid.
42 Letter of 20 July, in *Witness to Freedom: the Letters of Thomas Merton in Times of Crisis*, p. 278.
43 'Hagar the Egyptian's Flight to the Desert', in *Monastic Studies*, published by the Benedictine Priory of Montreal, no. 16, 1985, p. 93.
44 Seyyed Hossein Nasr, *'God' in Islamic Spirituality*, New York, Crossroads, 1987, p. 318. Quoted by Bonnie Thurston, 'Thomas

Merton's Interest in Islam: the Example of Dhikr, Merton and Sufism: The Untold Story', p. 318.
45 See Ibid., p. 47.
46 Thomas Merton, *Conjectures of a Guilty Bystander*, Sheldon Press, London, 1965, pp. 153–55.
47 An issue published in 1958–59, 57–71. Reproduced in Louis Massignon, *Opera Minora*, Beirut, Dar al-Maaref, 1970, vol. III, pp. 772–84.
48 Thomas Merton, *Conjectures of a Guilty Bystander*, p. 128.
49 See Sydney H. Griffiths, 'As One Spiritual Man to Another: The Merton-Abdul Aziz Correspondence', in *Merton and Sufism: The Untold Story*, p. 105.
50 See Sydney H. Griffiths, 'Merton, Massignon and the Challenge of Islam', in *Merton and Sufism: The Untold Story*, pp. 64–66
51 Louis Massignon, 1983, vol. II and vol. III of *The Passion of Al-Hallâj*, Herbert Mason (tr.), Princeton, NJ, Princeton University Press. See Dorothy Buck, 'Le Thème du Point Vierge dans Les Ecrits de Louis Massignon', in *Louis Massignon au Coeur de Notre Temps*, p. 281.
52 Letter dated 18 Sept., 1965, in Patrick Hart , 'Jean Leclercq and Thomas Merton: a Monastic Exchange of Letters', in *Monastic Studies*, no. 16, 1985, pp. 74, 75.
53 Journal, 10 July, 1964. See Sidney H. Griffiths, 'Un Entretien sur les Choses Humaines et Divines' au travers de la correspondance de Louis Massignon et de Thomas Merton', in *Louis Massignon au Coeur de Notre Temps*, p. 270.

Chapter 7

Francis and the Sultan: A model for contemporary Christian engagement with Islam

Steven Saxby

Introduction
Living and working in an area with a large Muslim population and a steady proliferation of new mosques and Islamic bookshops, I have naturally found myself challenged by Islam and challenged too by how to engage with it in a way that is faithful to my Christian convictions. Studying 'inter-religious dialogue' has left me dissatisfied with what the established models of 'exclusivism', 'inclusivism' and 'pluralism' have to offer and eager to explore alternatives. I hope this essay will be of some help to Christians who share my experience. My attraction to St Francis is personal, rooted in an encounter with the Anglican Franciscans who live in the street where I was born, but the story of Saint Francis and his encounter with the Sultan of Egypt seems to ring out with wider significance for our times. Within the 'post-modern context' of the threefold paradigm being open to question,[1] Francis seems to offer a model of engagement with Islam that is clearly rooted in the Christian tradition and yet able to display both respect and openness to 'the other'.

I shall explore the model in three steps: first, I shall pay close attention to the context in which the encounter took place; second, I shall seek to provide a relatively comprehensive and unbiased overview of the various accounts of

Francis' meeting with Malik al-Kamil; and, finally, I shall seek to discover what motivated the Saint to visit the Sultan. I shall conclude that Francis was motivated by a desire to witness to the Christian faith, even to the point of martyrdom, and that his approach represented a radically different relationship with Muslims from that of his contemporaries. Indeed, I shall argue that Francis was sufficiently open to the religious 'other' not only to learn from his experience but also to use it for the benefit of further Christian witness. In summary I shall suggest that St Francis' encounter with Malik al-Kamil represents a model for contemporary Christian engagement with Islam.

The context of Francis' encounter with the Sultan

Before considering the various early accounts of Francis' encounter with Malik al-Kamil, I shall attempt to enumerate the context within which the meeting took place. It is important to take stock of the wider developments that led to the encounter, as well as some of the specific circumstances and personalities that were involved, in order to fully appreciate its significance. First, of course, it will be useful to present even a bare sketch of the life of St Francis of Assisi up to the point of his encounter with the Sultan of Egypt. He was born in 1181/2 in the Umbrian town of Assisi, the son of a wealthy merchant and his French wife. He was nicknamed 'Francesco' (Frenchie) and as a young man dreamed of becoming a knight. However, when he suffered the ignominy of being captured and imprisoned while fighting for Assisi against the nearby city of Perugia, he returned a changed man and he took to caring for the poor, especially those with leprosy. In 1206 he had his most dramatic conversion experience when, in the Church of San Damiano in Assisi, he distinctly heard the words 'Go and rebuild my Church'. Francis took to this task, embracing a life of poverty and attention to the Gospel. Others joined him as brothers and they committed themselves to a very simple but stark rule of life, calling themselves 'friars minor'. The order grew rapidly, such that it had already spread throughout Europe by the time of Francis' death in

1226. Indeed Francis had already sent brothers to Syria and Morocco in advance of his own journey to meet the Sultan at Damietta in 1219.[2]

Next, it is necessary to very briefly remind ourselves of the history of Christian-Muslim enmity up to the period of the encounter between the Saint and the Sultan, a history within which the encounter itself was quite exceptional. As Hugh Goddard's *History of Christian-Muslim Relations* reminds us, it is by no means the case that these relations are inevitably adversarial. For sure, the relationship has been 'long and tortuous' and 'the balance of power between the communities has swung backwards and forwards', but as well as conflict 'history itself points to the existence of a more positive irenical way of thinking among both Muslims and Christians at certain stages of history'.[3] Within the complex and diverse history of this relationship, it is obvious that the Crusades mark the period of most bitter tension, indeed of outright war, between Christians and Muslims. Goddard charts the course of the first four Crusades in the following way. Pope Urban II preached the Crusade in 1095, responding to an appeal from the Byzantine emperor after the loss of most of his Asian territories to the Seljuk Turks in 1071. Urban II added the liberation of Jerusalem to the Crusaders' task, giving it a religious as well as a political dimension. Princes from all over Europe responded to the call and five armies of some 50–60,000 men set off for the Orient in 1096. They encountered some losses but also spectacular success, capturing Antioch in 1098 and Jerusalem in 1099. By 1144 the Crusaders had lost some of the territory they had gained leading to a call for a Second Crusade, this preached by Bernard of Clairvaux in 1146. Disaster struck in 1187 when Salah al din (Saladin), who had united Egypt and Syria under his command, captured Jerusalem and began extending his rule throughout Palestine. A Third Crusade (issued by Gregory VIII in 1187) saw Richard I (the Lionheart) take Cyprus, Acre and other coastal ports, but otherwise saw little success. The Fourth Crusade led further east to where the Frankish Crusaders sacked Constantinople in 1204.[4]

If the four previous Crusades set the warring context for further Crusades, there was also a developing religious justification for the Crusades that had particular importance in relation to the call for the fifth one. Innocent III had called for the Fourth Crusade in 1198, during the first year of his papacy. For him it had been a failure since it had done nothing towards the cause of restoring the Holy Land to Christendom. This is part of the context for Innocent III's call in 1213 for a renewed Crusade, the date of which was set for 1217 at the Fourth Lateran Council in 1215.[5] Indeed, Innocent went to unprecedented lengths for the papacy in publishing both theological justification and practical incentive for the Fifth Crusade in his Encyclical *Quia Maior*. Moreover, as Mico points out, Innocent III was calling for more than just the restitution of the Holy Places. Mico writes that Innocent saw Islam as 'essentially evil', in Innocent's words, 'a diabolical force and the irreconcilable enemy of Christianity'.[6] Riley Smith suggests that Innocent III was 'obsessed by the Crusades' and makes the important observation that

> The crusading movement is often treated as an eleventh- and twelfth-century phenomenon that went into rapid decline in the thirteenth. But in fact no period can equal the activity of the eighty-seven years from 1187 to 1274, in almost every one of which a crusade was being waged somewhere.[7]

Basetti-Sani even suggested that Innocent's contemporaries 'believed the Crusades were to destroy Islam and realize the prophecy of the Apocalypse – the number 666 was interpreted as being the allotted span of the Muslim religion'.[8] According to this view, the end of Islam would have been expected in 1277. As it happened, Innocent died suddenly in 1216 but Honorius III, appointed Pope two days after Innocent's death, was just as passionate about embarking on a Fifth Crusade.[9] Meanwhile, the Muslim leadership also changed when Saladin's nephew, Malik al-Kamil, (1180–1238) succeeded his father as Sultan of Egypt in 1218.

It was in 1218 that the Crusaders arrived in Egypt and began the siege of Damietta. The city stood on the east side of the Phatnitic branch of the Nile, near to its opening on to the Mediterranean Sea. The Muslim armies were camped directly outside the city, with the Crusaders camped on the opposite side of the river. The siege lasted for fifteen months and included several defeats for the Crusaders before they captured the city in November 1219 (only for it to be recaptured by Malik al Kamil in 1221, captured by the Crusaders again in 1249, surrendered by the Christians in 1250 and largely destroyed by the then Sultan in 1251). Some assume that Francis arrived directly in Egypt from Italy and was in Damietta as early as late July.[10] Roncaglia's research reveals the view that Francis left Italy on the Feast of St John (24 June) 1219, departing on board a fleet bound for the Crusades. He suggests the crossing lasted a month before reaching the Crusader-controlled port of Acre in Syria (where Francis may have met the brothers he had previously sent there) and then resuming its route to bring aid to the Crusaders at Damietta.[11] One of the defeats suffered by the Crusaders prior to capturing Damietta was on 29 August 1219[12] and most commentators agree that Francis had reached the Crusader camp by that time. Yet regardless of which route Francis took and in which month he arrived, it is clear that Francis' visit was to a place and at a time of considerable historical significance.

All accounts of Francis' time in Damietta agree that he set out with the deliberate intention of making contact with the 'Saracens'. Here I shall use the term Saracens consciously, only because Francis used it in his own writings. Hoeberichts points out that the etymological origin of the word is uncertain, but that from the sixth century it had been applied to the ethnic inhabitants of the Arab peninsula whether Christian or pagan. It was later applied to the Arabs after they had become Muslim without any negative connotations. It only became synonymous with the Muslims as enemies of Christianity after the repeated attacks by Muslims on Italy during the ninth century.[13] However negatively or otherwise Francis viewed the term, it was to the

'Saracens' that he felt compelled to go and tradition has it that he made other attempts to do so before 1219. Thomas of Celano's *First Life* of St Francis written in 1228–29 tells of a previous attempt to reach Acre, essentially the gateway to the Saracens.[14] This was said to be in the sixth year of Francis' conversion (probably 1212) but was frustrated by winds that blew in an opposite direction, bringing Francis ashore on the other side of the Adriatic in Dalmatia (present day Slavonia).[15] After returning to Italy, he made another attempt to reach the Saracens described by Celano in the same account. Celano writes that Francis set out on foot for Morocco to see the Muslim leader there, the Miramamolin, but fell ill in Spain and was once again forced to return to Italy.[16] Roncaglia and others speculate that this trip was in 1213.[17] Celano's account is repeated by Julian of Speyer in his *The Life of Saint Francis*.[18] Both attempts emphasize Francis' desire to go among the Saracen's, a desire only realized in 1219.

Lemmens' article *De Santo Francisco Christum Praedicante Coram Sultano Aegypti* of 1926 established what has become the widely accepted view about Francis' movements after arriving in Egypt.[19] Lemmens follows the accounts of Jacques de Vitry, Ernoul and the Bollandist Suyskenus that Francis entered the Muslim camp shortly after the defeat of 29 August 1219 and was with the Sultan in September. If so, the encounter, which we assume lasted no more than a few days, may have been during a three-week truce sometime between 29 August and 26 September in which the Sultan offered to negotiate terms with the Crusaders.[20] Alternatively, the encounter may have been one side of the truce, either when hostilities were ongoing or when they had recommenced. Lemmens rejects the theory of Iacopozzi – who follows Paulinus, Bishop of Puteolanus, writing a century after Francis' encounter – that Francis entered the Muslim camp after Damietta eventually fell to the Crusaders on 5 November 1219. Indeed, most modern commentators accept Lemmens' view that Francis visited the Sultan in September 1219 before returning to the Crusader camp and finally leaving the area some time after 5 November.[21] Most accounts also agree that Francis returned to Italy from Acre sometime in 1220, recalling Brother Elias from Syria to go with him and help respond to the news of problems within the Friars Minor back in Italy.[22] Accounts differ as to whether they left in the early spring or early summer and whether Francis used the time in between (as tradition would suggest) to visit the Holy Land, presumably having obtained some kind of permit from the Sultan to do so.[23]

At this point it will be useful to say a little about Malik al-Kamil, to be clearer about the person whom Francis encountered when he was in Egypt. Lemmens also deals with this topic, seeking to point out that by most accounts Malik al-Kamil was a good man. He mentions a letter of Oliver, chancellor of Cologne, who – even after the Crusaders' defeat at Damietta in 1221 – wrote to the Sultan praising his character.[24] As we shall see in the accounts, all testify to the willingness of the Sultan to listen to Francis and all comment on the way he received the Saint with kindness. Green points out that the two men were of similar age.[25] Yet beyond the encounter with Francis, Malik al-Kamil is important in Crusade history and characterized as a peacemaker. It was he who offered the aforementioned truce in the summer of 1219.[26] Indeed, he offered not only to cede the Holy City and lands west of the Jordan, but also to return part of the True Cross;[27] it was the Crusaders who resumed hostilities.[28] Moreover, it was Malik al-Kamil who negotiated with Frederick II for the return of Jerusalem to Christendom in 1228/9 on the condition that the Dome of the Rock and al-Aqsa mosque remain in Muslim hands.[29] This settlement was opposed by the new Pope, Gregory IX, who as Cardinal Hugolino had been charged by Honorius III to secure support in Italy for the Crusades.[30] This is interesting not least because Munir, a modern Muslim writer, testifies to similar Islamic opposition to the settlement and suggests that,

> The Sultan was occupied with the idea of peace so much that he has been captured in Islamic history as the Muslim who opposed those Muslims who were in favour of the Fifth Crusade. Instead, he preferred a pact with a Christian repre-

sentative. ... Such was the milieu of the man al-Kamil that St Francis of Assisi was allowed to visit him for the purpose of Christian mission in 1219.[31]

It should also be remembered (although scholars of Francis and the Crusades seem not to mention this) that Malik al-Kamil is unlikely to have been wholly ignorant of Christianity. Cannuyer, a scholar of Coptic Christianity, reminds us that the Christian faith was preached at Alexandria in Egypt as early as 43–48 CE and that Christianity took root and flourished in Egypt among the Coptic people.[32] The Coptic Church broke away from the Churches of Rome and Constantinople after the Council of Chalcedon in 451[33] but it continued as a form of Christianity and was tolerated after the Muslims conquered Egypt in 641.[34] Coptic Christians were influential in government during the second century of the Fatimud Dynasty, which ran from 969–1169 CE, as well as officials in Saladin's court after 1187.[35] Moreover, Coptic Christians actually fought for Malik al-Kamil alongside Muslims during the Fifth Crusade.[36] As Cannuyer puts it: 'the dialogue between Muslims and Christians was of long standing in Egypt'.[37] Mico does note that Malik al-Kamil received Franciscan friars at his court a decade *after* he had met Francis,[38] but the relevance of the Sultan's connection with Coptic Christianity *before* he met Francis seems largely unexplored.

Having reflected on the person Francis went to meet in the Saracen camp, one other person deserves some attention and that is the friar who accompanied him. We shall see that the accounts bear witness to Francis being accompanied by one other friar and that Bonaventure is the first to name him as Brother Illuminato. Bonaventure describes him as 'virtuous and enlightened'.[39] Roncaglia argues that Illuminato must have accompanied Francis for a reason and that he may have joined him from the 'convent at Acre' in Syria.[40] There is no evidence that Illuminato (confusedly from Arce near Assisi) knew Arabic but this does not mean that he didn't. Otherwise we may assume, with Cragg, that they communicated in French or with the Sultan's interpreters.[41] Mico's suggestion that the friars preached 'in a kind of sign-language that allowed the audience to get the general drift of their message'[42] would seem unlikely if we are to believe the level of dialogue that took place between Francis and the Sultan within the actual accounts.

The accounts of Francis' encounter with the Sultan

Now that we have had an opportunity to consider the context of the meeting between the Saint and the Sultan, we are able to turn to a consideration of the encounter itself. It is not easy from secondary sources to obtain a clear picture of what the various early sources related to Francis' encounter with Malik al-Kamil state about the event. Modern commentators display a certain amount of selectiveness as to which early accounts they choose to relate, as well as a degree of retelling the stories in a way that serves a particular interpretation of Francis' motives. I shall therefore attempt to present the early accounts in a relatively comprehensive and unbiased fashion, leaving discussion of the various interpretations of Francis' motives to later on. I shall begin with western sources from outside the Franciscan brotherhood and then present the Franciscan sources. It should be noted that dealing with both kinds of source in English has been greatly helped by the recently published, complete translation of the sources edited by Regus Armstrong, Wayne Hellmann and William Short.[43] The summaries and quotations below are all based on that translation. In addition to the aforementioned sources, I shall also comment on an interesting piece of research that reveals an Arabic source for the encounter between Francis and the Sultan.

The first non-Franciscan account of the encounter comes from *Historica Occidentalis* (*c.*1221/5) by Jacques de Vitry, sometime preacher for the Crusades and then Bishop of St John of Acre. The author recounts how he himself saw Francis in the Crusader camp at Damietta before Francis went to meet the Sultan, 'fortified only with the shield of faith'. Francis is captured by Saracens on the road and says: 'I am a Christian. Take me to your master.' The account tells how 'that cruel beast' the Sultan became gentle when he saw Francis and listened carefully as he preached the faith of Christ. However, fearing his soldiers would be converted, the Sultan sends Francis away with his protection. Before he leaves, the Sultan says to Francis: 'Pray for me, that God may deign to reveal to me the law and the faith which is more pleasing to Him.'[44]

The next non-Franciscan account is from the *Chronicle of Ernoul* (1227–29), a shield-bearer of one of the feudal lords of the Crusader states. It tells how 'two clerics' in the Crusader camp sought permission from a Cardinal [this would have been Pelagius, Cardinal-bishop of Albano, the papal legate who accompanied the Crusade] to go and preach to the Sultan. [The clerics' identity is not known to Ernoul but we are in no doubt he is describing Francis' encounter.] The Cardinal allows them to go but disclaims any responsibility, not wanting to give permission for them to go were he believes they will only be killed. The Saracen sentinels see the clerics and take them to the Sultan who asks if they wish to become Saracens or if they have come with a message. They respond that they would never want to become Muslims and have come with this message from God:

> If you wish to believe us, we will hand over your soul to God, because we are telling you in all truth that if you die in the law you now profess you will be lost and God will not possess your soul. It is for this reason we come. But if you will give us a hearing and try to understand, we will demonstrate to you with convincing reasons, in the presence of the most learned teachers in your realm, if you wish to assemble them, that your law is false.

The Sultan then summons the 'archbishops, bishops and good clergy of his law' and the clerics ask that they listen first, adding, 'then you can have our heads cut off'. However, the Sultan's council refuse to enter into discussion with the clerics and ask for their heads to be cut off anyway. The Sultan refuses to do so and instead offers land and possessions if the clerics will remain with him. The clerics refuse this offer, saying their only interest was in being listened to. They then receive food and safe conduct back to the Christian army.[45]

We should note that the *Chronicle of Bernard the Treasurer* (1229-30), a document heavily dependant on Ernoul, repeats the above story[46] and that there is a reference to Francis going to the army at Damietta and then staying in Syria in *The History of the Emperor Eracles* (1229-31).[47] However, neither account adds any more detail about the encounter than those already mentioned.

We can now turn to the Franciscan sources and initially to Thomas of Celano's *First Life* (1229), the first of the various biographies of Saint Francis. Celano recounts how, 'taking a companion with him, he was not afraid to face the Sultan of the Saracens'. Francis is beaten and insulted when he first enters the Saracen camp, but upon meeting the Sultan he is welcomed with gifts. The Sultan is overflowing with admiration for Francis when he refuses them and he listens carefully to Francis. However the story then ends abruptly with the words, 'In all this, however, the Lord did not fulfil his desire, reserving for him the prerogative of a unique grace.'[48] Commentators assume this reference is to Francis' desire for martyrdom, which Celano believed was denied in Egypt but fulfilled in a different way through Francis' reception of the stigmata. We should note that *The Life of St Francis* by Julian of Speyer (1232-35) draws heavily on Celano, but that his telling of the encounter between Francis and the Sultan is nothing other than an abbreviated version of that in the *First Life*.[49] Celano abbreviated his account himself for his *Legend for Use in Choir*.[50] Interestingly, there is hardly any reference in these versions of the story to Francis' time in the Crusader camp, this being in marked contrast with an episode in Celano's *Second Life* (1245-47). In the additional biography Francis is in the camp and confides in his companion that an impeding battle will not go well for the Christians. He then rushes 'to the Christians crying out warnings to save them, forbidding war and threatening disaster'. Francis is taken for a fool but in the event [of what we can assume was the fighting of 29 August 1219] the Crusaders are defeated and Francis witnesses the army retreat from a massacre that diminished the forces by six thousand.[51]

The *Versified Life of Saint Francis* (1232–9) by the poet Henri d'Avranches was written by a non-Franciscan but largely based on the *First Life* by Thomas of Celano. It was written in poetic form for the court of Pope Gregory IX and seems to modify the story slightly both for dramatic emphasis and theological acceptability. It tells of how Francis goes to Damietta and wishes 'to reach the presence of the King of the Persians, to whose ears the word of the Lord he intended first to convey'. He crosses the Nile in a small boat and is treated harshly before he is taken to the king who admires Francis' spirit and offers him gifts. Francis refuses any gift other than that of being heard and the Sultan summons his sages. The account then details a formal lecture by Francis on subjects such as the oneness of God, condemnation of Muhammad's teaching, Lucifer, Eve, and Baptism. This impresses the sages and the king so much that they cry, 'Often may he come among us'. However, Francis then abandons the work, feeling unable to convert such a multitude without help from others, and returns home.[52]

This first batch of writings about the Saint apparently led to an appeal for more information about Francis at the Friars Minor General Chapter of 1244 and it seems that three new episodes about the encounter came forward.[53] One of these episodes finds itself in the *Major Legend of St Francis* (1260–63) by St Bonaventure. In this account, Francis leaves the Crusader camp during hostilities, aware that any Saracen cutting off a Christian head will be awarded a gold piece. He is therefore fearful of, but nevertheless drawn to, the expectation of his death. As mentioned above, Bonaventure names Francis' companion as Brother Illuminato and describes him as 'a virtuous and enlightened man'. They begin their journey and see two lambs, calling to mind the text, 'Behold, I am sending you out as sheep in the midst of wolves' [from Matthew 10.16]. On encountering the Saracen sentries, they are beaten savagely before being taken to the Sultan. The Sultan asks who has sent Francis and he replies that he has been sent by God 'to announce the Gospel of Truth'. He preaches on the Trinity and Christ as Saviour, upon which the Sultan listens and asks him to stay longer. At this Francis issues the following challenge:

> If you wish to be converted to Christ along with your people, I will most gladly stay with you for the love of him. But if you hesitate to abandon the law of Muhammad for the faith of Christ, then command an enormous fire to be lit and I will walk into the fire along with your priests so that you will recognize which faith deserves to be held as the holier and more certain.

The Sultan, having seen one of his senior priests slip away, declares his priests would be unwilling to take up the challenge and Francis continues:

> If you promise me that if I come out of the fire unharmed, you and your people will come over to worship the Christ, then I will enter the fire alone. And if I shall be burned, you must attribute it to my sins.

The Sultan refuses the challenge and offers gifts, which Francis refuses. Again the Sultan offers gifts, this time subsidies for the churches and poor Christians, but Francis still refuses. He departs having made no conversions and deprived of his martyrdom.[54]

The fire episode represents the first of the three new episodes that may have come to light after the appeal of 1244. The two others which, according to Maier, 'have for a long time been disregarded by historians'[55] can be found in *A Book of Exemplary Stories* (*c.*1280–1310) and are the story of Francis walking on a carpet of crosses and a story in which Francis seems to defend the Crusade. These are worth relaying, not least for their persistence within the Franciscan tradition, but also in relation to issues addressed below. The text states that the anecdotes were passed on to the anonymous authors by the General Minister [Bonaventure]. It says they were anecdotes that Illuminato used to recount from his time with Francis and the Sultan. The first recalls that the Sultan wanted to test Francis' devotion and laid before him a carpet made up of a pattern of crosses. The Sultan then says to his attendants:

> Now fetch this man who seems to be an authentic Christian. If he comes toward me, he will have to tread on the crosses that cover this carpet, so then I will accuse him of insulting his Lord. But if he is unwilling to come toward me, I will ask him why he is refusing to approach me.

Francis comes in and is instructed by God what to do. He walks on the carpet and greets the Sultan, who then says: 'You Christians adore the Cross as a special sign of your God. Why then do you have the audacity to tread on those crosses?' To this Francis replies:

> You should know that along with our Lord, two thieves were also crucified. We possess the Cross of our God and Saviour Jesus Christ, and that Cross we adore and surround with total devotion. So, while that true Cross of God had been entrusted to us, you have been left with the crosses of the thieves. For among you there is nothing of the sacred Cross of the Saviour.[56]

The next anecdote is in the same account. After Francis' answer, the Sultan states that the Christians, who are taught not to render evil for evil, should therefore not invade his land. Francis replies that the Sultan has not read the whole Gospel and he quotes: 'If your eye is an occasion of scandal, pluck is out, and cast it away.' Francis continues:

> With this he wanted to teach us that even if every man should be a friend or a relative, perhaps as dear to us as the eye of our head, we should not hesitate to break off relations with him, to destroy or even eradicate him, if he should try to separate us from our faith and our love for God. It is for this reason that Christians have acted justly when they invade your land and fight against you, because you blaspheme the name of Christ and you have tried to keep people from worshipping him. But if you wish to recognize, confess, and adore the Creator and Redeemer of the world, we would love you as ourselves.

The account ends declaring that all the Sultan's attendants were amazed at Francis' answers.[57]

There is but one more story of the Saint and the Sultan, which should simply be noted. Whilst all the accounts above, both from within and without the Franciscan order, testify to the largely accepted view that an encounter actually took place between Francis and Malik al-Kamil, this last story clearly lacks any degree of verisimilitude. It a legend told in the *Deeds of Blessed Francis and His Companions* by Ugolino Boniscambi of Montegiorgio (1328–1337) and repeated in *The Little Flowers of Saint Francis* (a translated and re-edited version of the *Deeds* compiled after 1337). This legend, following a summary of the meeting and the proposed trial by fire, is that St Francis appeared to some friars in a vision instructing them to visit the Sultan on his deathbed, an event leading to the Sultan being baptized.[58]

The above legend is not to be confused with the accounts presented before it. It should further be recognized that the claims for an actual historical encounter between Francis and the Sultan have been greatly boosted by an Arabic source seemingly referring to the encounter. This evidence came to light through the research of Louis Massignon and comes from Ibn-Al-Zayyat, an Arab author of the fifteenth century. It mentions a mystic named Fakr-El-Din-Farsi who was influential in the court of Malik al-Kamil and whose tomb bore the epigraph, 'This man's virtue is known to all. His adventure with Al Malik-Al-Kamil and what happened to him because of the monk, all that is very famous.' Massignon and others concluded, with good reason, that the monk was St Francis and the incident that of the senior 'priest' in Bonaventure's account, Fakr-El-Din-Farsi himself, slipping away from the proposed challenge of the lighted pyre.[59]

The above account from an Arabic source along with those from within and without the Franciscan brotherhood all serve to support the historical likelihood of the encounter between Francis and the Sultan, even if some of the details within the accounts differ from each other. Yet however diverse the differences within the accounts as to what actually took place when Francis was in Egypt, these are comparatively insignificant when compared to the diverse opinions as to why Francis went to Egypt in the first place.

Francis' motivation for his encounter with the Sultan

The various commentators on the encounter between the Saint and the Sultan reveal a range of interpretations as to why Francis went to see Malik al-Kamil. I shall attempt to cover the main issues by discussing the main interpretations under three headings: 'Support for the Crusades?', 'Peace Mission? and 'Witnessing to the Christian faith?'

Support for the Crusades?
The proposal that Francis supported the Fifth Crusade and that his visit was motivated by that support is put forward by Christopher Maier in his book *Preaching the Crusades*.[60] Maier presents his theory very aware that it stands in stark contrast with the way it has been interpreted by 'the majority of modern commentators'.[61] He does so on the basis of a particular approach to the accounts of the meeting. In short, he dismisses the accounts of de Vitry, Ernoul, Bernard, Celano, Speyer and d'Avranches as ones that relayed the story although they had little detail as to what actually took place. Instead, Maier argues, they all relied on a pre-established narrative framework that would have been familiar to them through the biography of John of Gorze and the *Chanson de Roland*. This framework, or *topos*, followed the form of a Christian envoy entering a Muslim court, attempting to convert him and then refusing the offer of gifts. For Maier, the reliable stories about the encounter are those that reputedly came through Brother Illuminato to Bonaventure, the episodes of the proposed trial by fire in Bonaventure's account and the two other episodes in *A Book of Exemplary Stories*. The manner of Francis' discourse in these episodes convinces Maier that the Saint supported the Crusades. In particular, Maier believes the carpet anecdote reveals Francis' support of the Crusaders' belief that the largest part of the relic of the True Cross was not actually in the Sultan's possession. Maier also argues that Francis' comments on why the

Christians were invading the Sultan's lands represented typical justification for the Crusades. Maier concludes:

> Francis did not come to Damietta to stop the Fifth Crusade. On the contrary, his overall objective was the same as that of the Crusaders. Francis, like the Crusaders, wanted to liberate the holy places in Palestine from Muslim rule. What was different was his strategy: Francis went beyond the idea of simply expelling the Muslims from where they interfered with Christian life. He wanted their total submission to the Christian faith. Short of this total submission there would be no peace; short of this, for Francis too, was the necessity, if not the duty, to crusade against the enemies of faith.[62]

For Maier, Francis' reputed praise of Charlemagne and the heroes of Roncesvallles, revealed in a story reputedly told by Brother Leo (see below), is further testimony of the Saint's support for the Crusades.[63]

Maier's is a pithy argument, but it rests, by his own admission, on taking the three post-1244 episodes at face value and it stands in sharp contradiction with much of the other evidence surrounding Francis' attitude to the Crusades. Basetti-Sani argued that the reason the last two episodes were not included by Bonaventure was that they were 'apocryphal' stories emanating from anecdotes originally relating to a Coptic patriarch of Egypt and a non-Christian king and attributed by the anonymous authors of *A Book of Exemplary Stories to Francis*.[64] The story of Francis praising Charlemagne and other Crusaders as having 'a glorious and memorable victory, [finally dying] in battle fighting as holy martyrs' (this story found in *The Assisi Compilation or Legend of Perugio*)[65] may likewise, as Hoeberichts argues, be a story where the author's perspective is entirely contrary to that of Francis and what the Saint really would have said.[66] Indeed, a major reason for dismissing these anonymous, pro-Crusader texts as inauthentic of Francis' own voice is that there is a great deal of evidence to suggest that Francis was by no means a supporter of the Crusades.

De Beer, in his article 'St Francis and Islam', advances a number of reasons why he believes Francis' visit to the Sultan was not motivated by support for the Crusades and I shall briefly present his reasons below. First, his earliest attempt to reach the Saracens began even before the Fifth Crusade was announced.[67] Second, no positive reference to Francis being a 'crusader' appears in his own writings.[68] Hoeberichts points that there is no expressed support for the Fifth Crusade in Francis' writings, this in contrast with the very clear influence upon Francis' *Earlier Rule* of other statements made at the Fourth Lateran Council. The *Earlier Rule* shows the influence of the Council on topics as diverse as permission to preach, orthodoxy, penance and eucharistic reception, but no trace of any influence on the rule of that Council's extensive proclamations in support of the Fifth Crusade. Francis, so Hoeberichts concludes, was clearly 'selective with regard to papal documents'.[69] Third, de Beer points out that Francis did not send friars as preachers to the Crusade, indeed it was the latter that became friars.[70] Fourth, there is, in Francis' writings, no sense of superiority over the infidel; in all relationships Francis is a 'friar minor'.[71] Fifth, there is nothing in Francis' writings, in contrast to his contemporaries, which is negative towards Islam.[72] By contrast, de Beer mentions de Vitry's description of Saracens as 'sacrilegious disciples of the Antichrist'[73] and Hoeberichts shows how negative attitudes to Islam were openly expressed by Bernard of Clairvaux, Innocent III, and even such revered figures as Peter the Venerable.[74] Sixth, Francis did not go to Egypt in the role of 'military chaplain'.[75] Seventh, he seemed to make straight for the Sultan rather than deliberately spend time with the Crusaders.[76] Eighth, in 1217, he actually forbade the sending of missionaries to Muslims lands to 'prevent any ambiguity with Islam' during that first year of the Crusade. Later, after his meeting with Cardinal Hugolino, de Beer suggests that Francis' impulse to the infidels is awakened 'as though to counter the Crusade'.[77] Ninth, Francis goes to the Sultan with no other protection save the faith[78] (cf. de Vitry's account). Finally, we find Francis in Celano's *Second Life* trying to persuade the Crusaders not to fight.[79] This last point does not necessarily imply (as Hoeberichts argues after Powell),[80] that Francis opposed the Crusade, he may simply have been predicting defeat in that battle. Similarly, Francis' words 'I am a Christian' in de Vitry's account may not necessarily have been, as Hoeberichts argues,[81] an attempt to disassociate himself from the Crusaders. What is clear however is that there is no evidence in Francis' writings or actions – other than the later, anonymous sources mentioned earlier – to suggest that the Saint supported the Crusade. There were Christian voices that raised questions about the Crusades[82] but these were atypical. In general, open support for the Crusades was common in Francis' day and Francis' approach is such a marked contrast that de Beer is confident enough to say:

> It thus seems fully proven that Francis' action is the exact opposite of any Crusade mysticism. No sublimation is possible! Francis is not Bernard! And when Francis reached the Sultan no doubt was possible, as all the sources, almost in spite of themselves confirm: Francis did not come to Islamic territory on behalf of the Crusaders.[83]

Peace Mission?

If one accepts that Francis' visit to the Sultan was not motivated by support for the Fifth Crusade, is it necessary to accept that Francis did the opposite and that he went instead on a deliberate peace mission? Hoeberichts' major study *Francis and Islam* does a lot to clarify that Francis did not support the Crusade, but it goes much further, suggesting that Francis was motivated by an already worked out 'mission of peace' when he set off for Egypt. He writes, 'Francis ... without arms and possessions, in a nonviolent way, went to see the Sultan.'[84] He argues that this 'mission of peace' was worked out first in the context of wars between Italian cities and between the wealthy oppressors and exploited poor: it was only then extended beyond the boundaries of Christendom in a 'mission of peace' to Islam. He suggests the friars minor had developed the notion of 'being subject', being understood as *minoritas*, rather than as those associated with the rich and powerful.[85] This, he argues, is why they entered a house with the words 'Peace to this house'.[86] Hoeberichts writes:

Francis and his brothers were so convinced of the value and the significance of their way of life and action that, when they were confronted with the Crusades and became aware of the existence of the Saracens, they decided to move beyond the borders of the Christian world and to extend their peace mission to the world of the Saracens and Islam.[87]

Hoeberichts' principal argument for the proposal that Francis had developed a 'mission of peace' comes from his analysis of chapter 16 of the *Earlier Rule* or *Regula non bullata* of 1221. This is the chapter on 'Those Going Among the Saracens and Other Nonbelievers' that begins with the text 'The Lord says: "Behold I am sending you out like sheep in the midst of wolves." Therefore be prudent as serpents and simple as doves.' [Note the reference to this text earlier in Bonaventure's account.] The rule exhorts any brother who wishes to to go among the Saracens if given permission by the minister. It proposes two ways to 'live spiritually' among the Saracens: one, 'not to engage in arguments' but to 'be subject to every human creature for God's sake'; the other way, 'to announce the Word of God, whenever they see it pleases the Lord, in order that [unbelievers] may believe in almighty God...'. It then lists several texts that would encourage any who may experience persecution.[88] For Hoeberichts, the key 'mission of peace' phrase is 'be subject to every human creature for God's sake'. He sees the fact that this was left out of the *Later Rule* or *Regula bullata* of 1223, over which Francis had little direct influence,[89] as indicative of the 'clericalization' of the order and of its movement away from Francis' 'mission of peace' theology.[90]

However, there is an inconsistency in Hoeberichts' presentation that has implications for exploring Francis' motives for going to Malik al-Kamil. Hoeberichts gives the clear impression, as indicated above, that Francis' 'mission of peace' theology was already worked out when he left for Egypt. However he also says that chapter 16 of the *Earlier Rule* 'can be considered as the result of the position which Francis and his brothers, on the basis of their theology of church and world, adopted toward the Saracens and Islam after they had come into personal contact with them during their visit to the Sultan.'[91] Here we have a more plausible theory and one that makes more sense of Hoeberichts' admission that 'not much of Francis' peace vision emerges in the stories about his visit to the Sultan'.[92] Later Hoeberichts says this is 'for the simple reason that it did not fit the ideas of the biographers, or rather their prejudices about Muhammad and Islam'.[93] As we shall see, it seems clear enough that Francis did develop his ideas as a result of his meeting with the Sultan and that these were reflected in chapter 16 of the *Earlier Rule*. However, it seems somewhat programmatic – and not very consistent with the impression of St Francis in the early sources and the tradition – to believe that Francis was motivated to go to Egypt by an already worked out 'mission of peace' theology which he put into practice among the Saracens and then included in his rule. The truth is that Hoeberichts' study and his presentation, especially as the study continues into Part Two, is aimed at fostering present-day Christian-Muslim relations, creating an '*oumene* of peace where the greeting of peace which Jesus gave to is followers is answered by the Muslim wish of peace, *salaam* ...'.[94] This may be a laudable aim, but it is easy to form the impression that Hoeberichts' present-day intentions are transposed onto Francis' motivations for meeting Malik al-Kamil. Mico points out that 'most authors prefer to assign ... [chapter 16 of the *Earlier Rule*] to the time after Francis' return from the East'.[95] It would seem consistent with other post-Egypt developments in Francis' thought to suggest that even if he had worked out a 'mission of peace' theology before encountering the Sultan, that he did not actually make the application of this theology to going among the Saracens until after his experience in Damietta. If this is the case, we are still left asking, 'What motivated Francis to go to Egypt?

Witness to the Christian Faith?
All the accounts, without exception, of the Saint's encounter with the Sultan testify to Francis as a man of great faith and courage going into enemy territory and

presenting the Sultan with news about the Christian faith. They all emphasize that the Sultan listened carefully. Most tell of Francis presenting the Sultan and his people with a challenge to turn to the faith of Christ. For Maier, and his theory that Francis went to support the Crusades, the first stories of Francis' encounter simply followed a pre-established literary framework; the later ones confirm his theory. For Hoeberichts, and his theory that Francis went on a 'mission of peace', the sources simply betray the biases of their writers, revealing little which will support his theory. Hoeberichts implies, for example, that Francis did not preach to the Sultan at all and the accounts of this represent 'entirely the view of James of Vitry'.[96] Moreover, Hoeberichts goes to some lengths to diminish the import of Francis' other way of being present among the Saracens, namely that the brothers 'when they see that it pleases the Lord' should 'proclaim the word'.[97] Hoeberichts puts so much energy in to describing what he believes were the conditions surrounding 'when it pleases the Lord' that one wonders if the brothers would have been able 'to proclaim the word' at all.[98] In short, it would seem that both Maier and Hoeberichts have ready-made theories to explain why Francis went to the Sultan and that what the early accounts say about the event is, for them, inconsequential. Let us then assume for a moment that Francis did go to Malik al-Kamil to witness to the Christian faith and see how this framework fits with the account and with other interpretations of why the Saint set off to meet the Sultan.

I hesitate to suggest that Francis' witness to the Christian faith was principally a desire for his own martyrdom, for this runs the risk of presenting a misleading and crude image of Francis. The early lives of the Saint do not hesitate to suggest that this was Francis' major motivation, but always in the context of witnessing to the faith and never as a desired end of itself. The chapter in which Celano's account appears includes the words '... burning with the desire for the holy martyrdom ... he wished to preach the Christian faith and repentance to the Saracens and other unbelievers'.[99] Mico points out that Francis would have been raised on stories of the eleventh-century *Legends of the*

Martyrs written in Assisi.[100] All the Franciscan sources testify to Francis' desire for martyrdom, but all accounts are clear that Francis' expectation of martyrdom is in the context of witnessing to the Christian faith. Indeed, the accounts suggest that this witness was achieved even if the martyrdom he expected was not granted among the Saracens. Francis' joy on hearing the news of the friars martyred in Morocco in 1220 is an uncomfortable story for Hoeberichts, since Francis was aware that the martyrs had openly attacked Islam. Hoeberichts cites the *Chronicle of Jordan of Giano* to suggest that Francis actually found their martyrdom displeasing.[101] *The Chronicle* does recount how Francis asked one day that the reading be stopped, but the text goes on to explain that this was because Francis believed a brother should not glory in another's suffering but only in his own.[102] Basetti-Sani was not only of the opinion that Francis desired martyrdom, but also that the proposed ordeal of the lighted pyre had a symbolic meaning. He argued that it represented a taking up of the challenge that Muhammad had proposed in Mecca to the Christian delegation from Najran. In the quranic account, the Christians refuse to prove their faith upon Muhammad's suggestion of a trial by fire.[103] For Basetti-Sani, Francis' gesture:

> appears as a prophetic announcement of the new attitude which God now required of Christians with regard to Islam: reparation through suffering, witness to the faith through suffering and death, and Christian charity which judges no man but recognizes in all the gifts of God and loves the Muslims as brethren even to the point of martyrdom.[104]

De Beer makes an interesting observation on this subject of martyrdom. He too suggests that Francis was motivated by a desire to witness to the faith and that he expected to be martyred as a consequence of his going among the Saracens. However, de Beer also argues:

> Francis' boldness lay in thinking that his martyrdom would speak more to Islam than to the Church. Against the extravagance of the Crusade, Islam required a radical witness

which would be the radical opposite. Martyrdom is the conscientious objection raised against all those who support the intolerance of holy war; it is an anti-crusade.[105]

According to de Beer, had Francis had any knowledge of Islam, he would have known that the outcome of the meeting between Muhammad and the Christians of Najran was that the Quran subsequently condemned Muslim participation in activities designed to prove matters of faith:

> All the signs are that when he entered Moslem territory, Francis was not all that familiar with the religion he was confronting ... But Francis was so sure of his faith, of his conversation, of his truth that it was impossible not to believe a witness who had just let himself be murdered to save his killer.[106]

This proposal seems consistent with what we have learned about St Francis. He was not a Crusader and it seems more appropriate to view his journey to the Sultan as some kind of anti-Crusade gesture. However, it does not seem likely that Francis had a worked-out a 'mission of peace' theology that he took with him to Damietta. The notion that Francis anticipated his martyrdom as he went to witness to the Christian faith, perhaps in a radically alternative way to the Crusaders, seems to do justice to all the accounts of his journey and the way his encounter with the Sultan has been understood within the tradition. Indeed, two important conclusions flow from the fact that Francis' expectation was not realized. The first is that he and his early biographers believed that the martyrdom he had been denied in Egypt was fulfilled in a different way through Francis' reception of the stigmata. It has even been suggested that Francis in some way perceived his suffering as a gesture of love for Muslims and bore the stigmata for the salvation of Islam.[107] The second conclusion is that Francis was changed by the experience, indeed that he encountered things in Islam that informed his later thinking and practice. Lehmann has given particular attention to the *First Letter to the Custodians*, *A Letter to the Rulers of the Peoples* and the *Second Letter to the Custodians*, all of which

Francis wrote in 1220 after his return from Egypt.[108] These include several proposals that the Saint seems to have developed as a result of his experience in Egypt. For example, he proposes 'that the names and written words of the Lord, whenever they are found in dirty places, be also gathered up and kept in a becoming place'.[109] He also asks the rulers that 'every evening an announcement may be made by a messenger or some other sign that praise and thanksgiving may be given by all people to the all-powerful Lord God'.[110] It is hard to resist the view that Francis was affected by his experience of Muslim reverence for the names of God and by the Islamic call to daily prayer.[111] It would seem that Francis' journey to Egypt provided him not with the martyrdom he anticipated but with inspiration to further develop his own witness to the Christian faith.

As a final contribution on this topic, an interesting insight into Francis' missionary motivation comes from the Muslim writer Fareed Munir. He suggests that before the seventeenth century development of 'mission' as something to do with extending the geographical boundaries of Christianity, the Church's concept of mission was of every believer sharing their faith. He states that this concept is in line with the model of mission in Islam. To Munir, Francis' ability to share his faith while learning something of Islam is testimony to the Saint being 'a good Muslim' and, with the Prophet Muhammad, being 'one in a spirituality of mission'.[112]

Conclusion

I began by sharing my own experience of living in the midst of a large Muslim population and being challenged by how to engage with Islam in a way that is faithful to my Christian convictions. I also noted my dissatisfaction with what the established models of 'exclusivism', 'inclusivism' and 'pluralism' have to offer Christians in such a context. My own search for a model of Christian engagement with Muslims that is faithful to Christianity and yet open to the 'other' within Islam has led me to share the view that such a model is provided by the story of Francis and the Sultan.

It has been important to give sufficient space to a careful

consideration of the context of Francis' encounter with
Malik al-Kamil, of the accounts of that encounter and of the
main interpretations of it. This journey led toward a rejection of the view that Francis was motivated by support for
the Crusades, but likewise of the view that he went to Egypt
with a ready-made 'peace mission' theology. Rather, I have
preferred to accept the uniting theme of all the accounts
and the dominant historical interpretation of the
encounter, namely that Francis was motivated by a desire to
witness to the Christian faith, even to the point of martyrdom. I have nevertheless accepted that Francis' witness may
have been a radical anti-crusading gesture and that Francis
was changed by his experience, as evident in his later writings. Indeed, Francis showed a capacity to witness to his
faith and to use his encounter with the religious other of
Islam to develop his Christian witness further.

If the interpretation of Francis' encounter with the
Sultan is accepted, how applicable is this model to contemporary Christian engagement with Islam? Kenneth Cragg
suggests there was a tension in Francis' experience that
both ennobled and compromised his encounter with the
Sultan. Francis was both a representative of the faith with
which the Sultan was at war and an example of a radically
different Christian mission from that exemplified by the
Crusaders. For Cragg, 'The nobility lay in the effort to
displace force with love and power with poverty. The
compromise stood in the actual context of siege and
belligerence from which Francis was only symbolically
freed.'[113] Arguably, and in the light of very real and present
global tensions, Christian engagement with Muslims today
exists in a similar context. How can the Christian attempt to
convince the Muslim in Iraq, or even in London, that US
and UK actions in the Middle East are not motivated by a
Crusade mentality, especially when the American President
has used the terminology of the Crusades in justifying military action in the region?

O'Mahony has repeated, after David Burrell, that the real
challenge for European Muslims and Christians is how to
practise an inner journey that is neither assimilating nor
appropriating, in Burrell's words to develop 'discovery of

one's own faith in encountering the faith of another'.[114] O'Mahony offers as a model for such an approach the example of Louis Massignon.[115] Massignon and his friend Mary Kahil developed a shared sense of commitment to Islam that they ritualized by going to the church at Damietta in February 1934.[116] Massignon was a follower of St Francis, he became a member of the Franciscan Third Order and took the religious name of *Ibrahim* in recognition of the patriarch's role in the history of Christianity and Islam.[117] It was Massignon, as mentioned earlier, who discovered the Arabic reference for the meeting between Francis and the Sultan. It was also Massignon who fostered Basetti-Sani's interest in Islam, including the notion that the stigmata was in some way Francis' offering for the salvation of Muslims.[118] At Damietta, Massignon and Kahil vowed together to offer their lives for Muslims, 'not so they would be converted, but so that the will of God might be accomplished in them and through them'.[119] They termed the offering *badaliyya*, an Arabic term for spiritual substitution. In 1934, Massignon wrote to Kahil, 'I have promised God to tear myself away from everything gradually, gently, but implacably ... so as to be judged worthy of martyrdom in a Muslim land if God permits.'[120] The influence of Saint Francis on Massignon is undeniable. Massignon, hailed by O'Mahony as 'a witness for the future',[121] followed Saint Francis as a model for his Christian witness to and through Islam. If this essay is of no other value, it has affirmed me in my personal journey and led me to pray that I too may follow the example of Louis Massignon, Mary Kahil, Basetti-Sani and others in following a model of Christian engagement with Islam patterned after that historic encounter between St Francis and the Sultan.

Notes

1 See Michael Barnes, *Theology and the Dialogue of Religions,* Cambridge University Press, 2002, pp. 7–9 and D'Costa, G. in Ford, D. (ed.), *The Modern Theologians,* Oxford, Blackwell, 1997, pp. 624–44.
2 See numerous modern biographies of the Saint Francis, e.g.

those mentioned in J. Hoeberichts, *Francis and Islam*, Quincy, IL, Franciscan Press, 1997, pp. 269–74.
3 Hugh Goddard, *A History of Christian-Muslim Relations*, Edinburgh University Press, 2000, pp. 2, 4.
4 Ibid., pp. 84–89.
5 Hoeberichts, op. cit., p. 7.
6 Mico, J., 'The Spirituality of St. Francis: Going Among Non-Believers', *Greyfriars Review*, vol. 10. no. 2., 1992, p. 115.
7 L and J. Riley-Smith, *The Crusades: Idea and Reality, 1095–1274*, London, Edward Arnold, 1981, pp.19, 22.
8 Basetti-Sani, G., 'Francis of Assisi', *Concilium* no. 7, 1968, p. 9 and Hoeberichts, op. cit., p. 22.
9 Hoeberichts, op. cit., p. 28.
10 G. Basetti-Sani, *Muhammad and St Francis*, Florence, F. Francesco-Feiole, 1975, p. 27; Cragg, K., *The Arab Christian*, Oxford, Mowbray, 1992, p.106; C. Maier, *Preaching the Crusades*, Cambridge University Press: Cambridge, 1994, p. 9.
11 M. Roncaglia, *Saint Francis in the Middle East*, Cairo, Mondial Press, 1957, pp. 21–25.
12 Lemmens, L., 'De Santo Francisco Christum Praedicante Coram Sultano Aegypti', *Archium Franciscanum Historicum* vol. 19, 1926, p. 559. (I am grateful to Ivor Chapman for a personal translation of this text from the Latin into English.)
13 Hoeberichts, op. cit., p. 199, n. 7
14 R. Armstrong, W. Hellmann, and W. Short, (eds), *The Saint, Volume I of Francis of Assisi: Early Documents*, London, New City Press, 1999, pp. 171–79.
15 Thomas of Celano's *First Life* 1.XX in ibid., p. 229f.
16 Ibid., p. 230.
17 Roncaglia, op. cit., p. 20.
18 Armstrong et al., 1999, op. cit., p. 394f.
19 Lemmens, op. cit.
20 Roncaglia, op. cit., pp. 21–25.
21 Lemmens, op. cit., p. 564.
22 Roncaglia, op. cit., pp. 21–25; J. Green, *God's Fool*, London, Fount, 1983, p. 209.
23 Roncaglia, op. cit., pp. 21–25; F. De Beer, 'St Francis and Islam', *Concilium* no. 149, 1981, p. 18.
24 Lemmens, op. cit., p. 564; see also Hoeberichts, op. cit., p. 92.
25 Green, op. cit., p. 203.
26 Roncaglia, op. cit., pp. 21–25.
27 Maier, op. cit., p. 14.
28 Roncaglia, op. cit., pp. 21–25.

29 Goddard, op. cit., p. 88.
30 Hoeberichts, op. cit., p. 28f, p. 31.
31 F. Munir, 'Islam and Franciscanism: Prophet Mohammad of Arabia and St. Francis of Assisi in the Spirituality of Mission', *Spirit and Life*, vol. 9, 25–41, 2000, p. 34f.
32 C. Cannuyer, *Coptic Egypt: the Christians of the Nile*, Thames and Hudson, London, 2001, p. 16.
33 Ibid., p. 29.
34 Ibid., p. 61.
35 Ibid., pp. 66–69.
36 Ibid., p. 70.
37 Ibid., p. 74.
38 Mico, op. cit., p. 125.
39 Bonaventure's 'Major Life of Saint Francis' in Armstrong, R., Hellmann, W. and Short, W. (eds), *The Founder, Volume II of Francis of Assisi: Early Documents*. London, New City, Press 2000, p. 602.
40 Roncaglia, op. cit., pp. 21–25.
41 Cragg, op. cit., p.108.
42 Mico, op. cit., p.123.
43 For an Index to these sources see Armstrong, R., Hellmann, W. and Short, W. (eds), *Index of Francis of Assisi: Early Documents*, London, New City Press, 2002.
44 Armstrong et al., 1999, op. cit., p. 584.
45 Ibid., pp. 605–67.
46 Ibid., p. 607f.
47 In ibid., p.609.
48 Thomas of Celano's *First Life* 2.XX in ibid., p. 231.
49 Ibid., pp. 363, 395.
50 Ibid., p. 322.
51 Thomas of Celano's *Second Life or The Remembrance of the Desire of the Soul* 2.IV in Armstrong et al., 2000, op. cit., p. 265f.
52 Armstrong et al, 1999, op. cit., p. 423 and pp. 485–88.
53 Maier, op. cit., p. 12.
54 Bonaventure's *Major Life of Saint Francis* in Armstrong et al., 2000, op. cit., p. 602f.
55 Maier, op. cit., p. 16.
56 In Armstrong, R., Hellmann, W. and Short, W. (eds), *The Prophet, Volume III of Francis of Assisi: Early Documents*, London, New City Press, 2001, p. 799.
57 In ibid., p. 799.
58 Boniscambi's 'Deeds of Blessed Francis and His Companions' in Armstrong, XXVII, 2001, op. cit., pp. 490 , pp. 605ff.
59 De Beer, op. cit., pp. 14f.

60 Maier, op. cit.
61 Ibid., p. 8.
62 Ibid., pp. 16f.
63 Ibid., pp. 9–17.
64 Basetti-Sani, 1968, op. cit., pp. 211f, n. 7.
65 Armstrong et al., 2000, op. cit., p. 209.
66 Hoeberichts, op. cit., p. 87.
67 De Beer, op. cit., p. 15.
68 Ibid., p. 15.
69 Hoeberichts, op. cit., p. 4.
70 De Beer, op. cit., p. 15.
71 Ibid., p. 15.
72 Ibid., p. 15.
73 Ibid., p. 12.
74 Hoeberichts, op. cit., p. 15 and pp. 19–23.
75 De Beer, op. cit, p. 15.
76 Ibid., p. 15.
77 Ibid., pp. 15f.
78 Ibid., p. 16.
79 Ibid., p. 16.
80 Hoeberichts, op. cit., p. 97.
81 Ibid., p. 80.
82 See ibid., p. 205, n. 35 and Mico, op. cit., p. 117.
83 De Beer, op. cit., p. 16.
84 Hoeberichts, op cit., p. 42.
85 Ibid., pp. 52f.
86 Ibid., p. 31
87 Ibid., p. 58.
88 'Earlier Rule or Regula non bullata' in Armstrong et al., XVI, 1999, op. cit., pp. 74f.
89 See ibid., p. 106.
90 Hoeberichts, op. cit., p. 132.
91 Ibid., p. 43.
92 Ibid., p. 58.
93 Ibid., p. 75.
94 Ibid., p. 134.
95 Mico, op. cit., p. 125.
96 Hoeberichts, op. cit., p. 105.
97 'Earlier Rule or Regula non bullata', XVI, op. cit.
98 See Hoeberichts, op. cit., pp. 94–111.
99 'Thomas of Celano's First Life' in Armstrong et al., 1.XX, 1999, op. cit., p. 229.
100 Mico, op. cit., p. 120.
101 Hoeberichts, op. cit., p. 74.

102 See The Chronicles of Thomas of Eccleston and Jordan of Giano, *The Coming of the Friars Minor to England and Germany*, translated by G Salter, from the critical edition of Little and Boehmer, Dent & Son, London, 1926, p. 132.
103 Basetti-Sani, 1975, op. cit., pp. 21–30.
104 Basetti-Sani, 1968, op. cit., p. 12.
105 De Beer, op. cit., p. 16.
106 Ibid., p. 17.
107 Basetti-Sani, 1975, op cit., p. 30 and 1968, op. cit., p. 13.
108 L. Lehmann, 'Francis's Two Letters to the Custodes: Proposals for Christian-Islamic Ecumenism in Praising God', *Greyfriars Review* vol. 2, no. 3, 1988; See also Armstrong et al., 1999, op. cit., pp. 56–60.
109 Ibid., p. 56.
110 Ibid., pp. 58f.
111 See Hoeberichts, op. cit., p. 89.
112 Munir, op. cit., p. 38.
113 Cragg, op. cit., p. 107.
114 O'Mahony, A., 'Islam in Europe', *The Way*, vol. 41, 2001, p. 132.
115 Ibid., Gude, M. L., *Louis Massignon: The Crucible of Compassion*, Notre Dame, Indiana and London, University of Notre Dame Press, 1996, pp. 130ff.
116 Ibid., pp. 134f.
117 Ibid., p. 124.
118 Borrmans, M., 'In Memoriam Giulio Basetti-Sani', *Islamochristiana* 27, 2001, p. 9.
119 Gude, op. cit., pp. 134f.
120 Ibid., pp. 134f.
121 O'Mahony, op. cit., p. 130.

Chapter 8

'Our Common Fidelity to Abraham is What Divides': Christianity and Islam in the Life and Thought of Louis Massignon

Anthony O'Mahony

Louis Massignon saw Christianity and Islam through the lens of the tragic figure of the mystic al-Hallâj (857–922).[1] Al-Hallâj, who was 'martyred' in Baghdad for heresy, represented for Massignon a direct parallel to the suffering of Jesus on the Cross.[2] As Christianity had suffering and compassion as its foundation, so too, according to Massignon, did Islam. Indeed, he regarded suffering as fundamental to Semitic and Jewish tradition: 'This brings us to a fundamental problem of Semitic, and particularly Jewish psychology, in its most "Kirkegaardian" aspect: there is a hidden but divine good in suffering, and this is the mystery of anguish, the foundation of human nature.'[3] Massignon's mystical Catholicism belonged to the core and essence of his being, and it informed his entire understanding of Islam. It was 'commitment' to the other outside his own Christian faith which made Massignon such a powerful witness. The Dominican scholar Jean-Pierre de Menasce, OP states,

> If the attitude of Christians towards Muslims and Islam (and consequentially towards all the great religions) has changed in the last forty years, through objective understanding, through gripping the highest and most central values,

through a complete respect for people and institutions, and all this as a result of Christian intensity and not despite it, this is to a great extent owed to Louis Massignon'.[4]

Indeed, the explicit recasting of western missionary effort, by the French theologian and Cardinal of the Church, Jean Danielou, SJ after the Second World War, as one finding Christ even more then preaching him, can be traced directly to Danielou's association with Massignon.[5]

Christianity and Islam have been pitted against each other because of their overtly worldwide mission. There was for many centuries a territorial standoff between Islam and Christendom, with the attendant isolation of many of the Eastern Churches from the western lung of Christianity.[6] It would be difficult to find a longer, more sustained animosity than that between 'official' Christianity and Islam. For if the Jew was the 'other' in the midst of Christendom, Islam was the 'other' facing it, and with power at is disposal. Massignon came to the view that Islam was more resourceful spiritually than it ever had been militarily and that these resources could be mined by Christians to recover dimensions of their faith hitherto hidden.[7] The French Jesuit André d'Alverny, SJ observed of Massignon 'Everywhere, it is a man of prayer, one of the great men of prayer to whom believers of all religions relate and who give unbelievers themselves a secret and happy wound'.[8]

Massignon's keen sense of there being but one God, complemented by his careful delineation of the proper notes of each tradition which affirms that 'onenesss' as an article of faith, lead him to find resonances between the assertions of each tradition which other readers would fail to see. That is the very oneness of God leads him antecedently to suspect correlations between divergent traditions, while his respect for those divergences forbids him seeking commonalities in other ways.[9] Massignon's first understanding was that of the universality and unity of human reason. Wherever reason functions on data, which are analogous but which occur in different historical and social contexts, the result will be a parallelism which at first sight would seem to have its root in a borrowing or in an imitation, while in reality there is only the same functioning of reason in different individuals. Secondly to explain existing parallels in the idea of a certain realm of human imagination. The latter has to use certain images in order to represent non-material and non-rational realities and such images occur at different places and times, and in different social and cultural contexts. At a deeper level, however, they may be considered to be the expression of 'archetypes' which manifest themselves at singular points in history, which have an eschatological significance. Lastly is theological rather than philosophical and is meant to explain religious rather than rational or imaginative expressions in the realm of mysticism. Certain striking parallels, which can be established between religious or mystical vocations in different religious traditions, could be attributed to one divine grace operating in different minds and souls. It is thus assumed that authentic mystical experiences are due to a divine action, which gives birth to inspirations and vocations, leading to a certain personalization of the subject and to a direct if not intimate relationship between man and God. Massignon investigated a number of such vocations in Islam, of which he judged that of Hallâj to be superior to that of the others. One scholar has observed that 'yet the very exploratory character of his writings, and indeed of his often enigmatic prose, continues to draw from us something which mere scholarship can never do: a glimpse of the *spirit* which animated these classical works'.[10]

Massignon understood that his views were controversial to many in the Church. However, loyal to the fidelity of the Catholic faith, he always sought clarification from theologians and ecclesial authorities. In many ways what made his contribution to Christian thought on Islam so integral and profound, was that he held it was only by remaining close to the authority of the Church and authentically within the tradition that truth could be sustained.[11]

Louis Massignon: Life and Thought

Louis Massignon (1883–1962) was arguably one of the most important scholars of Arabic and Islam in the European tradition of the twentieth century.[12] He was a dominant presence in the field of Islamic studies, and whose career which begun in 1900, spanned more than sixty years.[13] However, distinguished as his career was, today his name would probably be known only within the scholarly world as related to Islamic studies, were it not for a life whose range defies easy categories.[14] He made a special contribution to our knowledge of Islamic mysticism, Sufism, and sociology and had deep and lasting influence upon Islamic studies in general, particularly in France.[15] However his most lasting contribution was to how Islam was to be understood and interpreted within the Christian tradition and in particular within his own Catholic Church.[16] By the force of his personality and the originality of his ideas Louis Massignon was perhaps the only Islamicist scholar who was a central figure in the intellectual life of his time.[17]

Abbé Harpigny in his important study *Islam et Christianisme selon Louis Massignon*,[18] divides Louis Massignon's life into three episodes: 'le cycle hallagien' – which ended with the submission of his doctoral thesis: *La Passion d'al-Hosayn-ibn Mansour al-Hallâj, martyre mystique de l'Islam* in 1922; '*le cycle abrahamique*' – up until his ordination as a priest in the Greek Catholic Melkite Church in Cairo in 1950; and '*un cycle gandhien*' – a period of political activism which ended with his death in 1962.

However we understand or measure the work and personality of Louis Massignon, there was a deep symmetry between his writings, his acts, and his beliefs.[19] At the centre of Massignon's scholarly endeavour was the search for what was, or is, original in a person, a society or a work. Authenticity, where present, was one of the qualities he sought: there took place what was worthwhile and essential. Such authenticity could lie in the subject matter, which was expressed, or in the way in which such subject matter was expressed. His interest was aroused by the particular traits pointing to a certain authenticity. Behind such originality or authenticity Massignon could detect, in some cases, a sensitivity to a testimony. This sensitivity was at the basis of his never-ending attention to expressions of the human soul, especially those of a religious connotation. Massignon's research constantly faced the methodological difficulty of proving that something was or was not a borrowing from something else.[20] This was particularly true in the debates between the Spanish Catholic priest-scholar Miguel Asín de Palacios and Louis Massignon on the Christian antecedents of Islamic mysticism.[21] However, if Massignon could not present strict evidence, he always attempted to discover hypotheses other than those of direct literary or historical derivation, in order to explain similarities between different phenomena without any apparent relationship. For example, he showed considerable interest in such coincidences as existed both in Islam and in Christianity and sought to link them with each other or find some connection between them at a deeper level. [22]

A clear record of how Massignon reconciled his scholarly work on Islam with his orthodox Christian and Catholic beliefs is found in *Les trois prières d'Abraham: Seconde prière*, which is a meditation on Abraham's prayer for Ishmael, as reported in Genesis. He stresses that Ishmael's exile took place after he had been circumcised and had received God's blessing in response to Abraham's prayer (Gen. 17:18–20). Massignon sees in Muhammad's own forced emigration, or *hijra*, from Mecca, a repetition of Ishmael's banishment at the instigation of Sarah. He suggests that, when Muhammad encountered the Jews in Medina, he therefore declared before God that he drew his inspiration from Abraham and claimed Abraham's entire spiritual and temporal heritage for the Arabs alone.[23] In later years, he became particularly interested in those phenomena which show a convergence or dialogue between Islam and Christianity: the meeting of Muhammad and the Christians of Najran, the cult of Fatima as a parallel to the veneration of the Virgin Mary, the veneration of the Seven Sleepers of Ephesus by Christians and Muslims alike,[24] vocations within Islam of mystical compassion and substitution like that of al-Hallâj. Massignon, who was very interested in biography, liked to plot on the graph of what he called *Curve de vie* or 'the curve of life' of the life stories which attracted his attention.[25] He also thought that there are 'Christic' figures within Islam who could ultimately play a role in bringing Muslims to confess the divine sonship of Jesus, the Christ, if only at the last judgement, such figures included Salmân Pâk,[26] al-Hallâj,[27] al-Ghâzali and others.[28]

The renewal of Massignon's Christian religious consciousness was directly linked in his own mind to Islam. Al-Hallâj, particularly, had moved forever beyond the realm of mere academic interest to become an actual guiding fraternal force. Their extraordinary friendship 'filled the heart of Massignon and shaped his mind so thoroughly that he can be seen as the greatest Muslim among Christians and the greatest Christian among Muslims'.[29] Massignon, with his involvement in the political issues of his time, Jerusalem, Palestine, Morocco, Algeria, was not just a radical activist, but a radical exemplar of a Hallâjian synthesis, old but little known in our world, of the heart and mind, *qalb* and *'aql*, unalienated from one another. This was his full achievement as a human being and the simplest, profoundest fruit of his friendship with al-Hallâj. In a letter to the American mystic and Trappist monk Thomas Merton, he wrote:

> My case is not to be imitated; I made a duel with our Lord, and having been an outlaw (against nature in love), against law (substituted to Moslems), and Hierarchy ... (leaving my native proud Latin community for a despised, brided and insignificant Greek Catholic Melkite church), I die lonely in my family, for whom I am a bore ... I am a gloomy scoundrel.[30]

He died during the night of 31 October – 1 November 1962.

In his childhood, Massignon had received his religious education from his mother, as his father was not a practising Catholic. Through his father, however, he came into contact with J. K. Husymans who was had 'reconverted' or rediscovered the Catholic faith. He also met E. Psichari and later Charles de Foucauld,[31] who had done the same.

Although the university atmosphere was anti-clerical, Massignon practised his religion, at least in his early student days, but by the time he arrived in Egypt, he did not.

It is, in the very nature of the case, impossible to know the inner development of a young man of so many decades ago, for which so little data exists. It seems important to us, that he had already taken up the study of al-Hallâj with ardour in March 1907, and that a fragment of February 1908 describes al-Hallâj as an example to follow. The particular inner experiences which Massignon underwent in May 1908, as a result of being arrested by the Ottoman Turkish authorities on suspicion of spying; an abortive attempt – according to some – to escape, and a dangerous fit of malaria could only be judged after careful investigation. Apparently, the person involved looked all this upon as providential.[32]

On returning to France in July 1908, Massignon having 'recovered his faith became once more a loyal member of the Catholic Church. He proceeded to destroy his writings of earlier years, informed friends and colleagues of his conversion, sought the company of persons who had taken the same step, and stood by his belief for the rest of his life'.[33] Louis Massignon's conversion, it should be stressed had taken place among Arabs and he had encountered a religious loyalty on the part of the Muslims in Mesopotamia. Private Muslim prayers were said when he was lying on what appeared to be his deathbed. Throughout his life, Massignon maintained solidarity with the Arab people.

The study of al-Hallâj already started came now in its full proportions: as the study of an 'intercessor' of a witness to 'the God of love' in Islam, representing on a mystical level what Jesus did in Judaism, albeit in subordination to him. Consequently, the Hallâj research became one of the most existential studies in Orientalism, having as its ultimate aim the discovery of the spiritual truth and reality of which al-Hallâj had been a witness and martyr.[34] The intense *soif d'absolu* of this *homme de prière et de désir*[35] was devoted to Christ basically, and then to al-Hallâj, the truth of the latter only reinforcing that of the former. It is with regard to Islam that one may speak of a 'vocation' of this scholar, which meant a transcending of age-old barriers. Reaching out towards an absolute, he arrived at a cruelly difficult position, not only culturally and politically but also intellectually and spiritually.[36] Massignon attempted to realize his 'vocation' through his work, the various aspects of which will now be highlighted and described.

In the first place, there is the scholarly research on the Islamic tradition. From the scholarly point of view, already before his conversion, Massignon had shown great ability, which was to bear fruit during the rest of his life. It is just as striking that his mind, being at all times on the frontline of research, working on so many and so very different subjects never enabled him to write a handbook or synthesis of his many findings. His devotion, then, went especially to Islamic spirituality through the Quran, the mystics and thinkers, without neglecting archaeology, sociology and socio-economic history. Through its spirituality, however, Islam as such had significance for him, a significance that, from time to time, determined his interpretation of particular phenomena. His interpretation of Islam suggests, therefore, a few remarks. Massignon pleaded for recognition of the 'conditional authority' of the Quran and he sought for a partial recognition of Muhammad as a prophet.[37] But Muhammad had declared the divine essence as absolutely inaccessible to man, rejecting doctrines like those of the Trinity and Incarnation, as well as of mystical union. It was only three centuries after Muhammad that such mysteries were opened up by al-Hallâj within Islam, and this 'fulfilment' of the work of Muhammad by Hallâj is at the core of Massignon's thought. Here. Already, one finds his conviction that Islam is not closed to the workings of grace, but that conversions 'from within' – as opposed to conversions *to* another religion – are possible, in particular through the saints, of whom Hallâj is the chief. This vision is put into a historical perspective, when the claim of Islam, to descend from Abraham through Ishmael is accepted as valid: Islam has indeed a share of the promise of God to Abraham and to

Hagar (Gen. 16:10–12 and 21:11–13, 18). The place of al-Hallâj within Islam, and the place of Islam with regard to Abraham, determine Massignon's theological interpretation of Islam. Islam is the monotheism of those who have been excluded from the privileges awarded to Isaac and so to Israel and the Christian Church, and it calls these two to account for the use made of their privileges. There is no question of an 'absence of God' in Islam with its 'Abrahamic' consciousness of God. Predestination works in Islam too, where hearts are called to a zealous faith in divine transcendence. Such a faith may burn with indignation against all idolatry of pseudo-absolutes, or it may turn into a mystical love. As already mentioned Massignon was particularly interested in those phenomena that show a convergence or dialogue between Islam and Christianity, particularly vocations within Islam of mystical compassion and substitution like that of al-Hallâj. His interpretation of such phenomena went beyond their immediate historical or sociological structure, and other phenomena, which fell outside this vision, could not but be neglected.

The attitude of Massignon to contemporary developments in the Islamic world, and the action he consequently took were of great importance. He was intensely sensitive to the effects on the Muslim mind of the clash between modern western and traditional Muslim society. Morally and religiously wounded, he runs the risk of becoming a *perte de l'âme*. So he found it necessary to participate in the reconstruction of Muslim culture, religion and personality – although this might go against 'colonial interest'.[38] As for the Church, Massignon pleaded for recognition of the religious vocations that take place within Islam and an acceptance of Islam into a common adoration of God. He advocated a broadening of the doctrinal position of the Catholic Church with regard to Islam, and had audiences with the Pope on several occasions. The new current formula of 'dialogue' with Islam may be seen as lying within Massignon's vision. He formed a Christian sodality on the basis of prayer and compassion with regard to Islam.[39]

It should be borne in mind, that it was in his Church and in contact with some great Catholic converts, that

Massignon found the way to the essential mystery of the self-communication of God to man, and the possible communion of man, through Christ, with God. Against this background, his personal experience and 'communion with the saints' became what amounted to a vocation. And gave him such grace as to make him acceptable to others. From a crucially difficult position 'between' Christians and Muslims, he strove first for sanctification and then for a dialogue with Islam, 'in the presence of God'. From this point of departure, his search for a theological formula for inter-religious relations can best be understood.

Although his spiritual experiences came to him through Islam, Massignon arrived at attitudes of thought and action, which went beyond a particular Arab and Muslim context. These can be studied separately as the spiritual content of the many situations and encounters, which he experienced. A number of themes run through his work, which may be called the components of Massignon's spiritual universe. Some of them represent such essential features of life, as speech, thought, friendship, hospitality, destiny, anguish, suffering, death, sacrifice, idolizing. Another group related to the realm of the spirit, comprised justice, truth, purity, vows, pilgrimage, predestination, compassion and substitution, vocation and witnessing. Mention is often made of God's transcendence, His mystical reality, His exclusiveness, His word and grace. This aspect of Massignon's thought could be greatly elaborated. His 'interiorist' approach to reality and especially religion, his study of the rules of the degree of authenticity of testimonies of any kind, were applied on the basis of internal criteria. A few words may perhaps be said on some values, which he considered especially important.

One such value is *hospitality*, which he considered a basic structure of human behaviour and a code of inter-human relations in a world where the 'other' tends to become foreign. Besides its importance for individual relations between societies or between society and the individual, it may also become an expression of a mystical relationship between God and man. Whereas hospitality is the admission of the 'other' unto one's self, *compassion* is reaching out to the 'other' and participating in his suffering. To be affected by the suffering of other men – whether one is aware of it or not – becomes an act whereby one man takes another's suffering upon himself by 'transference'. The effect is an alleviation of the suffering itself. If Islam brought hospitality to Massignon's mind, it was certainly Christianity – via al-Hallâj – in which he found the mysteries of passion and compassion. A further step is the idea of *substitution* where one person carries, both positively and negatively, the weight of another: a doctrine, which Massignon found in both Christianity and in al-Hallâj. So his thought developed on the theme of an 'apotropean' chain of saints in the history of mankind, an extension of the Catholic idea of the role of the saints in the Church.[40]

Massignon was influential in changing the attitude of the Catholic Church towards Islam.[41] He formed a group of Arabists highly qualified in the study of Arabic and Islamic civilization. He conducted numerous missions for cultural exchanges between France and the Islamic world. But it now appears that the bases of his action – and it no doubt could have been otherwise – were too absolutist to yield visible results in the political world. The apolitical character of his stand was interwoven with loyalties, which politicians on either side could hardly appreciate. The drama of colonization and decolonization was geared to a purely earthly logic.

Massignon participated in the drafting of the Sykes-Picot agreement and saw hopes for an Arab kingdom evaporate. He had to acquiesce in the dismemberment of Syria and to participate in the Algerian celebrations of 1930. He then came, more and more, to oppose and protest against political imprisonment after the Madagascar massacres (1947); the western attitude over the Palestine question (1948); the sending of Muhammad V in exile (1953); the repression in Morocco and Tunisia; and finally the Algerian killings. The Algerian drama was a special nightmare.

In those years, his intellect outraged, he resorted to prayer and to non-violent action. He had seen the value of this last in the example of Gandhi for whom he had the greatest respect. Since 1953, moreover, he kept a day of fasting once a month to be observed by both Muslims and the Christians who were members of his sodality 'Badaliyya'. Badaliyya was based in Paris, Rome and Cairo, including members of the Greek Catholic Melkite Church and those who were drawn to this circle. Massignon held a view of history, which sees the handing on of knowledge of God from one individual to another as the only significant process and therefore most deserving of study. Louis Massignon developed this theme of history in a series of letters to Paul Claudel between 1908–9 in which the meaning of history is to be found not in the impersonality of social evolution, but in the divine word in the individual seed. Such encounters can take place within the ordered framework of an established tradition: but they can also be sudden confrontations: the unexpected 'Other' breaks in on ordinary life, shattering and transforming it. In a moment of illumination a man can transcend his worldly images and see beyond them another beauty.

History is a chain of witness entering each other's lives as bearers of a truth beyond themselves, and a chain which can run across the habitual frontiers of different religions. Massignon believed that he himself had been drawn into this chain, in an event of which it is difficult to accept all the details as he described them, but which certainly decided the direction of his life. The event was his initiation as a witness, a participant in the mystery of substitution, by which a man can provide for others what they cannot obtain for themselves. Having acquired through Muslims the knowledge of transcendence, how could he himself serve as a channel through which they could come to knowledge of incarnation? For Massignon, the Arabic language had an ontological quality; language can give a grasp of reality, it liberates from space and time, and it gives the access to the world of ideas.[42] As a priest of the Melkite Catholic rite he would have said Mass in Arabic.[43]

Massignon used to speak about religion, ethics and personal experiences. He did not speak of a strictly personal 'vocation' which he had to fulfil, but rather of things which had overcome him. It seems to us, however, that his life, which would appear to the most biting cynic as exceptional, would show on closer investigation not only a strange destiny, but also the realization of a vocation. Using this word we deprive it of all its idealistic overtones: for how can we call it 'ideal' when a vocation as was his brought so heavy a burden.[44]

Louis Massignon's Theological Reflection on Islam

Over four decades ago Louis Massignon came to the end of 'his course', and was able to say – just like Paul the Apostle to the Gentiles – that he had 'fought the good fight to the end and kept his faith' (2 Tm 4:7). Since then, his disciples, colleagues and friends have not ceased to evoke his memory, to experience his presence and to question his work. Robert Caspar says in his well-documented study, 'Louis Massignon's vision of Islam and his influence on the Church',[45] the prophetic intuition of Massignon did not fail to bear fruit in the field of Muslim-Christian relations, especially through a close theological examination of the conciliar discussions and decrees of the Second Vatican Council. Paul VI, who was a close friend of Massignon's before becoming Pope and, as Mgr Montini, was a member of the Roman sodality of the Badaliyya established by Louis Massignon, and John Paul II, who was also inspired by it, have thus been able to inherit the courageous and generous openings provided by the thought of Massignon who justly reminded present-day Christians that in order to understand the Muslims, they have to mentally move away from the centre, just like Copernicus did and then, assuming that the problem has been solved, put themselves in the very axis of Muslim doctrine, that virgin point of truth which is at its centre and which makes it live, and from which invisibly and mysteriously everything else sustains itself.[46]

And is this not, strictly speaking, the very thing which Louis Massignon realized for himself first of all, after he was taken in hand again by the visit of the Stranger on 1–3 May 1908 when God touched his heart in Iraq, in the desert? As we mentioned above, Guy Harpigny in his study *Islam et christianisme selon Louis Massignon*, showed how Massignon's curve of life developed in three spiritual cycles whose masters were al-Hallâj, Abraham and Gandhi. Each of them reflected the very Jesus Christ whom his brother 'in the desert', Charles de Foucauld, like to call the 'unique model'. As Pierre Rocalve points out in his recent study on *La place et le rôle de l'Islam et de l'islamologie dans la vie et l'œuvre de Louis Massignon*,[47] the Hallâj cycle 1906–1922: study of the summits to which mysticism in Islam can lead; the Abraham cycle 1922–1950: repeat meditation on the primordial witness of monotheism in history; and the Gandhi cycle 1950–1962: witness for justice through non-violent action; were matched by three periods during which research was followed by reflection and commitment, where he pursued three fields of interest: First of all, medieval Islam, secondly eternal Islam, [and] lastly contemporary Islam. It is obvious that these kinds of categorization, because they are too abrupt, always contain an element of arbitrariness. Massignon's intellectual life and his spiritual life were profoundly united. With him, everything flows from Islam and the Muslims, as it is with them and for them that he has developed 'his vocation as the compatient and substituted one', whereby he 'gradually helps his secret vow come to the surface through his public life', because he was 'provoked to holiness'.

Louis Massignon had specialized in neither biblical exegesis nor Christian theology. He was familiar with the Muslims whom he visited at home or helped even in Paris, he was a professor of sociology at the Collège de France, but he was just as profoundly marked by his faith in Jesus Christ which he had found again: rooted in a spirituality where suffering and compassion have redemptive value, fraternally surrounded by a host of witnesses and saints, intellectually enriched by a thousand readings which opened up his Christian culture up to infinite horizons. He therefore found himself called to 'situate' in relation to the Christian history of salvation that which he discovered in Islam and which he perceived of its founder and book, and he was thus able to appreciate all the more the authentic values of the Muslim religious experience. It is therefore hardly surprising that during the fifty years of study, teaching and witness, the thought of Louis Massignon should have experienced growing maturity, albeit in the straight line based upon his own fundamental intution, all the more as for him this was never about a structured theological reflection but more like a contextualized existential perception into which the current problems experienced by the Muslims and the calls of his increasingly demanding spirituality were fed. This explains why – as one of his disciples, the Arab Catholic priest E. S. Sabanegh puts it – 'the value judgements made by Massignon with regard to al-Hallâj or the Muslim religion are the outpourings of an ardent faith and a passionate temperament for which effective and affective commitment are never very far from intellectual conviction'.[48] It is therefore only with this in mind that one should read his key texts on these subjects, in order to gain a better understanding of their intention of the moment and at the same time their real limitations.

Leaving aside the systematic study of Muslim dogmatic and mystical theologies, such as it was undertaken by Louis Massignon in *La Passion d'al-Hallâj* and the *Essai sur les origines du vocabulaire de la mystique musulmane,* those who have focused on the outlines of his 'spiritual vision' of Islam agree that there are four key documents on this subject. First the *Examen du 'Présent de l'homme lettré', par Abdallah Ibn al-Torjoman* (which is dated autumn 1917). Then there is the corpus of his thought on Islam which can be found in *L'Hégire d'Ismaël,* one of the prayers of Abraham which had already been edited by him from 1925 to 1927 and was published in *Les Trois Prières d'Abraham* in 1935. Thirdly, there is a long interview with a Franciscan review which was published in *Rythmes du monde* in 1948 and bore the significant title, 'Le Signe marial' . Finally, there is a personal letter published by Mrs R. Charles-Barzel in her book *Ô Vierge puissante* in 1958, which reproduces many passages from his letters to the Badaliyya. Of course, one could collect the thousands of thoughts, annotations and reflections contained in the whole of Massignon's work which give an idea of his thought and explain the reasons for his actions; however, these four texts can be deemed sufficient at present for us to ask questions about the theological aspects of his thought on Islam. What remains is the difficult problem of reading and interpreting these texts in a way which is faithful to the intentions of the author. Massignon was a poet and prophet as much as a sociologist and a linguist: it is not easy to distinguish in his writings between those parts where he describes Islam and the Muslim societies in an objective manner and those where he expresses his solidarity with the values which he finds and celebrates, and which are therefore subjective, with words which belong to the Christian vocabulary or even with neologisms which he endows with new and very personal meaning. Taking into account these real difficulties – which numerous disciples have interpreted in different ways – we will now look at the four documents mentioned above.[49]

L'Examen du "Présent de l'homme lettré"[49]
We know why Louis Massignon edited the Examen in autumn 1917 when he was in Egypt: he met up with a friend, a religious, whom the reading of *Tuhfat al-adib* (*The Present for the literary man*) by Ibn al-Torjoman, alias Anselmo Turmeda, an anti-Christian Muslim apologetic work dated from the fifteenth century and which had been translated into French, had shaken in his faith. In editing this work, Louis Massignon displayed a vast knowledge of the entire anti-Christian Muslim literature at the same time as a 'Christian sense' of the texts; plus a profound understanding of the richness of his Christian theology and spirituality. One may justly consider that his return to the Christian faith in May 1908 must have been followed by long years of rigorous research and that he was able to 'place himself' all the better in relation to anti-Christian Muslim apologetics. He thus became even more rooted in his faith in Jesus Christ which he had found again. All of this makes one think that the *Examen*, far from being a first outline of his thought, already expressed a fundamental synthesis where the confrontation of the two religions on

the level of faith, texts and founders led him to express his 'Christian vision' of Muslim realities.

The best version of the *Examen* has recently been published in Rome by the Pontifical Institute for the Study of Arabic and Islam and is therefore accessible to all. The *Examen* thus presents itself as a small treatise of comparative theology. Massignon starts off by describing the personality of the translator and that of the author of the *Tuhfat*; this he does not without a certain verve which is at time caustic. He then goes on to analyze in turn the method employed and finally the fundamental postulates of Ibn al-Torjoman's apologetics. The conclusion is a convivial dialogue between a Muslim and a Christian friend. A long appendix, which could be entitled 'Divine Providence', seems to suggest a spiritual foundation course for those who have questions of faith: where does God appear in the world? How do human beings become aware of his presence? Why does God present himself to each conscience as a question? Louis Massignon starts off by answering these three questions in an impersonal manner before explaining himself by means of very personal confidences, which are the outlines of his spirituality. Massignon, recognizing that all 'these polemicists are often of good faith because they judge according to Islam' and that 'Islam is a community of believers whose only sign of communion is a Book', then moves on to question the real scope of one and the other. In his chapter on the fundamental postulates of Muslim apologetics he notes that it is 'critical and trenchant (and not constructive or gradual, such as Christian apologetics) and only suggests to man to adhere through reason by the evidence of natural religion'.[51]

According to what he perceives of it,

> the aim of Koranic revelation is not to expose and justify supernatural data which were hitherto ignored, but to make intelligences, by reminding them in the name of God of the temporal and eternal sanctions, find again the natural religion, the primitive law, the very simple cult which God has prescribed forever, which Adam, Abraham and the prophets have all practised in the same way, by convincing the idolaters, Jews and Christians, of the evidence of that divine law

which they must recognize, engraved in their intelligence, once they have stripped it of all vain superstition

In doing so, Muslim apologetics shows itself to be

> literal and destructive whereas Christian apologetics are real and vivifying [...]. Its only aim is to make the intelligences find faith again by helping them access the texts of a book. Muslim apologetics does not have to specify its meaning, nor does it have to define dogmas, nor does it practise virtues. It simply draws some legal rules from the Book, from the external governing of society; it is only attentive to the intelligences and tolerates with indulgence the habitual miseries of the flesh, the hidden faults which do not lead to public disorder. It does not scrutinise the conscience. It demands as little as possible as revelation only provides the intelligence with a natural proof and only promises the body a limited reward.

All this is clarified in the relationship between Creator and creature:

> Islam sees the Creator in God; the creation of the world separates *ipso facto* the being of the creatures from the creative essence [...] Islam sees in all creatures one of the innumerable forms of obedience which divine thought pleases itself to conceive, and which the created being – which has been placed in interdict, excluded from the divine essence, forever exiled in the finite – has the mission to witness by that unbreakable separation from God, that He is the Only Master, and that all creatures are indistinctly His servants'.

Speaking about the Quran and Muhammad, Massignon notes that

> Muslim apologetics, which starts off from the rational impossibility of any relationship uniting God – the Creator – with Man – the creature, seals this prohibition by the very text which was revealed to Muhammad. Muslim apologetics interposes a permanent formal miracle between God and man, an obvious sign of separation and prohibition [...]: the text of the divine Word.

In doing this,

> the Koran is superior to Muhammad: the essential part of any new edition of the divine message reminding man of that natural religion which must guide all acts of their nature like an instinct of a social order, is not to show how to practise the Law by means of a personal and living example, but instead to remind man of the sanctions.

And further down:

> Muslim apologetics present the Koran as the authentic text of positive divine Law which it considers as fixed from the beginning and *ne varietur* for all peoples, especially through the law of Moses. It conceives the Mosaic revelation as a simple new edition of primitive revelation destined to all peoples.

As can be seen from these few passages taken from among many others

> the Koranic revelation finally is presented as the natural law, that is, the eternal law directing the acts and movements of men towards the end which is theirs, such as they are formulated for reason. This revelation calls itself, like the eternal law, universal, unmovable and absolute ... all human reason of natural law can decipher by itself, from the start, and proclaim the whole code of natural law, Decalogue of Sinai, or Sermon on the Mount, by beginning by its first article, reduced because it is a pure intellectual acquiescence, to the *shema Israel,* to the duty to proclaim divine unity. And this first article is the only one which is indispensable for eternal beatitude. The Koranic revelation reminds every man of the fact that they have engraved in their reason natural law, and that it is both necessary and sufficient.

It therefore follows

> that in Islam, God is unknowable in his essence and that all he asks of man is to accept the revealed terms which describe the divine attributes without seeing them as a means of understanding Him, and to practise throughout

their lives the revealed Law which expresses his orders without seeing this as a means of union with Him. The question as to what God is for Himself must not be asked.

What, then, is the role of Muhammad in such a context? For Massignon

> in order to be communicated to the others, the evidence with which he understood the divine Book simply demanded that human reason should follow his own constitutive Law. And this fundamental point in the psychology of Muhammad, his obstinate sincerity, explains to us why Muslim apologetics identified the Koran with natural law, the positive divine law, the Book of Judgement and the divine Word.

Louis Massignon explains this by describing 'the psychological development of the situation': 'The intelligence of Muhammad received the vigorous impression of an idea which is pure and simple, abstract and naked, i.e. one, that of divinity'. And

> this divine essence, pure and simple [...], Muhammad considers it at the centre of his intelligence and it makes him reconstruct the whole of natural religion thanks to everyday experience: creator, creature; believer, infidel; elected, damned [...]. The proclamation of divine unity is for Muhammad the essence of his reading of that divine Law which he knows is engraved in the reason of every being and has been entrusted to all prophets. He is therefore one of them because he has conceived of the thought.

Still according to Louis Massignon, Muhammad 'verifies the then subsisting editions of that Law among the Jews, the Christians and the Sabeans. There he finds the origins of his race, the vocation of Abraham, the birth of Ismail, the prayer of Agar'. Thus 'Muhammad has found his fathers and the Law of Abraham his great ancestor', convinced that his race, 'the race of Ismail', is no longer excluded from the divine promise but rather the elected people which has to be organized. And Massignon then analyzed the 'touch, enlightenment, spark' which in the end constitutes something like the developments of the reality of the Koran. At the end, he says, there is 'that proof of God, that "intellectual miracle", the *ayah* verse, the very essence of His message'.

By considering Islam thus, and by therefore respecting it as a return to the natural religion of the origins and giving the Quran and Muhammad all their possible value in doing so, Massignon does not fail however to question the 'role of Islam in the history of the world' (he even added, 'for the triumph of Christianity'). According to his intuition, there is a specific mission which is something like a threefold challenge. 'Islam', he says, 'wanted to prove against all idolatries that the primitive religion of the patriarchs, from Adam to Noah and Abraham, was sufficient for all the social needs of man, by ordering man's reason to adore the unique God of natural Law, through faith, forever'. What is more, 'Islam wanted to prove, like Judaism, that the Law of Moses was good for all peoples and all times and that faith was sufficient for observing its rigorous laws.' Finally,

> Islam wanted to establish against the Church that love was only wanted by God for humans in their relationship with each other, that love was something which had been too much prostituted among them for God to be wanted to be loved by them for Himself, forever. He wanted to exclude from the beatitude of the elected all-intuitive vision of the divine essence, and all-transforming union from their holiness, and finally he wanted to reduce their eternity to the contentment of the flesh and to the pure thought of intelligence; that is hell, with the pain of damnation without the pain of meaning.

This is therefore, according to Massignon, the anti-establishment or prophetic role which historical Islam has fulfilled for the last fourteen centuries and should fulfil in the future.[52]

'L'Hégire d'Ismaël' – the second of the 'Trois prières d'Abraham[53]
Planned at the end of the Hallâj cycle, edited and published at the heart of the Abraham cycle, the prayer of Abraham for the Muslims, titled *Hégire d'Ismaël* (1935),

which was framed by the prayer for 'Sodom, to the Philoxenia of Mambré', on the one hand, and the prayer to 'Moria, the place of the offering of Isaac', on the other, is of particular significance. In it, Massignon declares in his shorthand way of expressing himself that in 'Berseba, the well of the oath' where 'God imposed expatriation on Abraham, the "Hegira" of his first-born son, Ismail, Abraham consented to his exile in the desert provided that his descendants survive, that it should be provided by God in the world with a certain privileged perennity, marking this Ismaili, Arab race with a vocation, the sword, "the iron endowed with scathing power" (Q 57:25) which suspends its threat, once Islam was formed, on all the idolaters to which the holy war is declared, implacable for as long as they do not confess that there is only one God, that of Abraham, "the first Muslim". Militant claim of pure transcendence, mysterious resurgence of the patriarchal cult preceding the Mosaic Decalogue and the Beatitudes, denudation of the desert'.

Making what he said in his *Examen* of the *Tuhfa* more explicit, Massignon comes to consider that Islam 'is almost an Abrahamic schism, like Samaria and Talmudism were Mosaic schisms, like Greek Orthodoxy was a post-Chalcedonian schism'. It is 'a mysterious reply by grace to the prayer of Abraham for Ismail and the Arabs'. This intuition is one of the riches, but also one of the most adventurous once given the central place of Jesus Christ in the Jewish-Christian history of salvation. Massignon does not doubt that Christ accomplishes all promises made to the Fathers and to the prophets of Israel and thus completes the holy history of our humanity; but he also considers that Islam 'though a movement of temporal involution, through going back to the remotest past, inversely symmetrical to the growing Messianic expectation of the Jews from Isaiah to Herod, announces the end of revelation, the cessation of the waiting', because he comes 'before not just Pentecost but before the Decalogue': he expresses 'with a naiveté which is even more primitive than a child's' a message which presents itself as 'levelling at the margins of natural religion all supernatural dogmatic unfolding', ultimately reducing itself 'to the moral virtue of religion'. Islam is thus a 'natural religion revived by prophetic revelation'.

These forceful claims are corroborated by other thoughts, which are just as audacious: 'It is appropriate', he says, 'that it was in the Arab desert [...] that a voice from above was heard: it brought creation back to the origins to announce the Judgement, it formulated the protestation of the primordial angelic nature'. Massignon understood Islam to be a protestation of the excluded and a call for the 'Judgement of God' against the elected (Judaism and Christianity) who had been unfaithful witness to their calling. Islam has – according to Massignon, 'a positive mission: by accusing Israel of considering itself to be privileged to the point of expecting a Messiah born of its race, the race of David, according to a carnal paternity, he confirms that he has already been born, unrecognized, from a predestined virginal mother, that it is Jesus the Son of Mary and that he will return at the end of time, heralding the Judgement'. It follows that the Quran and Muhammad are granted unparalleled privileges. He defines the latter as a 'negative prophet' because, as Massignon was to say later,

> in order to be a 'false' prophet one has to positively prophesy wrongly. A positive prophesy is generally shocking for the understanding because it is a predicted reversal of human values. But Muhammad, who believed in a frightening way in this total reversal, can only be a negative prophet, and that he is very authentically. He never pretended to be neither an intercessor nor a saint (Q 7: 188) but he confirmed that he was a witness, the voice which cries in the desert of separation between the good and evil, the witness of separation.

He has come after Moses and Jesus and is the 'negative harbinger of the Judgement of death which will reach everything that has been created'.

This is why Massignon envisages 'the existence of an "inspiration" of the Koran', but the only proof which he quotes to justify his claim is of a linguistic order. For him 'revelation which has only expressed and modalized itself in Semitic languages grew in Hebrew, spread in Aramaic beyond the thorny hedges of Israel in the 'clothing' of the Messianic lily and then found itself mysteriously burned to ashes *in clibanum missa* with the Koranic *dhariyat'*, the burning breezes of the Judgement'. The very archaism of the Arab language therefore predestined it to this particular vocation. All in all, the quranic revelation which was transmitted in Arabic is considered by Louis Massignon to be

> a truncated Arabic edition of the Bible, an amalgamate of unpublished things, levelled at the descendances of Ismail, and it can be given the rule of conditional authority conceded to the decisions of the anti-Popes within the limitations of it [the Koran] constituting the 'scriptural rule' of the Abrahamic schism of the excluded Agarenians. The Koran is to the Bible what Ismail was to Isaac. [...] there is in the Islam of the descendants of Ismail, a path leading to salvation: it is the *hajj* (the pilgrimage) founded on Abraham [where] there is pure offering of the heart of the pilgrim: in Arafat, he offers himself for the whole Community. At that moment, the woman is equal to man [...]. The Muslim *hajj* in Mecca is essentially a spiritual offering in Arafat and the 'descent from mercy' does not wait for the immolated victims on the next day to procure the jubilee indulgence of which the great Hebrew doctor Maimonides admitted its 'Abraham validity' thanks to the intercession of some pure, humble and hidden souls.

Without taking sides between the many interpretations which the disciples of Massignon have undertaken of this 'Abrahamic' dimension of Islam, extending it to all promises made to Abraham himself or reducing it to a strict 'Ismailism' of the excluded, it is quite significant that it was at the very moment when he welcomed and generously integrated Islam, its Book and its prophet that Massignon measures its limits and refusals like never before.[54] Referring back to the meditation of the Muslim mystics on 'the nocturnal ascension' (*mi'raj*) of Muhammad he confesses that

> one has to note that, having remained on the threshold [of

the divine space], dazzled, he [Muhammad] did not attempt to go any further into the divine fire, and in doing so, excludes himself from understanding from within the personal life of God, an understanding which would have sanctified him. Upon being invited to pray for the great sinners he did not dare make an intercession for all of them, he kept to the boundaries of his roots, he only prayed for those from the Muslim community. Although he finds ingrained in his memory the tablet of God the Creator enjoining everybody to adore, he does not take from it the final meaning of the precept; his will does not dare adhere to the counsel of perfect life, it declines the mystical betrothal, the enigma of which he thus withholds under pain of death from all Muslims, from the future.

No one could better express the grandeur and ambiguity of the Abrahamic vocation which Massignon recognizes in Islam.[55]

The Marian sign[56]
In 1948, Louis Massignon granted the Franciscan review of *Rythmes du monde* an interview on the subject of his Abrahamic cycle, at a time when he was preparing to become a priest in the Greek-Melkite rite and when he was about to become more involved than ever in the events of his time following the example of Gandhi. This interview clarifies, confirms and completes what he had already told in the *Examen* and in the *Trois Prières d'Abraham*. He was asked, 'Do you believe in Islam?' He replied, 'I believe in the God of Abraham, real, imminent, personal, not in the ideal Deity of the philosophers and the Devil, and this is the first link between me and my Muslim friends because the religion of Abraham consists of two key commandments: only to worship God alone and to follow His holy will with all your soul.' Upon being asked about the person of Muhammad, he replied, 'I think that he was sincere and that you should not do unto others that which you would not like them to do to you.' He then went on to explain in more detail what he meant by 'negative prophet'. Insisting on the 'sign of the two' (that of Mary and of Jesus) which

was suggested by the Quran itself, in which he wants to see a presence and a promise, Massignon added, 'I do not say that by announcing this sign of contradiction, Muhammad believed in the divinity of Jesus; in front of the Christians of Najran, his answer to this question was to ask for an ordeal, a divine judgement. (*mubahala*, Q 3, 54). He is still waiting, even more so, the Koran says that this sign will not be given by God until the Last Judgement.' And he confessed, 'I do not say that that "sign of the two" which is sketched out in the Koran is much clearer for the Muslim reader than the "sign of the three" before Abraham in Mambré, for the Rabbinical reader of the Bible. But there is no doubt that Muhammad was a Witness to it before the Jews in Medina [...] and I can only admire the mission of Muhammad in Medina as witness of this Marian Sign.'

He then went on to talk about the Quran, its message and inspiration and admitted that 'it is difficult to express the "death of a God" in Arabic', alluding to the unsolved problem of the death of Jesus, adding that 'the Koran admits that divine generosity goes beyond nature (in its rewards) and does not tolerate that the free insertion, by means of grace, of the divine mystery in the creatures (unique mystery where the Christians discern three mysteries, the Trinity, the Incarnation, the Redemption) – an insertion which is supernatural – should be diminished by the ambiguous vocabulary of natural relation, by ambivalent denominations such as those of the communication of idioms'. So what 'meaning' can the Islam of the Muslims have for Christians? Louis Massignon says that here he can hear 'a summons of superhuman justice which springs from the disadvantaged, colonialized, despised Muslim believers; for forty years it has awakened the Christian in me [...]. It is the call of faith which is at the root of justification (if it is not sufficient for salvation) [...] and this naked, childlike, resigned faith, which is not uplifted by the Jewish hope, smouldering under the embers without the brightness of Christian dilection, this faith is the witness of the faith of Abraham which is revived in Muhammad by an undesertable ancestral conviction'.

And he adds, this is why there are saints in Islam: 'I have

met them, and now, after forty years, I can admit that my return to the Church is the child of their prayer and that therefore they are for me, their neighbour, not outside the Church which I have found again with them'. According to Massignon, therefore, Christians should always treat Muslims 'as brothers in Abraham, not born of the same blood (*nasab*), but of the same Spirit of faith and of sacrifice', as they have been sent away by the latter to the demands of the Rule of evangelical life, that *Rahbaniyya* (monastic ideal) of which the Quran says that God has put it in the heart of those who follow Jesus.[57] Massignon concluded the interview as follows:

> It can be said that Islam exists and continues to subsist because it is of Abrahamic faith, to force the Christians to rediscover a more bare, more primitive, more simple form of sanctification, which the Muslims admittedly only attain very rarely, but through our fault because we have not yet shown it to them in us, and this is what they expect from us, from Christ. As those who know about it will guess, this is the programme of the Badaliyya in a nutshell: compassion and substitution for a better spiritual emulation in loyalty to the demands of one's own faith.[58]

The letter quoted in 'Ô Vierge puissante'[59]

In 1958, Mrs R. Charles-Barzel published the principle sections of a letter by Massignon addressed to her, in her book *Ô Vierge puissante*. We know what enormous efforts Massignon made during the Moroccan and Madagascar crises as well as those at the very heart of the Algerian tragedy. Whilst denouncing the numerous Christian and French acts of infidelity he still maintained his personal 'vision' of Islam and of the Muslims on a theological level, this time detailing in a perhaps slightly oversimplified way that which he had so far only repeated. In his letter he wrote,

> You have to remember above all that the Muslims have not yet received from God all graces, private or sacramental, which it is the Christians' redoubtable privilege to have. Redoubtable for them if they misuse them by despising the Muslims to whom God has not given them.

In fact, in the history of humanity we have three religious periods: 1) the stage of nature blessed by the sin of Adam, which corresponds to the patriarchal period; 2) the legal stage which begins with the Decalogue of the Sinai; 3) the evangelic stage which begins with Christ and at Pentecost. It is absurd to discuss with a believing Jew as if he had arrived at the evangelic stage; he is still at the Law of fear. In the same way, it is absurd to discuss with a Muslim as if he had arrived either at the legal stage or at the evangelic stage.

He concluded by saying,

Islam is still at the patriarchal stage, at the time of Abraham. And the fact that Muhammad preached it 600 years after Pentecost, that the Koran names Moses and Jesus Son of Mary does not prevent Islam from being at the patriarchal, quite primitive stage where the moral conscience which is admirably enlightened on the obedience to God, first served, and on the prohibition of idolatry, is still embryonic when it comes to polygamy, concubinage, abduction, and war stratagems.'

Massignon knows from experience that time is required for some forms of spiritual growth. He admits that

The Christians, even those who have arrived at the evangelic stage, have been slow to disapprove of all these but they practise it, alas! Knowing that it is bad, whereas it is in contact with us that the Muslim masses also realise that they are bad, now [...]. It is not just moral conscience which slowly acquires the natural moral laws, but also Revelation which has slowly dispensed the divine positive rights to mankind. One always has to bear in mind that Muhammad was still at the patriarchal stage, ingeniously devising war stratagems and practising eye-for-an-eye revenge of the most atrocious kind with a clear conscience, whereas us Christians know that this is wrong.

In the same way, Louis Massignon considers that polygamy 'is for him the polygamy of the Patriarchs of before the

Law'. Later on he says that,

> Muhammad founded a temporal State, Jesus did not have a temporal State to govern. The Muslims accuse us of having a Law which cannot be practised. Theirs is more proportionate to the average man. Muhammad did not do this on purpose but through the ingenuity of a contemporary of the patriarchal period of Abraham, and he thought that he had received it from God.

So, how should Islam be looked at from a Christian point of view? The letter reminds its addressee that 'Islam is a great mystery of divine will, the demand of the excluded, chased from the desert with Ismail their ancestor, against those "privileged" by God, Jews and above all Christians, who have abused the divine privileges of Grace.' Furthermore, the author of this letter adds, 'There are certainly some Muslims with clean consciences, for whom Jesus and Mary and the Easter of Hajj are sources of inner sanctification – you have met them yourself – but they are not for them, like for the Christians, sources of public, sacramental sanctification.' As we can see, he says nothing which has not been said or written before, but here it is expressed in a simpler and clearer language, with the risk of offending some sensitivities: it is always as a Christian, in total coherence with his faith in Jesus Christ, that Massignon intends to include the great spiritual adventure of historical Islam and of those who have been nourished by it religiously.

His annual letters to the Badaliyya, that sodality of prayer and intercessions founded by him and Mary Kahil at Damietta (the place where historically Saint Francis challenges the Sultan) in 1947, explain more and more of it and thus clarify the thoughts which he has expressed in the four documents analyzed here. In the first (1947) he enumerates the five goals of the Badaliyya. Before setting out its means and organization, Massignon points out that for the Christians the task is to 'devote themselves to the salvation of their [Muslim] brothers, and in this hope, to give in the name of their brothers, to Jesus Christ, faith, adoration and love that an imperfect knowledge of the Gospels does not allow them to give themselves.' He adds that, 'salvation does not necessarily mean external conversion. Much is already gained by a larger number belonging to the soul of the Church, living and dying in a state of grace'. This is how he intends to ensure the convergence of the spiritualities whilst respecting the loyalty of others, by including them in his Christian vision of salvation, as privileged guests thanks to the spirit of compassion and substitution. The humble and key role of this spirit in preparing for world unity was to be particularly evoked in his letter of 1957.

In his letter of December 1959, Louis Massignon had the opportunity to come back to this subject and rejected the accusation of 'missionary activity in the disguise of scholarly Orientalism in higher education'. He wrote that, 'Yet Sheikh Bahy knows that the Badaliyya in no way aims at the "external conversion" of its non-Christian friends; it asks them to deepen their current denominational position through an "internal conversion", in line with the God of Abraham, by means of a meditative and renouncing way of life, which is likely to engender in them this Face "which Mary has formed herself of Jesus" in the depths of their Muslim heart.' And finally, how could we not quote that great expression of his thought in his letter of Easter 1962? In it he refers to the specific forms of the Abrahamic substitution, adding that it is

> essentially, a witness of the faith in the Last Judgement (where in Islam, a certain presence of Jesus shows through, which is associated with that *Yawm al-Din*). This Muslim Faith, which is entirely directed towards the past and towards the 'holy light once promised to Abraham' makes our Muslim brothers into 'catechumens', just as the Hope of the Messiah makes our Jewish friends into 'catechumens' *with whom* (and not just *for whom*) we have to pray, we to whom the plenitude of the Third virtue, Charity, has been given. It should be added, whilst 'subliming' the famous medieval parable of the Three Rings, that the three Semitic languages which convey these three Virtues – Hebrew in Judaism, Aramaic in Christianity and Arabic in Islam – in fact have a 'capacity to inspire' [...] We have therefore prayed with them, for them ...

And therefore prayer, fasting, almsgiving and pilgrimage have always been, for him and for the members of the Badaliyya, the choice forms of a spiritual convergence where the spirit of substitution is capable of hastening the rapprochement so desired by the souls which God calls to holiness everywhere.[60]

Final Reflections

These are the theological aspects in the thought of Louis Massignon concerning Islam, the Quran and Muhammad. For him, Islam is a 'natural religion revived by a prophetic revelation' which reclaims the religion of Abraham, the pure monotheist of patriarchal times. This is what Sabanegh pointed out in the witness quoted above. Without necessarily wanting to confirm the existence of a carnal filiation of the Arabs starting from Ismail – which both ethnology and onomastics put seriously in doubt – Louis Massignon's vision envisages for them and for the Muslims a spiritual Abrahamic generation which thus guarantees religious legitimacy for both. Thus Islam would be placed 'in the transhistorical alliance which concludes with the "Son of Adam", just as it is in the special history of revelation which began with Abraham. For Massignon, 'as a result, the Koran cannot not be "inspired", at least for the share of truth that it contains', but it only has 'conditional authority' because it occasionally 'separates from God'. Regarding Muhammad, he is not a false prophet and his sincerity is not in doubt. He is therefore 'an authentic prophet, but a negative prophet' in the sense where 'prophesy is the angelic annunciation to human nature of the superhuman consummation of its finality'.

Although his knowledge of Muslim theology and mystics is perfect, Louis Massignon did not consider that he had the right to pass a Christian theological judgement on them which is definitive: he refused to attribute or have attributed a theological scope to his intuitions. His words thus seem like 'transtheological breakthroughs' where all kinds mix and mingle so that they can prophetically challenge each other even better. But as Fr R. Caspar says, 'he was nevertheless above all suspicions of syncretism. In the eyes of some he might have preferred Muslim values. But he was aware to the highest degree of the irreducible originality of the two religions. It is precisely by exploring the crest of Islam that he was able to pinpoint the watershed so clearly.'[62]

It is because he discovered saints in Islam that he proposed the reinterpretation of salvation history, by proposing to Islam, to the Quran and to Muhammad the place which he could loyally award them in a history of salvation at the end of which his Christian faith always put Jesus Christ. His efforts should serve as a reminder that the time of *exclusions* is no longer acceptable, be they theological and spiritual or even political and cultural. If the Christians and Muslims together with the Jews want to help the modern political condition, our present-day Sodoms and Gomorrhas, to seek reconciliation with God and with themselves, should we not, instead of *excluding* other believers, aim to *include* them by respecting them with their specific characteristics, in a coherent theological version which has a place for all, which guarantees peaceful and brotherly cooperation between us at the same time as spiritual emulation on the paths to holiness which is worthy of the true sons of Abraham? This is what Louis Massignon would suggest – a new international order based upon belief and theological truth.[63]

Notes

1 Herbert Mason, 'Louis Massignon et al-Hallâj', *Presence de Louis Massignon. Hommages et témoignages.* Textes réunis par Daniel Massignon, Paris, Éditions Maisonneuve et Larose, 1987, pp. 105–12.

2 Roger Arnaldez, 'Hallâj et Jèsus dans le pensèe de Louis Massignon', *Horizons maghrébins. Louis Massignon. Hommes de dialogue des cultures*, no. 14–15 (1989), pp. 171–78.

3 L. Massignon, 'Nature in Islamic Thought', *Testimonies and Reflections: Essays of Louis Massignon.* Selected and introduced by Herbert Mason, Notre Dame, Indiana, University of Notre Dame Press, 1989, p. 83.

4 J-P. De Menasce, 'Reconnaisance à Louis Massignon', *Mémorial*

Louis Massignon, Cairo, Dar-es-Salam, 1963, p. 81. These views expressed by De Menasce are more surprising as he was deeply sceptical of Islam as a distinct religious tradition, 'Islam, without doubt, is to be ranked among the heresies. The biblical revelation, although poorly known, is not unknown and is formally rejected with respect to the essential truths: the Incarnation and the Trinity', 'La théologie de la mission selon Kraemer', *Neue Zeitschrift für Missionswissenschaft*, vol. 1, 1945, p. 251.
5 Françoise Jacquin, 'Pour une comprehension des cultures: Louis Massignon et l'abbé Monchanin', *Louis Massignon et le dialogue des cultures*, Paris, Les Éditions du Cerf, 1996, pp. 341–56.
6 See the essays in the various volumes edited by A. O'Mahony, *Palestinian Christians: Religion, Politics and Society in the Holy Land*, London, Melisende, 1999; *The Christian Communities of Jerusalem and the Holy Land: Studies in History, Religion and Politics*, Cardiff, University of Wales Press, 2003; *Eastern Christianity: Studies in Modern History, Religion and Politics*, London, Melisende, 2004; and *Christianity in the Middle East: Studies in Modern History, Religion and Politics*, London, Melisende, 2005.
7 Michael Burrell, 'Mind and Heart at the Service of Muslim-Christian Understanding: Louis Massignon, as Trail Blazer', *The Muslim World*, vol. LXXXVIII, no. 3–4, 1998, pp. 274–76.
8 A.d'Alverny, *Mémorial Louis Massignon*, Cairo, Dar-es-Salam, 1963, p. 2.
9 Michael Burrell, 'Louis Massignon, as Trail Blazer', p. 274.
10 Michael Burrell, 'Louis Massignon, as Trail Blazer', p. 268.
11 Massignon wrote in 1937, 'Trying to live among my Christian brethren, just as I live it among the others, my faith, hope and love, pregnant of the full dogma. My only way to love my friends is to love them personally, with all that may seem to them, in their R.C. friend 'queer, obsolete, or borrowed', with all that I recognize as the living structural personality of the R.C. Church: ecclesiastic hierarchy, sacramental realism, vows perpetual, all that warrants my irrevocable love; for me, and for them: immaculate in Her Conception, exclusive in Her infallibility, indissoluble in Her wedlock, wearing the threefold token of crowning union given by the Spirit to the Bride', *Opera Minora*, vol. III, p. 789.
12 Albert H. Hourani, *Islam in European Thought*, Cambridge University Press, 1990, pp. 43–49.
13 Since his death from a heart attack on the night of 31 October, 1962, many memoirs, appreciations, scholarly and biographical studies of Louis Massignon have appeared, attempting to capture and convey something of his range of ideas, interests, and

personal imprints on others. Because of the complexity of his life and thought, though he kept nothing of either secret from anyone, he remains richly elusive. And perhaps because of the devotion of his intellectual and spiritual disciples, anything approaching an objective, let alone full, biography is difficult to achieve; see, however, the following studies: *Présence de Louis Massignon: Hommages et témoignages*. Textes réunis par Daniel Massignon, Paris, Éditions Maisonneuve et Larose, 1987; Jean Moncelon, 'Louis Massignon', *La Vie Spirituelle*, vol. 680, 1988, pp 363–79; C Destremau and J Moncelon, *Massignon*, Paris, Plon, 1994; G Zananiri, 'Massignon', *La Vie Spirituelle*, vol. 138, No 659, 1984, pp. 226–31; and Mary Louise Gude's fine study in English: *Louis Massignon: The Crucible of Compassion*, Notre Dame University Press, 1996.

14 P. Rocalve, *Place et rôle de l'Islam et de l'Islamologie dans la vie et l'œuvre de Louis Massignon*, Thèse de doctorat, Sorbonne, 1990 which has now been published as P. Rocalve, *Place et rôle de l'Islam et de l'Islamologie dans la vie et l'œuvre de Louis Massignon*, Institut Français de Damas, Collection Témoignages et Documents, no. 2, 1993).

15 Edward Said is critical of Massignon. However, as has been pointed out by others, Said rarely engages with religious belief or discourse with sufficient rigour or understanding, 'Islam, the Philological Vocation and French Culture: Renan and Massignon', *Islamic Studies: A Tradition and its Problems*, Malcolm H. Kerr (ed.), California, Malibu, Undena Publications 1980, pp. 53–72; and idem: *Orientalism: Western Conceptions of the Orient*, London, Routledge & Kegan Paul, 1978, pp. 263–74. See the work of Roger Arnaldez as a counterpoint, 'La pensée et l'oeuvre de Louis Massignon comme clés pour l'étude de la civilisation musulmane', *Louis Massignon au Coeur de notre temps*, Jacques Keryell (ed.), Paris, Éditions Karthala, 1999, pp. 305–20.

16 Neal Robinson, Massignon, Vatican II and Islam as an Abrahamic Religion, *Islam and Christian-Muslim* Relations, vol. 2, 1991, pp. 182–205; Robert Caspar, 'La vision de l'Islam chez Louis Massignon et son influence sur l'Eglise', *L'Herne Massignon*, J-F Six (ed.), series Cahiers de l'Herne, no. 13, Paris, Editions de l'Herne, 1970, pp. 126–47; Maurice Borrmans, 'Louis Massignon, Témoin du dialogue islamo-chrétien ', *Euntes Docete*, vol. XXXVII, 1984, pp. 383–401.

17 Massignon also had a long relationship with Judaism and Jewish scholars see Dominique Bourel, 'Louis Massignon face à Israël', *Louis Massignon et le dialogue des cultures*, Paris, Les Éditions du Cerf, 1996, pp. 293–306; Jacques Nantet, 'Louis Massignon et le Judaisme', *L'Herne Massignon*, J-F Six (ed.), Paris, 1970, pp.

220–24; A. O'Mahony, 'Le pèlerin de Jérusalem: Louis Massignon, Palestinian Christians, Islam and the State of Israel', *Palestinian Christians: Religion, Politics and Society*, Anthony O'Mahony (ed.), London, Melisende, 1999, pp. 166–89.
18 G. Harpigny: *Islam et Christianisme selon Louis Massignon*, Louvain, Université Catholique de Louvain, 1981, pp. 27–28.
19 For an attempt to assess Massignon's mysticism see J Keryell, *Jardin Donné, Louis Massignon à la recherche de l'Absolu*, Paris-Fribourg, Éditions Saint-Paul, 1993.
20 See the following works by Jacques Waardenburg who seeks to make a general assessment of Massignon as a religious thinker and as an Islamicist: 'Louis Massignon's study of religion and Islam; an essay *á propos* of his Opera Minora', *Oriens*, vol. 21–22, (1968–69) pp. 136–58; 'Massignon: notes for further research', *The Muslim World*, vol. 56 (1966). pp. 157–72; *L'Islam dans le miroir de l'occident*, Paris, Mouton, 1963; 'Regard de phénoménologie religieuse', *L'Herne Massignon*, J-F Six (ed.), Paris, 1970, pp. 148–56; 'L'impact du travail de Louis Massignon sur les etudes islamiques, *Louis Massignon au Coeur de notre temps*, Jacques Keryell (ed.), Paris, Éditions Karthala, pp. 295–304.
21 Mikel de Epalza, 'Massignon et Asin Palacios: une longue amitié et deux approches différentes de l'Islam', *L'Herne Massignon*, J-F Six (ed.), Paris, Éditions de l'Herne, 1970, pp. 157–69.
22 Louis Massignon's bibliography as a scholar is impressive. For the complete bibliography, see Youakim Moubarac, *L'Oeuvre de Louis Massignon;* Pentalogie Islamo-Chrétienne I, Beirut, Éditions du Cénacle Libanais, 1972–73. Amongst his studies, the first place must go to his two doctoral theses of 1922: *La Passion d'al-Hosayn-ibn Mansour al-Hallâj, martyre mystique de l'Islam*, Paris, Geuthner, 1922, First Edition, 2 vols. Massignon continued to work on a new edition of this work until his death in 1962. After his death, the new edition was assembled by a group of scholars working together with the Massignon family and friends, which was published as: *La Passion de Husayn ibn Mansur Hallâj, martyre mystique de l'Islam*, Paris, Gallimard, 1975, Second Edition, 4 vols. The second edition was translated into English by Herbert Mason as: *The Passion of al-Hallâj: Mystic and Martyr of Islam*, Bollingen Series XCVIII, Princeton University Press, 1982, 4 vols. An abridged version appeared as: *Hallâj: Mystic and Martyr* edited and translated by Herbert Mason, Princeton University Press, 1994. And *Essai sur les origines du lexique technique de la mystique musulmane*, First Edition, Paris, Geuthner, 1922; Second Edition, Paris, Vrin, 1954; Third Edition, Paris, Vrin, 1968, translated into

English by Benjamin Clark as *Essays on the origins of the technical language of Islamic mysticism*, University of Notre Dame Press, 1999; one important edition to this bibliography is *Testimonies and Reflections: Essays of Louis Massignon*, Selected and translated by Herbert Mason, University of Notre Dame Press, 1989. We also have three volumes of *Opera Minora*, (OM), containing some 207 of Massignon's articles *Opera Minora*, Abbé Y. Moubarac (ed.), Beirut, Dar al-Maaref, 1963 and Paris, Presses Universitaries de France, 1969.

23 Sidney H. Griffith, 'Sharing the Faith of Abraham: the 'Credo' of Louis Massignon', *Islam and Muslim-Christian Relations*, vol. 8, no. 2 (1997) pp. 193–210; Roger Arnaldez, 'Abrahamisme, Islam et christianisme chez Louis Massignon', *L'Herne Massignon*, J-F Six (ed.), Paris, Éditions de l'Herne, 1970, pp. 123–25.

24 A. O'Mahony, 'Louis Massignon, the Seven Sleepers of Ephesus and the Christian-Muslim Pilgrimage at Vieux-Marché, Brittany', *Explorations in a Christian Theology of Pilgrimage*, Craig Bartholomew and Fred Hughes (eds), London, Ashgate, 2004, pp. 126–48.

25 See for example Massignon's relations with Thomas Merton: Sidney H. Griffith, 'Thomas Merton, Louis Massignon and the Challenge of Islam', *The Merton Annual*, vol. 3, 1990, pp. 151–72; S. H. Griffith, 'Mytics and Suffi Masters: Thomas Merton and Dialogue between Christians and Muslims', *Islam and Muslim-Christian Relations*, vol. 15, no. 3 (2004) pp. 299–316.

26 Jean Moncelon, 'Salmân Pâk dans la spiritualité de Louis Massignon', *Luqmân*, Téhéran, autumn–winter (1991–1992) pp. 53–64.

27 R. Arnaldez, *Hallâj ou la religion de la croix*, Paris, Plon, 1964; Herbert Mason, *Al-Hallaj*, Richmond, Curzon Press, 1995; and Herbert Mason, *The Death of al-Hallaj: a dramatic narrative*, Notre Dame, University of Notre Dame Press, 1979.

28 A. O'Mahony, 'Mysticism and Politics: Louis Massignon, Sh'ia Islam, Iran and Ali Sharia'ti', *University Lectures in Islamic Studies*, vol. 2, 1998, pp. 113–34; 'The Image of Jesus and Christianity in Shi'a Islam and Modern Iranian Thought', *A Faithful Presence: essays for Kenneth Cragg*, David Thomas and Clare Amos (eds), London, Melisende, 2003, pp. 256–73; 'Mysticism, Politics, Dialogue: Catholic Encounters with Shi'a Islam in the Life and Work of Louis Massignon', *Catholics and Shi'a in Dialogue: Studies in Theology and Spirituality*, Anthony O'Mahony, Wulstan Peterburs and Mohammed Ali Shomali (eds), London, Melisende, 2004, pp. 134.

29 Ibrahim Madkour, Louis Massignon, *L'Herne Massignon*, op. cit.,

p. 68.
30 Louis Massignon to Thomas Merton, 31 December 1960, Thomas Merton Study Centre, Bellarmine College, Louisville, Kentucky quoted in Sidney H. Griffith, 'Thomas Merton, Louis Massignon and the Challenge of Islam', *The Merton Annual*, vol. 3, 1990, pp. 151–72.
31 There was a close contact between Massignon and De Foucauld: see the text from 1960 (OM III, 772–84) and the letters gathered by J-F. Six, *L'aventure de l'amour de dieu. 80 lettres inédites de Charles de Foucauld à Louis Massignon*, Paris, Éditions du Seuil, 1993.
32 Daniel Massignon, 'Le Voyage en Mésopotamie et la Conversion de Louis Massignon en 1908', *Islamochristiana*, Rome, vol 14, 1988, pp. 127–99, reprinted under same title by Éditions du Cerf, Paris, in 2001. The letters by the Iraqi Carmelite priest who cared for Massignon now published also give us a greater insight to this episode; *Autour d'une conversion, Lettres de Louis Massignon et ses parents au père Anastase de Bagdad*, Paris, Daniel Massignon (ed.), Éditions du Cerf, 2004.
33 Massignon's distress about his father, who died suddenly from a stroke while working in his sculptor's studio, without receiving the last sacraments, should be noted. Jacques Waardenburg 'Massignon: notes for further research', *The Muslim World*, vol. 56, 1966, pp. 162.
34 Michel Allard, SJ, 'Au coeur de l'oeuve de Massignon', *Travaux et Jours*, Beirut, no. 8, 1963, pp. 23–32.
35 Waardenburg, 'Massignon: notes for further research', p. 163.
36 Ibrahim Madkour, in his commenoration speech before the Academy of the Arabic langauge in Cairo, on 20 December 1962, called Massignon '… the greatest Muslim among the Christians and the greatest Christian among the Muslims', cited in Jean Morillon, *Massignon*, Paris, Éditions universitaires, 1964, p. 25.
37 David H. Kerr, '"He Walked in the Path of the Prophets": Toward Christian Theological Recognition of the Prophethood of Muhammad', *Christian-Muslim Encounters*, Yvonne Yazbeck Haddad and Wadi Zaidan Haddad (eds), Gainesville, University Press of Florida, 1995, pp. 426–46.
38 Waardenburg, 'Massignon: notes for further research', p. 166.
39 Jacques Keryall, *Louis Massignon, L'hospitalité sacrée*, Paris, Nouvelle Cité, 1987, pp. 387–402.
40 Waardenburg, 'Massignon: notes for further research', pp. 167–68.
41 Christian Troll, SJ, 'Changing Catholic Views of Islam' , *Islam and Christianity. Mutual Perceptions since the mid-20th Century*, J.

Waardenburg (ed.), Leuven, Peeters, 1998, pp. 27–28.
42 Paul Nwyia, SJ, 'Massignon et une certaine vision de la langue arabe', in *Studia islamica*, vol. L, 1979, pp. 125–49.
43 Albert Hourani, 'Islamic History, Middle Eastern History, Modern History', *Islam in European Thought*, Cambridge University Press, 1990, pp. 97–98.
44 Albert Hourani, *Islam in European Thought*, Cambridge University Press, 1990, pp. 44–46.
45 Robert Caspar, 'La vision de l'Islam chez Louis Massignon et son influence sur l'Eglise', *L'Herne Massignon*, J-F Six (ed.), Paris, 1970, pp. 126–47.
46 Maurice Borrmans, 'Aspects théologiques de la pensée de Louis Massignon sur l'Islam', *Louis Massignon et le dialogue des cultures*, Paris, Les Éditions du Cerf, 1996, pp. 110.
47 P. Rocalve, *Place et rôle de l'Islam et de l'Islamologie dans la vie et l'œuvre de Louis Massignon*, Institut Français de Damas, Collection Témoignages et Documents, No. 2, 1993.
48 E. S. Sabanegh, 'Le Cheminement exemplaire d'un savant et d'un chrétien à la rencontre de l'Islam', *Présence de Louis Massignon: Hommages et témoignages*, Paris, Éditions Maisonneuve et Larose, 1987, p. 122.
49 Borrmans, 'Aspects théologiques de la pensée de Louis Massignon sur l'Islam', pp. 112–14.
50 Louis Massignon, *Examen du 'Présent de l'Homme Lettré' by Abdallah Ibn al-Torjoman* (following the French translation published in *Revue de l'Histoire des Religions*, 1886, vol. XII), with a preface by Daniel Massignon, introduction by Père Henri Cazelles and observations by Père Albert (M. J.) Lagrange. Collection 'Studi arabo-islamic del PISAI', no. 5, Rome, PISAI, 1992.
51 These thoughts are taken up by Jacques Jomier, the great Dominican Islamicist: 'Islam is a natural religion in which the religious instinct which is present in the heart of each man is protected by a way of life, with obligations and religious observations imposed in the name of one who is, for the Muslim, the Quran revelation. It is a patriarchal religion, spiritually pre-dating the biblical promise made by God to Abraham, but which conserves the episodes of the life of the Patriarch involving his struggle against his father's idols and his voluntary submission to God, even his sacrifice of his own son. Islam re-presents Abraham (Father of the Prophets) as its great ancestor.' 'Le Coran et la Liturgie dans l'islam', *La Maison-Dieu*, no. 190, 1992, pp. 121–27, p. 121.
52 Borrmans, 'Aspects théologiques de la pensée de Louis

Massignon sur l'Islam', pp. 114–20.
53 *Les Trois Prières d'Abraham*, edition intégrale hors commerce, imprimée à trios cents exemplaires, Tours, Arrault et Cie, 1935. Reprinted as L. Massignon, *Les Trois Prières d'Abraham*, Paris, Éditions du Cerf, 1997, pp. 129–148.
54 The Church Fathers at the Second Vatican Council rejected the notion that Islam is descended from Abraham. Number 16 of the 'Dogmatic constitution on the Church' *Lumen Gentium* declares: 'But the plan of salvation also embraces those who acknowledge the Creator, and among these the Muslims are first; they profess to hold the faith of Abraham and along with us they worship the one merciful God who will judge humanity on the last day.' The study of the proceedings of the Council makes it clear that it did not want to state an objective link between Islam, Ishmael and the biblical revelation. The reference to Abraham is put on the subjective level: 'they profess ...'. Islam is situated first among the non-biblical, monotheistic religions and it is audaciously affirmed that the Muslims adore the same God as the Christians. For Massignon, Islam is an Abrahamic schism, as it were, preceding the Decalogue which founds Judaism, and Pentecost which founds Christianity. Whereas, on the one hand, the Second Vatican Council's positive description of central aspects of the Muslims' faith and practice and its new outlook on Islam would be unthinkable without Massignon's insight and commitment; on the other hand, the Council, as had been shown, refrained from adopting key elements of Massignon's idiosyncratic theologico-prophetic vision of Islam and its prophet. It was careful not to let the privileged position that Islam occupies among the other great religions in the history of salvation, overshadow the originality of the Judeo-Christian revelation with its culmination, in the eyes of the Christian faith, in the divine-human person of Jesus Christ. The Council also was convinced that the historical descent for the Muslims from Ishmael, as claimed by the Muslims, is far from having been proven from the available evidence.
55 Borrmans, 'Aspects théologiques de la pensée de Louis Massignon sur l'Islam', pp. 121–25.
56 An interview with Louis Massignon, 'Le Signe marial', *Rythmes du monde*, 1948–1949, pp. 7–16.
57 A. O'Mahony, 'Christian Monks and Monasticism in Islam', *The Merton Journal*, vol. 11, no. 1, 2004, pp. 20–26.
58 Borrmans, 'Aspects théologiques de la pensée de Louis Massignon sur l'Islam', pp. 125–27.
59 R. Charles-Barzel, ' *Ô Vierge puissante*', Paris, La Colombe, 1958, pp. 59–61.

60 Borrmans, 'Aspects théologiques de la pensée de Louis Massignon sur l'Islam', pp. 128–32.
61 L. Massignon, 'L'Homme parfait et son originalité eschatologique', *Eranos Jahrbuch*, vol. XV, 1947, pp. 289–91.
62 Robert Caspar, La vision de l'Islam chez Louis Massignon et son influence sur l'Eglise, *L'Herne Massignon*, J-F Six (ed.), Paris, 1970, p. 146.
63 Borrmans, 'Aspects théologiques de la pensée de Louis Massignon sur l'Islam', pp. 133–35.

Part Three

Christian Dialogue with Asia

Chapter 9

Monastic Interreligious Dialogue in India:
Henri Le Saux, OSB (Abhishiktananda) and Bede Griffiths, OSB Cam.

Judson B. Trapnell

To approach the topic of Western Christian monastic engagement with India, we will be working with extended passages from Henri Le Saux and Bede Griffiths set in the context of their relationship to each other. Specifically, we will begin and end with portrayals by each figure of *sannyasa* – a Sanskrit term central to Hindu spirituality that literally means a total, wholehearted laying aside or abandoning, a term usually translated as renunciation.[1] *Sannyasa* is especially significant for our conference theme as an orientation to the world, to the self, and to the divine that both Griffiths and Le Saux adopted from Indian culture to redefine their identities as monks. Between these passages on *sannyasa* or renunciation we will look at three 'moments' in which the lives of Le Saux and Griffiths creatively intersected, each moment suggesting an important issue for monastic interreligious dialogue.

Griffiths on the *Sannyasi*
In Griffiths's *The Marriage of East and West* (1982), he describes what it meant to him to be a *sannyasi* or one who renounces – an identity, he writes, to which he was brought

by the same 'golden string' that led him to become a Catholic and a monk at Prinknash Priory in Gloucestershire. He begins by defining the sannyasi as 'one who renounces the world to seek for God'– 'world' in the challenging comprehensive sense of the whole field of appearances or signs, a broader sense than most Christians would recognize as the first quote illustrates:

> The Church ... belongs to this world of 'signs'. The doctrines and sacraments of the Church are human expressions or signs of the divine reality, which are likewise destined to pass away. So also Christ himself is the 'sacrament' of God; he is the sign of God's grace and salvation, of God's presence among men, and this sign also will pass, when the Reality, the thing signified, is revealed. Finally God himself, in so far as he can be named, whether Yahweh or Allah or simply God, is a sign, a name for the ultimate Truth, which cannot be named.

Many Christians will feel themselves pushed here beyond their conventional way of conceiving the personal God of prayer and toward the Presence before whom words, even names, even the name of Christ, fail. As Griffiths continues, the vocation he is describing may begin to sound less familiar, less appealing, perhaps less Christian, even to the monastic:

> Thus the Sannyasi is called to go beyond all religion, beyond every human institution, beyond every scripture and creed, till he comes to that which every scripture and ritual signifies but can never name.[2]

Here we begin to sense the direction in which Griffiths's encounter with India has propelled him. There is something foreign in the radicality of this renunciation, is there not, for most of us? If you feel that distance from the viewpoint expressed in these statements, you have a sense of the risk involved in such interreligious encounters, and not only in India – a risk that Griffiths's and Le Saux's friend and student, Raimundo Panikkar, has described not as a risk *of* faith, but a risk *in* faith.[3]

Two further points are essential to Griffiths's sense of *sannyasa*:

> Yet when we say that the Sannyasi goes beyond religion this does not mean that he rejects any religion. I have not felt called to reject anything that I have learned of God or of Christ or of the Church. To go beyond the sign is not to reject the sign, but to reach the thing signified ... But equally fatal is to stop at the sign, to mistake the sign for the ultimate reality. It is this that sets one religion against another and divides Christians from one another, from people of other religions and from the rest of the world. This is essentially idolatry.[4]

Here then are two principles: First, while called to go beyond all symbols, all religion, the sannyasi nonetheless remains respectful of the legitimate need for them. Second, the *sannyasi* is one who reminds us that we must not mistake the symbol for the reality to which it points, lest violence toward the religious 'other' or idolatry before God result.

I am not sure that Fr Bede ever said anything more radical than he has here, anything more indicative of how serious engagement with another religious ideal, such as Hindu *sannyasa*, can transform one's point of view. With this image of monastic renunciation in mind, we turn to consider three moments in which Griffiths's life intersected with that of Henri Le Saux, moments that illustrate the diverse challenges faced when one identifies with a foreign religious ideal.

Shantivanam, Christmas 1957

The two Benedictines first met in Bangalore in 1955, not long after Griffiths had arrived in India and made his initial attempt to found an ashram or spiritual community along a Hindu model. Le Saux had himself been in India for seven years, having emigrated at age thirty-eight from France, after nearly twenty years in the Benedictine Abbey of St Anne de Kergonan. With his predecessor and fellow French priest, Jules Monchanin, Le Saux had founded Saccidananda Ashram or the Hermitage of the Most Holy

Trinity at Shantivanam in Tamil Nadu in 1950 – a contemplative community shaped by both the Rule of St Benedict and the Hindu ashrams they had visited. In the tradition of seventeenth-century Jesuit missionary Roberto de Nobili and nineteenth-century convert Brahmabandhab Upadhyay, Monchanin and Le Saux had adopted the lifestyle of the Hindu *sannyasi*. Taking on this identity entailed an observation of poverty as close as possible to that of the nearby villagers, a strictly vegetarian diet, the wearing of a saffron cloth or *kavi*, and the assuming of a new name – Le Saux's being Abhishiktananda or 'Bliss of the Anointed One' – a name by which he would be known in India for the rest of his life and which I will use for him from now on.

Griffiths, too, came to India after about two decades in Benedictine houses here in England. He was four years older than Abhishiktananda, a more public figure, his popular autobiography, *The Golden String*, having been published in 1954. And significantly, Griffiths was a convert to Catholicism from Church of England, had been educated at Oxford, and had first been introduced as a school boy to a contemplative receptivity through mystical experiences in nature. He visited Abhishiktananda and Monchanin at Shantivanam, and was impressed enough by their *sannyasic* lifestyle to adopt it for his own community, first in Bangalore and then with a Belgian Cistercian Francis Mahieu at Kurisumala Ashram in Kerala.

The first intersection that I want you to see occurs about the time of Griffiths's move south to join Fr Mahieu and a couple of months after Fr Monchanin's death in 1957. Abhishiktananda invited Griffiths, along with Fr Raimundo Panikkar and Fr Dominique van Rollenghen, OSB, to share a week with him at the ashram over Christmas – the ashram at this time being little more than few huts and a chapel built in a palm grove near the sacred river Kavery. It was the first of several such meetings, eventually growing larger in size and more diverse, held elsewhere than Shantivanam.[5] At this first meeting, their daily observance was simple and Benedictine, including the chanting of the offices and the Mass.[6] But these services would not have been quite like the observance in England or France, for these men were deeply conscious of their non-European surroundings and of how those surroundings were affecting their experience of the traditional rites.

And thus a first quote from Fr Bede – from a lecture given the year before at the All-India Study Week in Madras. Here he draws upon his experience of the Hindu temple which he elsewhere describes as a 'sacrament, a representation of the divine mystery', concluding that there is much for Christianity to learn from the symbolic life of such settings.[7] By the time of this first Christmas meeting in 1957, the Indian Church was seriously pondering the question of what is now called inculturation, or how to clothe the essential teachings and sacraments of Christianity in forms that will be meaningful to and draw upon non-European cultural contexts such as India. A few excerpts from Fr Bede's lecture:

> Is there any way by which Hindu conceptions, Hindu symbolism and Hindu forms of expression can be introduced into the Christian liturgy? To this I can only reply that in the present state of things none of this seems to be possible. You cannot simply transfer a symbol from one system of thought to another.[8]

Griffiths's qualification, 'in the present state of things', is significant. For what did not seem possible in 1956 did become reality at this same ashram in the years after Vatican II, when an Indian liturgy that did incorporate readings and symbols from Hinduism was practised with the approval of the bishop. Nevertheless, as Griffiths continues, it is clear that his own sense of symbols and of the divine mystery to which they point has been enriched by his encounter with India:

> What, then, is there that can be done? ... In the first place we have to try to recover our sense of the Christian mystery ... As we have seen, all Hindu religion is rooted in the idea of a transcendent mystery, something inexpressible, unimaginable, inconceivable, which is yet the goal of all human thought and striving. If we are to have any under-

standing of Hindu thought we must approach it with reverence as something essentially mystical both in its origin and in its goal. In this way our study of Hinduism will lead us not only to a grasp of the inner meaning of Hindu thought and practice, but also to a deeper awareness of the mystery of Christianity itself and to a theology which is not merely dogmatic and moral but mystical, a theology which is 'wisdom' in the ancient sense of the word.

Before any assimilation of Indian symbols into Christian liturgical practice can be attempted, Christianity must reawaken its own sense of God as a mystery beyond all thought, feeling, and symbol. Only once this mystical foundation is restored can one legitimately rebuild a liturgy and theology that are shaped by cultural values and religious symbols other than those which the Church has providentially inherited from western sources over the preceding centuries. Griffiths's second point follows from here: that Christianity can learn from Hinduism's 'most profound sense of sacramentalism' to recover it own receptivity to the power of symbols. Griffiths's experience of the Hindu temple and of the highly symbolic quality of Indian life as a whole accentuated his awareness of his own tradition's need for such a heightened sacramental sense. But he remained convinced, one might even argue to the end of his life, that Christian symbols such as the Trinity and the Mass, especially in their historical character, fulfil the aspirations represented by the less complete symbols of other traditions, including Hinduism.[9]

As Griffiths, Abhishiktananda, and their colleagues worshipped together, Griffiths did so with this theological framework in mind – a framework gradually being reshaped by his encounters with Hindu religious practice and Indian culture. Out of such meetings, then, a key issue for monastic interreligious encounter arose: To what degree can one assimilate the spiritual riches of the religious 'other' and still remain true to one's own tradition? Are liturgical symbols interchangeable between traditions in the shared quest for knowledge and love of God?

While Abhishiktananda participated in this same 1957

meeting, he experienced their daily observance through a somewhat different theological orientation, shaped by different experiences. In a letter, Abhishktananda described this gathering as follows: 'Long and deep discussions on *advaita* and Christian mysticism.'[10] To clarify:

Advaita is a Sanskrit term meaning literally 'not-two', and so it is used by Hindu philosophy to describe the non-dual relationship between the eternal aspect of the human and absolute Reality itself, the relationship between the Self and the Absolute, between Atman and Brahman. Abhishiktananda, and like him Monchanin and Griffiths, spent much of their lives in India articulating a Christian theology of *advaita* or nonduality, exploring what Jesus intended when he said 'I and the Father are one' (Jn. 10.30) – a one that is 'not one' because comprised of two in relationship; yet also a relationship that is 'not-two' because of the depth of love between the partners.

Yet *advaita* did not remain only an intriguing theory for either Abhishiktananda or Griffiths. In the nine years prior to this 1957 meeting at Shantivanam, Abhishiktananda had spent weeks at a time in the caves of a sacred mountain, Arunachala, practising nondiscursive meditation and experiencing nonduality as an 'abyss'. In this 'abyss' he underwent a radical shift in his identity, from being one before God, to one in God – to use perhaps too crude a distinction. The following passages from a letter of this period convey how these experiences of nonduality might have affected his sense of the liturgies shared at the 1957 meeting.

This letter was written in 1956, just after a two-week retreat with a Hindu guru, Sri Gnanananda, an experience Abhishiktananda described as 'time in a totally Hindu-Brahmin-Shivaite setting, not merely alongside them, but living with them as one of them' – a depth and length of immersion that I don't believe Griffiths ever experienced.[11]

> The attraction of this advaitin abyss, the abyss of Arunachala [the sacred mountain in whose caves he meditated], is stronger than ever ... What a conflict, when one has deeply lived the Christian *sacrament*. Here you are 'torn away' from signs. No reading, no prayer, no *puja* [Sanskrit, 'worship']

...; only sustained *dhyana* (meditation without thought) for those who are capable of it. Naturally no Mass here, and the breviary said entirely privately in an hour at midday. Once the *res* (the thing, the reality) is attained, the sacrament recovers all its meaning; but when you are all alone in the undefined space between the sign and *res*, irresistibly attracted by the one, and not feeling justified in abandoning the other ...[12]

As involved as he would become in the very process of creating an Indian rite of the Mass, Abhishiktananda never stepped outside the tension described in this passage, this standing between the rich signs of Christianity to which he maintained by his own admission a 'visceral attachment' and the reality to which those signs point, a reality to beyond which he felt 'irresistibly attracted'. One can imagine how this tension affected his worship at the 1957 gathering at Shantivanam, a state of conflict that would endure for most of his life.[13]

Abhishiktananda's internal conflict raises another important question for our broader discussion: To what degree is it appropriate and advisable for one to assimilate not only the symbols but the spiritual practices of another tradition, given the fact that such practices like symbols bear with them frameworks of meaning that may or not be compatible with Christianity?

Shantivanam, August 1968

We jump ahead over a decade to 1968, through and beyond the years of Vatican II – an event with immediate repercussions for the projects of inculturation and interreligious dialogue in India, and thus for both Abhishiktananda and Griffiths. During these years Abhishiktananda divided his time between the ashram at Shantivanam in Tamil Nadu and a hermitage he eventually acquired in the north of India near Uttarkashi in the Himalayan region, in addition to increasing travels to visit friends in other ashrams, to lead retreats, and to attend meetings related to church reform. It was also during this decade that he composed his best known works. During these same years Griffiths remained at Kurisumala Ashram in Kerala, writing a continous stream of articles, primarily published in the West where he began to make regular trips.

Shantivanam remained a solitary hermitage for Abhishiktananda most of the time, failing to attract other permanent members. Finally in 1968 he decided to move to the north and to turn over responsibility for the ashram to Fr Bede. Abhishiktananda and Griffiths had planned to meet at the ashram for a formal transfer of this responsibility in August, but the meeting never took place. Abhishiktananda had left prematurely for Madras, revealing how painful this leave-taking was for him. [14]

That the ashram would eventually attract vocations and grow to become a well-respected contemplative centre for retreats and interreligious dialogue is itself revealing of the different charisms of these two Christian *sannyasis*. Abhishiktananda's gift was for plunging to the depths of *advaitic* experience, come what may, in faith that only the Truth he knew as the universal Christ could await him there (Jn. 14.6).[15] Griffiths's charism, on the other hand, was for integration, always balancing mystical depth with rational analysis – carefully distinguishing the differences between the traditions and affirming how these distinctions diminished toward convergence at a mystical centre. These different gifts are further reflected in their different styles of negotiating the dialogue between Hinduism and Christianity, as the following passages will illustrate.[16]

It was during this period before he left Shantivanam that Abhishiktananda completed his account of the early meetings with Griffiths and others, published in 1965 as *La Rencontre de l'hindouisme et du christianisme* and in English in 1969 as *Hindu-Christian Meeting Point: Within the Cave of the Heart*. Here, as in his major theological work *Saccidananda: A Christian Approach to Advaitic Experience* (1965, 1974), he wrestled with how to articulate a theology of religions that is true to the experiential witness of both traditions to the divine mystery:

No solution can be found to these [comparative] problems

if we confine ourselves to the conceptualizatons of Christian theology, useful and even necessary as these are in their proper place. It is from within that we must seek to comprehend this double experience, trying to realize simultaneously in the depths of our own being that experience of the ultimate 'non-duality' which the Vedantin regards as the final goal of human life and experience of divine sonship in the unity of the Spirit which lies at the heart of our Christian faith. Only so will we be able to formulate an adequate theology of the presence of God at the very source of man's personal existence, and so become capable of fruitful dialogue with our Hindu brothers. Solutions cannot be imposed *a priori*.

Abhishiktananda is clearly advocating an approach to the theology of religions that corresponds to his own journey, one in which his early compelling experiences of nonduality removed the possibility of imposing *a priori* solutions, experiences that nevertheless had to be reconciled with his Christian experience of the Trinity. He continues:

> The instinct of our faith may indeed lead us to sense, at the very beginning of our effort to understand, that the experience of non-duality by its very nature tends towards the experience of the Father. But we are not thereby dispensed from pursuing our inquiries – not so much rational as intuitive – until the formulations of our conceptual thinking at last harmonize with the mystery which is revealed in our inmost being. Only then will we be able to show our Hindu brethren that the Christian experience does not fall short of that of the Vedanta, but that, without in any way threatening the essential values of the Hindu experience, it reveals within it even greater depths of the unfathomable mystery of God.[17]

From one's faith one may first derive a sense of how to compare the two experiences, but one must not rest here. Rather, one must patiently wait until one's conceptualizations fully cohere with one's 'double-experience' of the divine mystery, in his case, the *advaitic* and the Trinitarian. Such coherence would reveal, he believed at the time, not only the parity of Vedantic and Christian experiences but would show that the Christian realization discloses 'even greater depths' of the divine mystery.

Here in subtle form is what he called a 'fulfilment theology' of religions, a position that assumes 'the convergence upon the historical Christ and the Church, of all the religious and spiritual experiences of mankind.'[18] It was around the time of his departure from Shantivanam that Abhishiktananda became consciously dissatisfied with this framework.

We have already seen another version of this same 'fulfilment theology' in Griffiths's account of how the Christian Trinity and the Mass complete the longings represented by Hindu symbols. On the bases of the theological reforms encouraged by Vatican II and of his own deepening contemplative experience at the time of his move to Shantivanam, Griffiths would begin to experiment with other ways of characterizing the relationship between the religions. Here is an example, from one of the many short articles he sent for publication to *The Tablet,* this one from the year after his move, 1969. He is reporting upon his impressions of a conference on 'India's understanding of man' in which Hindus, Parsis, Muslims, and Christians took part. He begins by affirming as a general consensus the belief that one 'can be saved in any religion, and even without any religion, provided that he follows his reason and conscience', concluding that 'every religion has its place in the divine plan of salvation'. This not uncontroversial theology of religions is supported, he argues, by the kind of 'concrete meeting of people of different religions' in which he has just participated – an interreligious basis for theological reflection that complements Abhishiktananda's primarily intra-religious one just discussed. As both *sannyasis* would agree, the monastic encounter of non-Christian religions must proceed at both levels, the interpersonal and the intrapersonal. He continues by acknowledging the tendency within all traditions to claim its own superiority and yet proposes that an objective study of how members of different traditions compare in their religious and moral observance would conclude otherwise.[19]

These are substantial admissions in the light of his formation within a church outside of which salvation was not believed to be possible, but also in the light of the communalist conflicts that were present in his day in India as in ours. His further conclusion is none the less startling:

> If we believe that Christ is really the Saviour of all mankind, must we not admit that in some sense Christ must be said to be present in all religion? Does this not mean that in some sense the Truth – that is, not a mere speculative doctrine, but the final truth of salvation, of man's ultimate relation to God, the supreme Being – is in some way present to each religion? ... The one eternal Truth is reflected in different cultural and social forms, none of which is completely adequate, since the final Truth transcends all human expression, and the ultimate truth of Christianity no less than of other religions will only be revealed at the last day: that is, at the Parousia, when Christ, the eternal Truth, is manifested no longer under the earthly signs of doctrine and sacrament, but in his absolute reality.[20]

The interesting move is made here to identify Christ outside Christianity and present in non-Christian religions a Christ who, as Truth, transcends all particular formulations or truths since these are inevitably conditioned by their cultural setting, whether that be Rome or Delhi. Clearly Griffiths was not the first to express this theology of religions, itself a variation of a fulfilment schema, given the Christocentric language he uses. What is instructive is how he bases this conclusion upon his concete experiences of dialogue with Hindus, Parsis, and Muslims in India – giving it an empirical sense similar to Abhishiktananda's intra-religious approach.

Both of the passages we have just examined, then, prompt further questions that must arise within in any encounter with the religious 'other': How does one move from the experience of a challenging intra- and inter-religious encounter to the creation of new conceptual frameworks, that is, from praxis to theory? How does one evaluate such frameworks – on the basis of *a priori* principles derived from faith (a process of deduction), or on the basis of personal experience and objective observation (a process of induction) – or can one somehow use both processes? And is the monastic, as Griffiths and Abhishiktananda individually and together seem to exemplify, in a privileged position to formulate a theology of religions from such encounters? Those of you who are monastics could certainly answer this question far better than I. Perhaps this, too, we could consider.

Shantivanam 1990

The final significant intersection between the lives of these two Christian *sannyasis* that we shall consider is in 1990, again at Shantivanam. Abhishiktananda has died seventeen years earlier at age sixty-three. Griffiths is now eighty-three, still the head of the ashram, which has grown steadily under his care. It is here that he has written his books of the past two decades. And it is here that he convalesces after a stroke that occurred during his early morning meditation in January 1990, a stroke that fortunately does not leave him seriously impaired and that sparks a spiritual awakening he would describe as 'the greatest grace I've ever had in my life'. In the immediate aftermath of this physical crisis he feels himself open to a fuller awareness of the nondual divine reality as a 'communion of love', and to an abiding sense of unity that accompanies his consciousness of diversity. In response to an invitation heard a few days later in prayer to 'surrender to the Mother', he is overwhelmed by a deep 'breakthrough to the feminine', balancing what had been all his life his predominant rational side.[21]

It was sometime during this period, sensitized by this spiritual awakening or by his intensifying intimations of it, that he read James Stuart's biography of Abhishiktananda based upon correspondence. The letters of Griffiths's predecessor's later years disturb him, a point he will raise in some of his final lectures and interviews. This intersection of their two lives is deepened by the fact that Abhishiktananda had also experienced a spiritual awakening associated with a physical crisis – a heart attack in Rishikesh in July 1973 that he compared to the discovery of the grail. Set alongside each other, the effects of their respective awakenings evoke provocative comparisons.

Abhishiktananda attempted to portray the impact of his heart attack in a number of revealing letters to friends during the following five months. One such correspondent was Murray Rogers, who had shared in some of the early dialogue meetings noted earlier. Abhishiktananda writes of having discovered a powerful sense of the nonduality between his being and that of Christ's 'I AM', a discovery so immediate that it silenced the numerous formulations of theology that would normally mediate such an experience in the mind.

> [W]hat would be the meaning of a 'Christianity-coloured' awakening? In the process of awakening all this coloration cannot but disappear (the atomic mushroom). If at all I had to give a message, it would be the message of 'Wake up, arise, remain aware', of the Kena Upanishad. The coloration might vary according to the audience, but the essential goes beyond.

In the burning light of his awakening, all such 'coloration', Christian or otherwise, has been thoroughly if briefly eradicated; he has seen all the revered theological understandings disappear before the presence of Christ. The move from theory back to praxis, from mediating language back to immediate experience, can be devastating for even the most insightful and articulate conceptualizations.

> The discovery of Christ's I AM is the ruin of any Christian theology, for all notions are burnt within the fire of experience. Perhaps I am a little too Cartesian, as a good Frenchman. And perhaps others might find a way out of the atomic mushroom. I feel too much, more and more, the blazing fire of this I AM, in which all notions about Christ's personality, ontology, history, etc. have disappeared.[22]

Perhaps others might be able to sustain the meaning of theological speculation in light of such a fiery awakening, but Abhishiktananda, for one, cannot.

But lest one conclude the experience is totally destructive, a complete obliteration of the distinctions that constitute perceived reality,[23] there is in the letter a further step after this powerful apophatic moment, a rediscovery, a reperception:

> And I find his real mystery shining in every awakening man, in every mythos ...[24]

What does he mean here? He finds Christ's 'mystery shining', that same fire that has deeply transformed his consciousness and relativized all tiny sparks of thought and language; he finds that same fire of 'Christ's I AM' to be what he himself is; he finds it shining, alive where? in every person (who is not in the process of awakening?) and in every sacred narrative or religion.

But Fr Bede, in the light of his own experience, finds imbalance in these later letters, too much of an urge to 'go beyond' the world of distinctions, an incomplete intuition of *advaita* in contrast to his own experience in which all distinctions are transcended but then found reintegrated within that nondual reality – a reintegration that valorizes the world of created reality, of distinct selves, and of diverse religious symbols.[25] In a remarkable interview just a few days before a second, far more debilitating stroke at his ashram in December 1990, Griffiths describes his own ongoing experience of transformation and his resulting concern for incomplete understandings of nonduality, like Abhishiktananda's, that deny the value of the world.[26] One may argue with Griffiths's interpretation of his predecessor on this point, but this same interview also records striking affinities between their two awakenings:

> One thing that came through to me in that stroke experience was the death of Christ. We hear 'My God, My God, why have you forsaken me?' Jesus was dying on the Cross and he had been rejected by his people. He had been persecuted by the Roman government. He was physically in pain and psychologically in distress, and he had to face the darkness of death. He had to go through the total darkness. He had to lose his God, in a sense. Any god is a projection, and

eventually we have to get rid of all projections. The mind has to go; then, beyond the mind, we enter into the darkness, which is the darkness of love.

Whether the metaphor is fire or darkness, there is a similar explosion of all projections, of all notions in Griffiths's and Abhishiktananda's accounts. Griffiths accepts the necessity of this:

> As it is something a person has to go through, as I did, he must not reject it. One has to simply accept it, totally. Jesus on the Cross was my model there. I felt convinced that he went through this stage of total death, of annihilation. He let go of everything, and only then could he, as a human being, become total love.[27]

Clearly Griffiths does not shy away from Christian coloration in his account; it aided his understanding of his experience, while for Abhishiktananda theological categories such as the Cross or even love somehow reduced the fullness of the experience. This difference is significant and parallels their different charisms discussed before. However, as certainly as both drew upon the mystical writings of their tradition, so both also experienced through engagement with Hinduism, especially its monastic ideal of *sannyasa*, an unexpected depth to their realizations.

There is again a question here for our broader discussion: interreligious encounter and mystical awakening appear to cause a similar relativization of religious language for Griffiths and Abhishiktananda, though different in degree. Is this heightened awareness of the limitations of religious language an inevitable and valuable effect of the monastic encounter of another tradition?[28]

Concluding reflections – Abhishiktananda on *Sannyasa*

One of the final projects upon which Abhishiktananda worked was an essay entitled '*Sannyasa*', that has been called his 'spiritual testament'.[29] The following passages from it creatively augment Griffiths's account discussed at the beginning of this talk and also serve as a fitting invitation to our own discussion of Christian monastic engagement with India:[30]

> The call to complete renunciation cuts across all dharmas [all paths of righteousness, all religions] and disregards all frontiers. No doubt the call reaches individuals through the particular forms of their own dharma; but it corresponds to a powerful instinct, so deep-rooted in the human heart, *nihitam guhayam* [hidden in the cave (of the heart)], that it is anterior to every religious formulation. In the end, it is in that call arising from the depths of the human heart that all the great dharmas really meet each other and discover their innermost truth in that attraction beyond themselves which they all share.

As Raimundo Panikkar has developed more fully, Abhishiktananda is sketching here the universal archetype of the monk from the inside out, from the 'powerful instinct', and 'call', outward to its various forms in the religions.[31] He concludes:

> It is therefore perfectly natural that monks of every dharma should recognize each other as brothers across the frontiers of their respective dharmas. This follows from that very transcendence of all signs to which all of them bear witness. There is indeed a 'monastic order' which is universal and includes them all ... It is enough that they should recognize each other whenever they happen to meet, and in fact those who are genuine do infallibly respond to each other. Despite all differences in observance, language and cultural background, they perceive in each other's eyes that depth which the One Spirit has opened in their own hearts. They sense the bliss, the light, the ineffable peace which emanate from it; and when they embrace each other, as they so often spontaneously do, it is a sign that they have felt and recognized their innate 'non-duality', for in truth in the sphere of the *ajata*, the unborn, there is no 'otherness'.[32]

Griffiths and Abhishiktananda leave us with questions, creative questions, ones perhaps better lived than theorized about. Here are a few: What degree of immersion in, and assimilation of, the symbolic world and spiritual practice of the religious 'other' is appropriate for the Christian? Does the monastic have a special calling and a special capacity for such interreligious exploration? What theology of religions emerges from the praxis of interfaith dialogue? Does the Christian necessarily bring *a priori* principles to such formulations that no amount of experience, either intrapersonal or interpersonal, can contradict? How do we reconcile the experience of the Christian *sannyasi* who bears witness to a reality beyond all signs, and who undergoes the relativization of all religious language, with the sacramental nature of his or her tradition? Again, does the monastic, especially the contemplative, have a special calling and a special capacity to address such issues? Finally, what in the engagement of these two Benedictines with India is generalizable for our ongoing reflection on monastic interreligious dialogue? What in their experience is universalizable for our understanding of a monastic archetype? Does the monastic, like the *sannyasi*, by witnessing to the convergence of various religions upon a silent core hold the only viable key to interreligious understanding?

Notes

1 Jesu Rajan, *Bede Griffiths and Sannyasa*, Bangalore, Asian Trading Corporation, 1989, p. 10. Rajan distills the various meanings of *sannyasa* as follows: 'Summing up all these *sannyasa* could be defined as a state of life in which a person is totally detached from everything in the universe and at the same time intensely attached to the ultimate Reality. Intense attachment to the divine and utter detachment from everything else is the core of *sannyasa*', p. 11.
2 Bede Griffiths, *The Marriage of East and West: A Sequel to The Golden String*, Springfield, Illinois, Templegate, 1982, pp. 42–43. For other passages by Griffiths on *sannyasa*, see his *Return to the Center*, Springfield, Illinois, Templegate, 1976, pp. 9–15. See also Jesu Rajan, *Bede Griffiths and Sannyasa*, Bangalore, Asian Trading Corporation, 1989. See Swindells, 77.
3 Panikkar describes 'multireligious experience' as follows:
    He starts by making a real, heartfelt, unselfish effort – a bold

and hazardous one – to understand the belief, the world, the archetypes, the culture, the mythical and conceptual background, the emotional and historical associations of his fellows from the inside. In short, he seriously attempts an existential incarnation of himself into another world – which obviously involves prayer, initiation, study and worship. He does this not by way of trial but rather with a spirit of faith in a truth that transcends us and a goodness that upholds us when we truly love our neighbor ... It is not experimentation but a genuine experience undergone within one's own faith. Consequently that experience is forbidden, or rather does not become possible, unless he has established in himself the distinction between his faith (ever transcendent, unutterable and open) and his belief (an intellectual, emotional and cultural embodiment of that faith within the framework of a particular tradition that, yes, demands his loyalty, but not that he betray the rest of mankind ... Morever, this risk of faith must be understood as emerging from one's own faith itself not from doubting what one believes, but deepening and enriching it. This risk should not be understood as an intellectual or religious curiosity but as a dynamic of faith itself, which discloses another religious world in one's neighbor that we can neither ignore nor brush aside, but must try to take up, integrate into our own. What is more, when faith claims universality, the faith of the neighbor automatically becomes a problem that cannot be evaded (Raimundo Panikkar, *The Intrareligious Dialogue* (New York, Paulist Press, 1978), pp. 12–13).

4 Bede Griffiths, *The Marriage of East and West: A Sequel to The Golden String*, pp. 42–43. We should note that the power of this ideal is due as much to the internal simplicity and freedom it denotes as well as the external. See Bruno Barnhart (ed.), *The One Light: Bede Griffiths' Principal Writings*, Springfield, Illinois, Templegate, 2001, pp. 249–59. On freedom and simplicity, see also Griffiths, *Return to the Center*, pp. 11–15. *Sannyasa* is also not simply an abandoning of externals but a profound renunciation of one's inner possessions, one's ideas and emotions, and more fundamentally one's ego or self-will as well. And from the Bhagavad Gita, Griffiths received the further refinement that *sannyasa* is more precisely detachment than renunciation. One may abandon or give away possessions but still be attached to them; and one may have possessions but not be attached to them. For Griffiths as for the Gita, it is detachment as an interior state that is liberating; by detaching from external and internal possessions one may

surrender more totally to God. See Bede Griffiths, *River of Compassion: A Christian Commentary on the Bhagavad Gita*, New York, Continuum, 1995, pp. 105–108 (commenting on 6.1–4).

5 Abhishiktananda discusses these meetings between 1957 and 1963 in his *Hindu-Christian Meeting Point: Within the Cave of the Heart*, rev. edn., Delhi, ISPCK, 1976.

6 Abhishiktananda, *Hindu-Christian Meeting Point*, p. 9.

7 Bede Griffiths, 'Catholicism and the East,' *The Commonweal* 68/11 (13 June, 1958), p. 273 (reprinted in idem, *Christ in India: Essays towards a Hindu-Christian Dialogue*, Springfield, Illinois, Templegate, 1966, 1984, p. 99). See also idem, *The Marriage of East and West*, pp. 13–15.

8 Griffiths continues: 'A symbol is an image of great power, which crystallizes in itself a whole world of thought and feeling. Before a symbol can pass from one system of thought to another it must be divested of all the associations of thought and feeling which it has in the first system; it has in a sense to be re-created. In other words for Hindu thought and feeling to become Christian, it must die and be reborn; it must itself suffer the mystery of the Cross and the Resurrection.' Griffiths is close to Monchanin's viewpoint here: 'Hindu thought, so deeply focused on the Oneness of the One, on the kevalin in his kevalatva, cannot be sublimated into trinitarian thought without a crucifying dark night of the soul. It has to undergo a noetic metamorphosis, a passion of the spirit' (from Monchanin's 'The Quest of the Absolute' [1957], in J.G. Weber, (ed. and tr.), *In Quest of the Absolute: The Life and Work of Jules Monchanin*, Kalamazoo, Michigan, Cistercian Publications, 1977, p. 132.

9 Bede Griffiths, 'Symbolism and Cult,' in *Indian Culture and the Fullness of Christ*, Madras, Madras Cultural Academy, 1957, pp. 58–61. He continues: 'In the second place we have to recover our sense of symbolism. The doctrine of the ancient world was that God himself is an inexpressible mystery, but that He manifests himself in natural forms, and these forms are what we call symbols – that is manifestation of God. In Hinduism in particular we have the doctrine that God is not only manifested in nature, but that from time to time he has manifested himself in a human form – an avatara. Rama, Krishna and Siva, these are all *symbols* of God, signs of God's goodness and love and grace. ... Now when we confront Rama, and Krishna and Siva with the person of Christ, we have no need to reject or despise them. We have only to show that they are shadows of the reality. They are symbols which have been realized in Christ – He alone is the historic

fulfilment of all man's dreams of a saviour: He alone answers the deepest need of the human heart and reveals the ultimate truth of the divine love.' Thus he concludes in a missionary tone: 'Now the Hindus, we know, have the most profound sense of sacramentalism, of God's presence in the world, in the temple, in the sacred image. Is it not for us to show how the Christian Sacrament fulfills this longing of the Hindu soul to see and to touch God? ... If the Hindus found in our Churches this sense of mystery, of a living presence of holiness, would they not see in this the fulfilment of their deep piety which seeks so intensely and yet so pathetically to reach God by material means?'

10 James Stuart, *Swami Abhishiktananda: His Life Told through His Letters*, Delhi, ISPCK, 1989, p. 122.
11 For Abhishiktananda's fuller account of this retreat, see his *Guru and Disciple: An Encounter with Sri Gnanananda, a Contemporary Spiritual Master*, rev. edn., Delhi, ISPCK, 1990.
12 In conversation, Griffiths responded to the passage just quoted in the text as follows: 'I don't experience it in the same way. I know what he's saying ... I never felt the tension he did between the abyss and the sacrament. Obviously he wouldn't let go of either, and he was right ... But I've been more fortunate perhaps' (Interview by the author, tape recording, Gethsemani, Kentucky, August 1991).

See also Abhishiktananda's further comments in Stuart, 124: 'Liturgy and advaita are on two different planes ... Liturgy is on one particular plane, and on this plane it is marvellous (...). Advaita places you on another plane, and says that all the other planes are a game, *lila, maya*. And the advantage of Shivaism is that it very readily accepts that it is a game which has to be life behind ('When I was a child, I thought as a child ...'); while in the Church the plane of sacraments, liturgy, Church, is treated as an absolute in itself.' See also Stuart, p. 292.
13 Excerpts are all from letter of 3 March, 1956 from Abhishiktananda to Joseph Lemarie, in Stuart, pp. 100–101.

Abhishiktananda uses the term 'Greek', as did Monchanin, as shorthand for their western theological and philosophical conditioning. When Monchanin could not accept the radical explorations of Abhishiktananda's early collection of essays *Guhantara*, both acknowledged that it was due to Monchanin's 'Greek' mentality. When Abhishiktananda criticized his own *Sagesse hindoue mystique chretienne*, he would note his own Greekness (Stuart, pp. 81; see also letter by Monchanin quoted in Sten Rodhe, 'Christianity and Hinduism: A Comparison of the Views

Held by Jules Monchanin and Bede Griffiths', in *Jules Monchanin (1895–1957) as Seen from East and West*, Delhi, ISPCK and Saccidananda Ashram, 2001, p. 173.
14 Stuart, p. 228.
15 Ibid.
16 See the author's 'Two Models of Christian Dialogue with Hinduism: Bede Griffiths and Abhishiktananda', *Vidyajyoti* 60/2–4 (February–April 1996): pp. 101–110, 183–91, 243–54.
17 Abhishiktananda, *Hindu-Christian Meeting Point*, p. 9. Cf. Henri de Lubac's advice to Monchanin during their last meeting before Monchanin's departure for India: '[T]o rethink everything in the light of theology and to rethink theology through mysticism, freeing it from everything incidental and regaining, through spirituality alone, everything essential ... He believes that it is in coming into contact with India that I will be able to rework theology much better than by going into theological problems in themselves' (Weber, p. 25).
18 Abhishiktananda, *Saccidananda: A Christian Approach to Advaitic Experience*, rev. edn., Delhi, ISPCK, 1984, p. xv. Here he describes his approach as based upon 'an inner symbiosis within the human heart between the advaitic experience of self-awareness and the contemplation of the blessed Trinity at the very source of the soul'. On how this framework shaped most of his earlier writing as well, see Stuart, p. 321.
19 Bede Griffiths, 'The Meeting of Religions', *The Tablet* 223/6745 (30 August, 1969): p. 856: 'If an impartial commission were to be set up in India to study the behaviour of the different religious communities – Hindu, Parsee, Moslem and Christian – in regard to their religious observance and their moral character, their standards of public worship and private devotion, their concern for the poor and the sick, for education and social service, as well as their standards of personal integrity, of honesty, kindness and sexual morality, I think that it would be found that there is no great difference between them.'
20 Bede Griffiths, 'The Meeting of Religions', *The Tablet* 223/6745 (30 August, 1969): p. 856.
21 J. Trapnell, 'Bede Griffith, Mystical Knowing and the Unity of Religions', *Philosophy and Theology*, vol. 7, no. 4 (1993), pp. 355–79.
22 J. Trapnell, 'Bede Griffiths' Theory of Religious Symbol and Practice of Dialogue: Toward Interreligious Understanding', Ph.D, Washington, DC, Catholic University of America, 1993, p. 456, no. 143.

23 Stuart, p. 349.
24 Ibid.
25 J. Trapnell, 'Bede Griffith as Culture Bearer: An Exloration of the Relationship between Spiritual Transformation and Cultural Change', *Ameircan Benedictine Review*, vol. 47, no. 3 (1996), pp. 260–83.
26 'In a way, I never feel separated from the earth or the trees or people or whatever. It is all one, and yet the differences remain. This is so important. The danger of *advaita* is that it tends to minimize the universe, and even to deny it. It is *maya*, an illusion, or it is just a play and not taken seriously. In this true *advaita* [that he contrasts to this dangerously incomplete one] everybody and everything has its own unique reality; but the divine reality is present in every plant, every animal, every atom, every proton. The divine is totally present in each one ... Each part represents – makes present – the whole', (John Swindells (ed.), *A Human Search: Bede Griffiths Reflects on His Life, an Oral History*, Liguori, Missouri, Triumph Books, 1997, pp. 92–93. Griffiths late in life was very intrigued by the similar nature of the hologram.
27 Swindells, pp. 95–101.
28 Abhishiktananda, *Ascent to the Depth of the Heart*, p. 380: 'One who knows several mental (or religious or spiritual) languages is incapable of absolutizing any formulation whatever – of the Gospel, of the Upanishads, of Buddhism, etc. He can only bear witness to an experience – about which he can only stammer ...'
29 This essay originated in 1970 but was expanded in light of his experiences with his disciple Marc Chaduc's initiation into *sannyasa* in 1973. Chaduc has affirmed that the finished essay represents Abhishiktananda's 'spiritual testament' (Foreword to Abhishiktananda, *The Further Shore: Three Essays by Abhishiktananda*, Delhi, ISPCK, 1984, p. x). The biographical background of the essay is significant. It was written, revised, and expanded during the final three years of his life when he realized the unsatisfactoriness of the theological frameworks supporting most of his earlier writings; he found in *sannyasa* a principle that transcends religious differences, just as the *sannyasi* represents one who stands outside the religions. These were also years in which he intensified his meditation upon the Upanishads in light of the Gospel with his close disciple Marc Chaduc and in which he collaborated with Swami Chidananda of Sivananda Ashram on a ceremony of initiation into *sannyasa* for Chaduc. These were also years when he experienced intimations of his own final going beyond. We should note that Griffiths also objected to this

late writing of his predecessor at Shantivanam as well, specifically in its emphasis upon the legitimacy of an a-cosmic vocation for the *sannyasi*. Yet see Stuart 327 where Abhishiktananda relates *sannyasa* to both *advaita* and the Trinity in a way that are close to Griffiths's sense of both terms. Compare also Abhishiktananda's description of the parallels between Hindu *sannyasis* and the itinerant messengers of the Gospel in his *Saccidananda*, pp. 8–10.

30 The quoted passages below begin as follows: '[I]n every religion and in every religious experience there is a *beyond*, and it is precisely this 'beyond' that is our goal. Sannyasa is the recognition of that which is beyond all signs; and paradoxically, it is itself the sign of what for ever lies beyond all possibility of being adequately expressed by rites, creeds or institutions.' The scope of these synthetic statements is familiar from Griffiths. Abhishiktananda probes further, highlighting the specific Indian contribution to their understanding of monasticism: 'Terms like "Hindu sannyasa", "Christian" or "Buddhist monasticism", despite their convenience, should be used with caution, since they only have meaning on the phenomenological level (the level of appearance). No epithet or qualification, religious or other, can rightly be attributed to the core of what in India is called sannyasa and elsewhere monasticism.' We hear Abhishiktananda's characteristic skepticism about the delimiting effects of language, a tendency present in Christian negative theology but accentuated by his encounter with India – though recall that he has affirmed that *sannyasa* itself is a potent sign for 'the beyond'. He explores a level of meaning for *sannyasa* and monasticism beyond the phenomenological.

31 See Raimundo Panikkar, *Blessed Simplicity*.

32 Abhishiktananda, *The Further Shore*, pp. 26–27.

Chapter 10

Through a Glass Darkly:
The Jesuit Encounter with Buddhism in Tibet

John Flannery

The Portuguese *Descobrimentos* ('Discoveries'), the spectacular maritime expansion given impetus by Prince Henry the Navigator (d. 1460), are celebrated in the epic work of the national poet, Luis de Camões, *Os Lusiadas*. This work reinforced the image of the Portuguese as a nation of sailors with sea water coursing through their veins. This notion has tended to obscure the fact that these explorers also left their ships to cross vast continents on foot, on horseback, or even on camel. One such was the Portuguese Jesuit António de Andrade, the first European to cross the Himalayas into Tibet. Following a brief biography and account of his travels, this chapter will attempt a psychological and theological profile of Andrade the Jesuit in his early seventeenth-century *milieu*, examine his policy of evangelization 'from within', and consider the influence exerted by Islam in the Christian encounter with Tibetan Buddhism. The final section will ask what evidence modern scholarship can provide to support Andrade's conviction that the religion of Tibet contained vestiges of Christianity.

A brief biography of Andrade[1]
Born in 1581 in the Portuguese town of Oleiros, António de Andrade entered the Jesuits at Coimbra in 1597, and

completed his novitiate in Lisbon. In 1600 he set sail from Lisbon, arriving six months later at Cochin. After completing his studies at the College of St Paul in Goa, he was ordained, and sent to the Mogul mission in Agra.

In 1624, accompanying the Mogul king Jahangir (1605-1627) on a journey to Lahore, he discovered a group of Buddhist pilgrims at Delhi on their way to the great pagoda of Badre, some forty days distant, and close to the great desert lying between Hindustan and Tibet. Andrade seized this opportunity to visit the mysterious land of Tibet and set off with the pilgrims. Their route was the most direct but also the most difficult, climbing from 200 metres above sea level at Agra to 4750 metres at Tsaparang, capital of the Tibetan kingdom of Gugé. Disappointed at first to be told that the missionaries were not, as he had thought, wealthy merchants seeking trade, the king soon showed himself well disposed to the Jesuits, granting them a royal charter, including the freedom to preach their 'law'. After only twenty-five days Andrade returned to Agra, having spent seven months on the journey. The account of this trip is given in a letter to the Jesuit Provincial at Goa, in which he narrates not only the incredible ardours of the trip and some description of Tibet and its inhabitants,[2] but makes great claims for the potential of this new mission field. Andrade's letter was published in Lisbon in 1626 and aroused great interest throughout Catholic Europe.

Andrade returned to Tibet in August 1625, and a letter of 1626 relates his reception at court, the work involved in founding the mission, his theological debates with the lamas, and the construction of a church in Tsaparang. It is uncertain how long Andrade remained there: by 1630 he was in Goa as Provincial, and a letter of 1633 refers to his sending four Jesuits to the Tibetan mission in 1631. Having completed his term as Provincial, Andrade became rector of the College at Goa. He had always wanted to return to Tibet, and it was during preparations to do so that he died from poison in 1634.

Unfortunately, the promise of this new mission field was not to be fulfilled. In 1630 the king of Gugé was overthrown by the king of neighbouring Ladakh, who ordered

Christian converts to be transported to Ladakh. The opposition of the conqueror to Christianity may not have proved insuperable, but there had always been considerable opposition among the Jesuits at Goa to the Tibetan mission, and it is clear that the missionaries sent to Tibet after the death of Andrade to assess the situation were men lacking the zeal, spirit and vision of the mission's founder. The mission appears to have been abandoned by 1650.[3]

The memory of the king of Gugé, so well disposed towards Christianity, and the Christian presence there, seem to have been almost completely obliterated from the historical record.[4] Nor did a British expedition of 1912 find any physical evidence of Christianity at Tsaparang.

Andrade: a theological profile

Andrade's published letters provide us with few clues as to his theology. He initially believed that the Tibetans practised a version of Christianity which had been distorted or corrupted through time. This is clear from his conversation with a friendly lama, where his question as to whether the Son of God was the same as the Father is aimed at detecting Arian heresy in Tibetan beliefs, and his question about the Mother of God is designed to discover whether, following Nestorius, the Tibetans rejected the teaching of the Council of Ephesus in 431 that Mary was *Theotokos*. His concerns for christological orthodoxy also arise in connection with what he understands as the identification of the Sacred Book of the Lamas with the Second Person of the Trinity. For Andrade it is the *incarnation* of the divine Word which must be accepted and he rejects the notion of *inbibliation* which he understands the Buddhists to hold.[5] If this rejection of a holy book come down from heaven no doubt owes something to controversy with Muslims over the status of the Quran, then Andrade's insistence that 'Without good works, no-one goes to heaven'[6] would seem to echo the 'faith versus works' controversy with the Reformers.

Although never to prepared to compromise Catholic dogma, Andrade's approach in Tibet shows that he shared with de Nobili and Ricci a particular 'theology of history'.

His approach to evangelization in Tibet was not that of tabula *rasa favoured* in the Mexican mission, nor the creation of separate neophyte communities favoured by Francis Xavier in the South of India. If these approaches can be seen to represent a neo-Augustinian severity regarding everything outside the Church, those who advocated acculturation and inculturation of the Christian faith in India and China simply chose to use another, equally venerable, theological tradition which recognized the widespread dissemination of 'seeds of the Word', and saw the thoughts and writings of pagan philosophers as a kind of *praeparatio evangelii.*

While the early Fathers insisted on the entire newness brought about by the coming of God in the flesh, '*omnen novitatem attulit seipsem afferens*',[7] they also continued to insist on the universal active presence of the Word of God prior to the incarnation. In the view of the early Fathers, Christianity was destined to integrate, purify and transform whatever was good in the religions of the nations. The Word of God had been heard throughout the whole world – but had been eroded by the passage of time. Belief in a total evangelization of Asia came naturally to those who believed that in the beginning all was perfection and that the passage of time represented degradation. The Word of God had been spoken into creation twice, after the appearance of the First Adam, and that of the Last Adam. While today we see the Church as existing from the time of the Christ-event, Augustine spoke of the ecclesia *ab Abel,* the first just man.[8] The truth of Christianity presupposes its absolute antiquity. It was this perception of the substantial conformity between the religions of the first humans, and the teachings of the Church of Christ that enabled all the sacred traditions to be seen as more or less alterations of the original. The original unity of peoples and civilizations was taken as a given by Andrade and his confrères.[9]

Andrade – a psychological profile

The man in his setting
Throughout Andrade's life the Spanish Hapsburgs ruled Portugal. By the time of the death of Philip II of Spain (Philip I of Portugal) in 1598, Spanish unification was complete, and Spain dominated the world from the West Indies to the East Indies. The Portugal of Andrade was part of a multinational, multicultural empire. Although born in something of a backwater, Andrade would have been exposed to culture and scholarship at both Coimbra and Lisbon. While having a particularly Jesuit flavour (emphasizing the *Spiritual Exercises*), Andrade's training would have followed the norms laid of the Council of Trent, emphasizing Thomistic theology, and the Aristotelian philosophy which inspired it.

The information reaching Andrade and his fellow novices from the Jesuit missions overseas was probably patchy. Much missionary information was directed to the General of the Order in Rome, and while lines of communication between Goa and Lisbon were relatively good, news from the Chinese and Japanese missions must have taken a long time to reach Europe (one letter from Macau reached Rome seventeen years later).[10] It is likely that the teachers at the novitiate would have made full use of edifying accounts of missionary success to foster zeal in their charges. We know that edifying letters from 'the Indies' were included in the readings at dinner in the professed houses of the Society.[11]

The Jesuit
The Jesuit order of 'clerks regular', established formally in 1540 by Paul III, can be seen as arising from pressure for reform of the clergy *within* the Church. This was acted on by Clement VII (1523–1534), accelerated under his successor Paul III and continued as an important part of the work of the Council of Trent (1545–63). Retaining elements of the earlier monastic orders, the Jesuits were given freedom to exercise their ministry by being dispensed from the Office in choir and frequent chapter meetings, making

them available to work in any part of the world at the wish of the Pope.

The Order founded by Ignatius, essentially missionary in nature, had ties to Lisbon which predate its formal establishment. From Lisbon they first set off in the wake of the 'Discoveries'. Here too, was the first house belonging to the order and the first house of formation. Portugal was also the first administrative province to be established. Significantly, the establishment of general teaching establishments was forbidden during the first twelve years in Portugal on the basis that 'by their very nature, they would tend to weaken the freedom of spirit and openness to the world' needed for the missionary endeavour.[12]

Andrade's Lisbon was at the epicentre of the missionary endeavour which followed in the footsteps of Francis Xavier, who reached Goa in 1542. This charged atmosphere must surely have served to increase the zeal for souls which would drive him to undertake his remarkable journeys at enormous personal risk.

Knowledge of other religions
Centuries of Muslim presence in the Iberian peninsula had left their mark on the language, architecture, agriculture and even the appearance of its inhabitants. (Andrade has no difficulty in passing himself off as a Muslim traveller).[13] We can be sure that the age-old Muslim – Christian polemic regarding the doctrines of the Trinity, and Incarnation, the inspired nature of the Quran, the charge of falsification of scriptures by Jews and Christians, and the prophethood of Muhammad, were as familiar in Lisbon as at the Mogul court. Andrade will employ Muslim objections to Christianity in his debates with Tibetan Buddhists.

The extent to which Buddhism was known or understood in the West is more problematic. Some missionaries, who spent twenty or thirty years in Japan, are likely to have developed a good understanding of Buddhist doctrine in the process of refuting it. Catechisms produced with the aid of lay converts from Zen Buddhism could reasonably be expected to display a sound knowledge of at least some

Buddhist teaching. Although we have no systematic accounts of Buddhism from this period, there are numerous references in missionary correspondence. As we have already indicated, such correspondence was at least as much for edification as information: 'Take care not to write about matters which are not of edification', warned Francis Xavier.[14] The need for such knowledge may have appeared superfluous in the Indian missions to which Andrade would be sent, since Islam had displaced Buddhism from its birthplace by this time. The words of Frois, the chronicler of the Japanese mission, have something of a prophetic ring in the context of Andrade's Tibetan mission: speaking of theological debates with Buddhist monks he says,

> the form of their arguments and their ways of proceeding in them are very different from what we learn in our studies. As many of them ... are most eloquent in speech, anyone who did not know the basic principles on which their religion is founded might often think that both we and they are preaching the same thing.[15]

In addition to these direct influences on Andrade, there were other, more nebulous ideas embedded in the European psyche. One of the strongest of these was the idea of 'lost Christianities' in remote parts of the world, now effectively cut off from Christendom by *dar-al-Islam*.

The archetype of the lost brother

Andrade and his 'lost brother'
In 1624 in Srinagar, Andrade and his companion are subjected to hostile questioning, to which he replied that he was Portuguese, going to Tibet 'in search of a brother of mine ...'[16] This subterfuge provides an important key to understanding the inspiration of Andrade to reach Tibet whatever the personal cost, and his interpretation of what he found there. Andrade's words can be seen as a kind of parable of his mission, based on the archetype of the 'lost brother'.[17] Andrade and other Jesuits of the provinces of both Goa and Cochin did all in their power to maintain

belief in the existence of 'hidden Christianities', something which can be understood in two complementary ways: the existence in Asia of Christian kingdoms analogous to those of Europe, and the possibility of re-Christianization 'from within' of peoples who had formerly been Christian. This myth, so powerful in Europe at the end of the Middle Ages and beyond, was as much responsible for the advance of the *caravelas* of the 'Discoveries' as the favourable winds which filled their sails.

The Christian Priest-King Prester John and the Land of Cathay
The legend of the mysterious land of Cathay had a basis in fact: the expansion in the thirteenth and fourteenth century of Mesopotamian Christianity through Asia and to the Far East. The amplification in the legend of this phenomenon reflects the level of frustration felt in the West on account of the expansion of Islam in the Mediterranean basin, Asia, the silk and spice routes, and even in Europe itself. It was shortly before the second Crusade (1149–1174) that the legend of Cathay or the Kingdom of Prester John appeared. This told of 'Presbyter Joannes', a great priest-king, descendant of the Magi, who ruled a rich and powerful Asian empire. In a letter to the Byzantine Emperor, supposedly written by Prester John, which began to circulate in 1165, the 'Ruler of the Three Indies' claims that he is going to destroy the Saracens marching on Jerusalem. The prophecy contained in this forgery is based on two factors, both real enough, if somewhat recent; the spread of the Church of the East among the Mongols and Turks, and their expansion at the expense of the Muslim peoples of Eurasia. After the disastrous Crusade of 1248, Saint Louis dreamed of a joint Euro-Mongolian holy war against Islam, and sent first André de Longjumeau as ambassador to the court of the Great Khan, and then Guillaume de Rubrouck who crossed the Eurasian continent in 1253–4. De Rubrouck's report helps us to understand the mechanism whereby Western Christians invented brothers or half-brothers in faith beyond the Muslim world, and recognized, or believed they recognized, vestiges of Christianity in the Far East. He was overwhelmed by the Mongol court where almost all the

peoples of the empire and their diverse religions were represented. While confused by the absence of images of Christ on crosses in the Church of the East, what he saw of the lamas was at once strange and apparently familiar. Unlike the married clergy of the Church of the East, these *'sacerdotes idolorum'* took a vow of celibacy like the Latin priests, they rang bells, sang offices in choir, said the rosary, and were clean-shaven. Unlike the priests of the Church of the East these 'idolatrous priests' prayed with their hands joined, like the Roman priests.

Entering one of their 'churches' he thought that the 'main idol' resembled St Christopher, seeing images of what he believed to be bishops on the walls, their hands raised in blessing, and even the archangel Michael. At first sight then, Buddhism was interpreted as a mixture of Christianity and paganism.

Was it a Christianity which had been corrupted by the prevalence of paganism, or a paganism which had taken inspiration from the Church of Christ? De Rubrouck was already asking the same question to which Andrade would later attempt to respond.

Implicit in this view of Buddhism as a semi-pagan or half-forgotten double of Christianity is the belief in a large-scale evangelization of Asia in ancient times. A recently translated liturgical text of the Syro-Malabar Church for the Office of Saint Thomas, included the following: 'With Saint Thomas, the splendours of life-giving doctrine reached the whole of India. With Saint Thomas, the Kingdom of Heaven was taken and brought to the Chinese.'[18] Shortly after the publication of this remarkable hymn, two Portuguese works offered a synthesis between the western legends of Prester John and Cathay, and that of Saint Thomas. Both João de Barros in his *Décadas da Ásia* of 1563 and Gouveia in the 1606 *Jornada do Arcebispo de Goa Dom Frei Aleixo de Menezes* are insistent that the contemporary popular identification of the 'kingdom of Prester John' with Abyssinia was erroneous. There were said to be vast numbers of Christians beyond the mountains in the North, to whom the term should properly be applied. Both books also repeated confused and imprecise information about

Christians still to be discovered, which had been transmitted by Jesuits at the court of Akbar. This information would motivate various Portuguese expeditions to the interior of the Asian continent, including that of Andrade in 1624.

Muslim accounts of 'Christianity' beyond the mountains
In 1581, three Jesuits (Acquaviva, Montserrat and Henriques) at the court in Agra heard tell of Christians beyond the Himalayas. In 1582 Acquaviva refers to the land of the Tibetans as 'Bottan' (from the Hindi *Bhotanta*), saying 'They are white men, and there are no Muslims among them'.[19] In his compendious work on geography and history of 1590, Montserrat writes that 'this Empire of the Indies, which the Turks call *Hindustan,* was formerly governed by Christian kings'.[20] After their conquest by the forces of Islam, however, the same author tells us only a Christian remnant remains 'on the slopes of the *Imao* (the Himalayas)'. Accompanying Akbar on a trip to Kashmir in 1597, three other Jesuits, Xavier, Pinheiro and Goís, heard Muslim travellers speak of a country called *Tebat* with churches, monks and bishops. In the following year the Jesuit Jerome Xavier, nephew of Francis Xavier, met a Muslim merchant from Central Asia returning from making the pilgrimage to Mecca. He spoke of a vast, rich, Christian land to the northeast of Agra, or Lahore, with the name *Xatai,* which resembled *Cathay.* On the strength of this conversation Xavier mounted an overland expedition to find Cathay or Xatai. In 1602 this expedition set out under the charge of the Jesuit lay brother, Bento de Goís, who spent three years on a journey which ended with his death from exhaustion at Xuxhou, in the extreme West of China. During his adventures[21] he had the opportunity to visit the former king of Ladakh in the dungeons of the Sultan of Yarkand, communicating with him through a Muslim Tibeto-Persian translator. From this conversation he was led to conclude that the people of Tibet prayed not in mosques but in churches, had a celibate clergy, fasted during Lent, and had the *Injil* or Gospel as their holy book.[22]

Unfortunately, the sacrifices of de Goís had been in vain,

Cathay *(Xatai)* was none other than the China reached almost a century earlier by Portuguese sailors.

The confusion of Buddhism with Christianity, however, was not unique to Muslims. The same error was made by a poorly catechised European layman. Shortly after the departure of de Goís, a Portuguese merchant, Diogo de Almeida, asked for an audience with the archbishop of Goa and told of his experiences while living in Tibet, or more precisely, Ladakh.

What he had seen there confirmed the western hopes of finding, at last, a powerful Christian land in the centre of Asia. According to Almeida, the Tibetans 'have many richly decorated churches, with altar panels and images showing Our Lord Jesus Christ, Our Lady and the Holy Apostles. They have many priests and these, like ours, observe the law of celibacy, they also dress similarly, the only difference being that they completely shave their heads. They have a bishop they call '*lamão*'.[23]

Three and a half centuries later the uneducated merchant, Almeida, and the learned Jesuit lay brother, de Goís, never having met, were in agreement with Guillaume de Rubrouck that the Tibetan lamas belonged to the category of 'Christian'. Although unjustifiable in terms of scientific history, de Rubrouck's perception of Buddhism in the thirteenth century was to have a future. It was just this concept which was reasserted by Andrade.[24]

Evangelization 'from within'– Christian-pagan hybrids

Andrade's approach was to work for a 'christianization' from within, working to reform and purify traditional beliefs and practices It may be no great exaggeration to claim that Andrade and his compatriots 'wished that [Tibetan society] should one day wake up to find itself Christian, without ever having the impression of denying its true self, or of having completely broken with its rites and traditions'.[25]

While Ricci became a mandarin to bring Christ to the Middle Empire, and de Nobili a renunciate and *brahman* to bring the Gospel to the Hindus, Andrade had the remarkable stroke of good fortune to be elevated to the rank of Grand Lama by the king of Gugé, Thi Tashi-Dagpa, during his first brief stay in Tibet. [26]

Andrade's new position could only serve to reinforce the supposition on the part of the Tibetans that the European priests were a kind of *bonze*. Since they were used to seeing only their Muslim and Hindu neighbours, the Jesuits from far off India to the South of the Himalayas, were seen as following in the footsteps of predecessors, such as Atisha (982–1054), a reformer of Tibetan Buddhism, and Tsong Khapa (1357–1419), who reformed Lamaism. Andrade accused the Tibetan monks of laxity, as if the purpose of ascesis was the same for the Jesuits as for the Lamas.[27] He also questions them about the propriety of novices taking part in ritual dances, something that would not be considered acceptable in Europe.[28]

Andrade made use of real and imagined analogies between Buddhism and Christianity; the cult of relics, veneration of the '*double-vajra*' which so resembles a trefoil cross, and pictorial illustrations of the process of conversion or of destiny in the after-life. On hearing that the Sanskrit mantra *Om mani pad me hum,* so ubiquitous in Tibet, was inexplicable, he did not hesitate to tell his neophytes to continue using it 'as it would be morally impossible to tell them to stop saying it, since it was their habit and custom', albeit first attributing a Christian interpretation to it.[29] A careful reading of the Second Letter shows that the people of Tsaparang, before any kind of Christian initiation, were able to pray in the new church.[30]

The belief of the Jesuit missionaries to Asia in the sixteenth and seventeenth centuries, in the widespread existence of pagan/Christian hybrids, reflects exactly the Islamic view of the non-Islamic world. Muslim travellers discovered numerous pagan-Christian, or better, pagan-monotheist hybrids. Islam shared the view of India and of Europe of old that considered the beginning of history as a time of perfection, and the passing of time as a kind of degradation. Islam represents a renewal of the original religion of mankind, seeing both Judaism and Christianity as deformations of the true religion, as practised by Noah,

Abraham, Moses and Jesus. Christians, as one of the people of the book (*Ahl al-Kitab*), fall into an intermediate category, neither Muslim nor pagan, although always liable to paganising. The Islamic view of Buddhism shows the same ambivalence, seeing it as an idolatrous paganism,[31] or, more indulgently, recognizing in the Buddha another Divine Envoy of former times whose original message conformed to that of Islam. In its current form, of course, Islam considered Buddhism as, at best, a degenerate pagan-monotheist hybrid.

In India Andrade had spent some time defending Christian faith in an essentially Muslim environment. The understanding of lamaistic Buddhism which comes across in his texts was complicated by interminable Muslim-Christian polemic and by the influence this had on the particular mentality of Catholic missionaries sent to Muslim countries. Between the Islamic view of Christianity as a pagan-monotheism, and that of Buddhism as a pagan-Christianity, common to de Rubrouck, Ricci and Andrade, there is a play of mirrors, which sheds an illusory light on a subject which in fact is most obscure, the true identity of far-off peoples.[32] It was this which authorized the equally illusory hope of a gradual conversion of these half-Christians or half-pagans and dictated a particular strategy of evangelization 'from within' in Tibet: a stretegy which would prove vain.

Andrade's theological discourse: Christian perceptions of Buddhism as seen through the lens of Islam

That Islam should play an important part in the Christian perception of Tibetan Buddhism is hardly surprising; it may indeed be fairly claimed that without the tendency of Islam to confuse Christianity and Buddhism, Andrade may not have set off for Tibet.[33] At Jahangir's court the Jesuit missionaries were immersed in an essentially Muslim environment, where the language of communication was Persian. It would be the same language which Andrade used to communicate on his arrival at Gugé, depending initially on the services of a Kashmiri Muslim interpreter.[34] This would be highly significant, given that Persian, although an Indo-European language, uses Arabic orthography, and shows considerable lexical evidence of Arabic, the one and sacred language of Islam, and that as a consequence of its use, cultural and religious categories based on the Quran were insinuated into what Andrade believed he was learning about Tibet.[35]

Although Andrade clearly states early in the Second Letter that 'these are not Christian lands, but seem to once have been',[36] he continued to find analogies between Tibetan religion and his own. Such analogies were artificially augmented by the linguistic limitations occasioned by the only language common to some members of Thi Tashi-Dagpa's court and the Jesuits.[37] The Three Jewels of Buddhism could only be rendered by the Persian word, also Arabic and Quranic, used to designate the Christian Trinity, *Tatlit*. To refer to the Buddha, Andrade uses the term 'Son of God', since no interpreter could call him *but* in Persian without appearing to insult him.[38] The *lhas* of the Tibetan pantheon are understood as angels rather than gods, due to the (mis)translation sequence *lha – malak – anjo* (where *malak* is the Persian for angel, and *anjo* the Portuguese equivalent).[39]

In view of the complexity of the language and the lack of tools for learning it, it is improbable that Andrade had already been able to dispense with the services of an interpreter during a friendly encounter with a Buddhist monk related in a letter of February 1626.[40] In Andrade's words:

> One of the lamas (their ecclesiastics) came to visit us and we questioned him closely as follows:
>
> 1. How many gods do you worship?
> R. One only, who is three.
>
> 2. Does God have a Son?
> R. Yes, and this Son was made man, and then died and went to heaven where he still is, with the Father.
>
> 3. Is this Son God, like the Father?
> R. Yes, but also man.

4. Did he have a mother or not?
R. Yes, and she was so good that she went to heaven, and is still there.

The conversation, which continues in a similar vein, is based on an error in translation.⁴¹ When the lama wishes to refer to one of the Jewels of Buddhism, or rather to one of the foundations of its wisdom, *conjoe* in Portuguese orthography (*dKon mc'og* in erudite transcription), Andrade is given to understand *Xuda* or *Allah* in Persian, which is rendered in Portuguese as *Deus* (God). Andrade had no way of knowing that the concept of a creator God, Lord of the world and of mankind, shared by Christianity and Islam, is completely absent from Buddhism. This initial error would never be overcome. Some indication that Andrade and his Buddhist interlocutors are discussing different religious universes is given in the second letter where he states 'in the first [discussion] we discussed what God is. They said that God is one and three. But, in order to explain this, they added ridiculous ideas'.⁴² In Andrade's letters there is no reference to the fundamental beliefs of Buddhism: universal emptiness and the inter-relatedness and insubstantiality of all things and all beings. The erroneous sequence *Conjoe-Allah-Deus* is also at the root of Andrade's defective understanding of Tibetan iconography, which led to his seeing Buddha as 'Son of God' and representations of Transcendental Wisdom as 'Mother of God' (the mistranslation of *lha* as 'angel', referred to above, also had a part to play). What completely escaped Andrade was the fact that,

> While the Christian sees in his sacred images the reflection of a real history of salvation with real and subsistent beings, since he Believes in a divine *ego*, on which is based the human *ego*, in his the disciple of Shakyamuni sees, or supposedly sees, concretisations of universal emptiness, the froth of nothingness and the ephemeral. For the latter, any *ego* is illusion.⁴³

Interestingly, in dealing with the sacred book of the Lamas

(the *Prajnaparammitasutra*) Andrade makes use of the accusation so familiar from Muslim-Christian polemic, of falsification of scripture. or *tahrif*.[44] It is the teaching of metempsychosis contained in the text which leads Andrade to declare that what had formerly been a book from God had been interpolated and contaminated by ideas from their pagan neighbours, '... if your book does say this, which is so contrary to reason, it can easily be seen that it is not from God, because the book of God does not contain teaching which contradicts reason: and if your book was once the book of God, it has gone astray ...'[45]

As if the linguistic and historical problems Andrade had to contend with in dealing with the beliefs of the Tibetan lamas were not enough, there was a further source of difficulty. Christianity claims theological uniformity on the basis of the *Credo,* which is the same for the most learned theologian and for the humblest believer. Things are different, however in the 'religious' traditions to the East of Islam, and particularly in the case of Tibet, so strongly marked by the esoteric tradition of India. In the defunct Buddhism of North India, as in its Tibetan successor, essential teachings are protected from non-initiates by the use of a crepuscular language (*sandhyabhasa).* Neither written texts nor public speech reveal all. A double hermeneutic runs through all language, enabling it to be understood in a 'vulgar' way, or in a hidden, mystical sense. While a document of the Jesuit Roman Archives tells of an unnamed priest able to easily read the Tibetan sacred book,[46] it is improbable that the newly arrived missionaries had already been initiated into such well-guarded secrets, even if they were able to read the 'surface' text.[47] Occasional hesitation on their part noted by Andrade in his discussions with the lamas reflects the basic divergence between the fundamental criteria of truth, being, and existence which characterize Buddhism and Christianity. For Andrade and his companions, schooled in Plato, Aristotle and the teachings of the Scholastics, it must have been difficult, if not impossible, to grasp that for the lamas 'the sacred truths are neither true nor false'.[48]

In view of the continuing difficulties in dialogue between

Christianity and a Buddhism which is at once a *gnosis and* an agnosticism, we can but sympathize with Andrade in facing the enormous task of understanding the beliefs of the lamas, lacking access not only to any systematic exposition of Buddhist thought, but even to books of grammar or dictionaries, and led further into a maze of miscomprehension by the linguistic difficulties he experienced, and the historical, theological and cultural preconceptions to which he was both heir and hostage.

Traces of Christian influences on Tibetan Buddhism: a basis in fact, or merely self-delusion?

It is easy for us, informed as we are by comparative studies in religion, to dismiss as naive Andrade's belief that Tibetan Buddhism showed clear signs of Christian influence, and that by eliminating what he saw as pagan accretions, a lost or hidden Christianity could be restored. Before dismissing out of hand his belief in Christian influences, however, it may be useful to ask whether evidence exists to support his case.

Before doing so, we do well to note[49] that it is not enough to draw attention to simple, purely ornamental motifs in the form of a cross, or drawings in the form of a swastika. Nor can we base our findings on the dubious analogies which some explorers claim to have found between Christianity and lamaistic Buddhism.

There is, however, clear evidence of Christianity in Central Asia at an early date.[50] Prevented from expansion in its homeland as a consequence of the growth of Islam, the Church of the East went through a period of remarkable missionary activity, reaching as far as Malaya and Indonesia by the first quarter of the eighth century.[51] Tibet had a Church of the East metropolitan in the late Middle Ages, implying the existence of bishops and possibly of local clergy. In the second half of the seventh century, Tibetan tribes may have been included in the apostolate of a Chinese general called A-lo-han (Abraham). This Church of the East Christian from Persia governed the savage tribes on the border of Tibet, where he erected a stone tablet.

A Sassanid cross appears on a sheet covered with exercises in Tibetan among the documents taken by Pelliot[52] from Tuen-huang. The document indicates that Christianity had reached at least as far as the Tibetans of Central Asia, where they were trying to establish an empire. and can probably be dated to 760–782.

That Christianity had penetrated into Tibet is confirmed by two archaeological discoveries. A. H. Francke (1870–1930) discovered a cross of iron and bronze alloy around the neck of a body from the area near lake *mThsomo-riri* in Ladakh, and Shawe and Toussaint discovered inscriptions carved in the rock face at *Dran-Tse*, on the caravan route connecting Kashgar, Bactria and India with central Tibet. Above one of three typically Church of the East crosses can be read the Sogdian word for Jesus. The inscription speaks of a man from Samarkand who has come to Tibet and can be dated 825–6. Other crosses at Schalskukul are accompanied by depictions of doves and may also have Christian significance.

From the inscriptions, it would appear that the evangelization of Tibet took place from Central Asia rather than from China, and it would seem that Christian communities in Tibet probably included Tibetans as well as other nationalities. In addition to the evidence from the Church of the East, we have that of the Arab geographer, ben Muhalhil, who accompanied a Chinese embassy to Central Asia in 940. He speaks of a tribe called *Tubat* (Tibet). In their town, he says, there were Christians, alongside Muslims, Jews, Mages and Hindus. The demise of these Christian communities was likely to have been caused by the persecution of 'foreign' religions led by nobles and *Bon* sorcerers around 840.

If artefactual evidence for possible Christian interaction and influence on Buddhism must be treated with caution, it is perhaps even more important to remain objective when examining possible influence between one culture or religion and another as reflected in the texts of the traditions. Jean Dauvillier is unwilling to go beyond admitting that there appears to have been an exchange of legends between Christianity and Buddhism, for instance those of

Barlaam and Josaphat, and for 'some contamination of secondary doctrines' such as the belief in the reincarnation of animals noted by de Rubrouck in 1254.[53]

In a specifically Tibetan context, however, Marcelle Lalou draws attention to a document brought back by Paul Pelliot[54] and entitled '*Exposition of the way of the dead; a guide to the holy country of the Gods*', One section refers to the salvific action by *Bodhisattvas* on behalf of beings who have fallen into hell. The manuscript no doubt forms part of a funeral rite, where the deceased is guided on his way by direct discourse. These *post-mortem* instructions by the officiant supply the knowledge which the deceased has failed to acquire in life by ascesis or yoga. The retributive automatism of *karman* is decisively interrupted through the saving action of the *Bodhisattvas*. The *Bodhisattva* saviour will (must?) act if invoked. The fatal law of *karman* is mollified by a doctrine of mercy and redemption due to the action of a third party. Certainly, *Bodhisattvas* are generally seen to be characterized by an attitude of fraternity, but this is not normally seen as *post-mortem*.

Even so, Lalou asks, is it not strange to discover in 'The Vehicle of the *Bodhisattvas*', where it is taught that they prefer the salvation of others to themselves, two contradictory notions; that of the judgement of the dead by a god, and the automatism of *karman*. In the admittedly non-canonical text from *Tuen-huang*, the dead can escape both judgement and the retributive law of *karman*. Lalou goes as far as to propose that 'it does not seem absurd to suggest that this document bears traces of the Christian doctrine of redemption'.[55]

Where there is such paucity of evidence for Christian influence on Tibetan Buddhism, any plausible suggestion merits serious consideration. Tucci argues that lamaistic liturgical prescriptions to free the dead person from the fate prepared for him by his own deeds, while basically Indian in origin, and following the plans of Tantric ritualism, do have a particularly Tibetan flavour. While both Mahayana and Vajrayana schools had found ways to circumvent the inflexibility of the law of *karman* in connection with the living, Tibetan belief in the possibility of having an influence on the fate of the dead was a general belief extending beyond the *Bar do thos grol* (Book of the Dead) liturgy.[56] Having taken this step, it seems to me perfectly reasonable to suggest that the notion of *post-mortem* activity by *Bhodisattvas* may well show Christian influence as Lalou proposes.

Study of other Central Asian texts has led to a recognition of a number of 'catalytic influences', such as the coming into prominence of the Buddhist notion of self-sacrifice as Christianity made itself felt further and further to the east of Persia beginning in the fifth century, the idea of Buddha giving his life as a ransom (*uruncaq*) or receiving living beings as a forfeit, and the strong consciousness of sin and guilt giving rise to confessions and confessional formulae, even for laymen. Both Buddhism and Christianity are soteriological religions, and it is hardly surprising that, as Gillman puts it, 'It was, then, especially the pluralistic milieu of the oasis towns of the Silk Road that had a deep influence on Buddhism as it passed along this route from India to East Asia, where such originally 'foreign' ideas were developed further.[57]

Tragically, Buddhist documents which may have balanced the one-sidedness of the Jesuit accounts of the Tibetan mission are now beyond recovery. In his account of his journey to Western Tibet, Young describes the library of the abandoned monastery at Toling as 'knee deep in loose papers ... the leaves tumbled anyhow onto the floor'. We can only imagine the content of these 'masses of indigo-tinted sheets, with writing on them, sometimes in gold, sometimes in gold and silver in alternate lines'.[58] Didier refers to the shelves and cupboards full of crumbling books photographed by Jurgen Aschoff at Tsaparang itself, books which may have shed further light on the theological discussions between Andrade and the lamas, and possibly also on earlier Christian influences in Tibet.[59]

Conclusion

The brief period of the first Jesuit mission to Tibet must be characterized as one in which a process of acculturation rather than inculturation was taking place.[60] While it was too soon for parallels to the incorporation of Confucian rites into Christian worship to have emerged in Tibet, Andrade's approach is characterized by a remarkable openness to the religion of the lamas. His approach of 'Christianization from within' looks back to Origen, Clement of Alexandria and Justin Martyr, with their respect for pagan philosophies as natural religion,[61] and anticipates the statement of Vatican II that the Church 'rejects nothing of what is true and holy', and 'has a high regard for the manner of life and conduct, the precepts and doctrines' of the religions.[62] The conflict between this view of a Christianity accomodative to other religions and a rigid view of salvation history which denies any value to them would be fought out in what is known as the 'Chinese Rites Controversies'. We can only speculate as to whether a 'Tibetan Rites Controversy' would also be exercising scholars today if Andrade's mission had taken root. I suspect it would.

In view of the fact that it was to end in failure, it is easy to dismiss the first Jesuit mission to Tibet as an ill-thought-out enterprise largely driven by the single-mindedness of its founder, whose name and exploits remain little known[63] even in his native country. In view of Andrade's lack of accurate information about Tibet and its religion, it is not surprising that he allowed the superficial similarities between lamaistic Buddhism and Christianity to assume an importance which from our perspective seems unwarranted. In spite of the difficulties he experienced, difficulties exacerbated as we have seen by the influence of Islam, he stands firmly in the Renaissance tradition of Christian humanism of Ricci and de Nobili, and arguably deserves the same status in the annals of the history of missions. Esteves Pereira rightly praises the 'courage, perseverance, resignation to suffering, and apostolic zeal' shown by Andrade on his travels to Tibet, showing himself in his written accounts to be not only a zealous missionary, but also ' an intrepid explorer and far-sighted observer'.[64]

There is also a salutary reminder in Andrade's story for those engaged today in interreligious dialogue. While we no longer have to brave hostile terrain in order to enter into dialogue with other religions, we do well to endeavour to recognize to what extent our own religious and cultural conditioning may colour attempts to enter the religious universe of 'the other'.

Notes

1. Drawn largely from the biography of Andrade by Francisco Maria Esteves Pereira, *O Descobrimento do Tibet pelo P. António de Andrade da Companhia de Jesus, em 1624*, Lisbon, Academía das Sciencias de Lisboa, 1921. Pereira appends the two important letters by Andrade to his superiors in Goa which relate his travels to Tibet and missionary endeavours there. References to the First and Second Letters are taken from this edition.
2. Whom he described as 'people inclined to godly things', First Letter. p. 70.
3. Esteves Pereira, p. 15.
4. G. M. Young, 'A Journey to Toling and Tsaparang in Western Tibet', *Journal of the Punjab Historical Society*, vol. VII, no. 2, p. 187.
5. Hughes Didier, *Os Portugueses no Tibete – Os Primeiros relatos dos jesuítas*, Lisbon, Comissão Nacional para as Comemorações dos Descobrimentos Portugueses, 2000. Originally published as *Les Portugais au Tibet (1624–1635)*, Paris, Chandeigne, 1996, pp. 57–59.
6. Second Letter, p. 102.
7. Irenaeus *(adv. Haer. IV, 34)*.
8. The Mass continues the sacrifice of Abel the Just, *munera pueri tui justi Abel* says the canon of the Tridentine rite. See Jacques Dupuis, SJ, *Toward a Christian Theology of Religious Pluralism*, Maryknoll, New York, Orbis, 1997, pp. 34–35.
9. Ibid., p. 48.
10. W. V. Bangert, *A History of the Society of Jesus*, St Louis, Institute of Jesuit Sources, 1986, p. 250.
11. J. W. O'Malley, *The First Jesuits*, Cambridge, Mass., Harvard University Press, 1993, p. 358.
12. António Lopes, 'História da Província Portuguesa da Companhia de Jesus' in *A Companhia de Jesus e a Missionação no Oriente*, Lisbon, Brotéria/Fundação Oriente, 2000, pp. 35–52 .
13. Esteves Pereira, p. 47.
14. Michael Cooper, 'The Early Jesuits in Japan and Buddhism' in *Portuguese Voyages to Asia and Japan in the Renaissance Period*, *Renaissance Monographs* no. 20, Tokyo, The Renaissance Institute, Sophia University, p. 43.

15 Cooper, 'The Early Jesuits', p. 50.
16 First Letter, p. 51.
17 Hugues Didier, 'Interférences Islamochrétiennes dans les Représentations du Bouddhisme' in *Islamochristiana*, vol. 16, Rome, 1990, pp.115–38.
18 M. Ricci, N. Trigault, *Histoire de l'expédition chrétienne au royaume de la Chine* Paris, Desclée de Brouwer, 1978, pp. 181–82.
19 G. Toscano, *Alla Scoperta del Tibet*, Bologna, Editrice Missionaria Italiana, 1977, p. 28.
20 Op. cit., pp. 38–40.
21 For an account of his travels, cf. Neves Águas (ed.), *Viagens na Ásia Central em Demanda do Cataio*. Mem Martins, Publicações Europa-América, 1988.
22 F. Guerreiro, 1609 *Relaçam annual das coisas que fizeram os Padres da Companhia de Jesus nas partes da India oriental*, Lisbon, pp. 165ff.
23 António de Gouveia, *Jornada do arcebispo* ... Coimbra, 1606, p. 3, cited by H. Didier, *Os Portugueses no Tibete* p. 36 (my translation).
24 Esteves Pereira, p. 79.
25 See Hugues Didier, 'Le Découvreur du Tibet: António de Andrade SJ' in *Christus*, vol. 40 (1993) pp. 371–81, pp. 374–75.
26 Esteves Pereira, p. 64,'whom we take as our Grand Lama'.
27 H. Didier, *Os Portugueses no Tibete*, p. 42.
28 Letter 2, p. 83.
29 'Lord, forgive me my sins', Second Letter, Esteves Pereira, p. 103.
30 But not to be present at the Eucharist, cf., Second Letter, p. 113.
31 Hugues Didier, in *Os Portugueses no Tibete*, p. 50 suggests that this view is reflected lexically in the Persian *but* (idol) and draws attention to Iranian poets frequent rhyming of *but* with *Tubit* (Tibet).
32 H. Didier, *Os Portugueses no Tibete* , p. 52.
33 Which he did dressed as a Muslim! Esteves Pereira, p. 47.
34 Esteves Pereira, p. 61.
35 H. Didier, *Os Portugueses no Tibete*, p. 54.
36 Esteves Pereira, p. 79.
37 H. Didier, *Os Portugueses no Tibete*, p. 55.
38 For the etymology of the term (*al-Budd* in Arabic) see Daniel Gimaret, 'Bouddha et les Bouddhistes dans le tradition musulmane', *Journal Asiatique* (Paris), vol. 257, 1969, pp. 273–316, here p. 275.
39 H. Didier, *Os Portugueses no Tibete*, p. 55.
40 *Archivum Romanum Societatis Jesu* Goa 73, folio 48, cited in H. Didier, *Os Portugueses no Tibete*, 2000, p. 56.
41 Didier accepts however that the oddities of the discussion cannot be entirely attributed to linguistic difficulties: it may, indeed

point to some knowledge of Jesus in Tibet. Cf. Didier, *Os Portugueses no Tibete*, p. 57.
42 Esteves Pereira p. 95.
43 Didier, *Os Portugueses no Tibete*, p. 56.
44 Hugues Didier suggests that this may be one of many *palaeo-Christian* concepts inherited by Islam. The Early Church, during the period when it exclusively used the Greek Septuagint rather than the Hebrew texts of the Old Testament, levelled the charge of falsification of scriptures against Judaism. Cf. Didier, *Os Portugueses no Tibete*, p. 60 and n. 110.
45 Esteves Pereira, p. 100.
46 Referred to in Hugues Didier, *Os Portugueses no Tibete*, p. 63, n. 120.
47 The Gospel parables have something of this quality: cf. Matt. 13:11.
48 Henri de Lubac SJ, *Amida*, Paris, 1955, p. 302 n. 83, cited in Didier, *Os Portugueses no Tibete*, p. 63.
49 Cf. Jean Dauvillier, 'Témoignages Nouveaux sur le Christianisme Nestorien chez les Tibetains' in Dauvillier, J., *Histoire et Institutions des Églises Orientales au moyen Age*, London, Variorum, 1983, pp. 163–67.
50 This survey of evidence of Christianity in Central Asia and Tibet is drawn from the collection of articles in Jean Dauvillier, 'Les provinces Chaldéennes 'de l'exterieur' au Moyen Age', in *Histoire et Institutions des Églises Orientales au moyen Age* I, 261–316. With particular reference to evidence from Syriac documents see also Hunter E. C. D., 'The Church of the East in Central Asia' in *Bulletin of the John Rylands University of Manchester*, vol. 78/3 (1996) pp. 129–42.
51 See the fine series of articles by Brian E. Colless: 'The Traders of the Pearl: The Mercantile and Missionary activities of Persian and Armenian Christians in South-East Asia', *Abr-Nahrain*, vol. IX (1969–70), pp. 17–38; vol. X (1970–71), pp. 102–21; vol. XI (1971), pp. 1–21; vol. XIII (1972–73), pp. 115–35; vol. XIV (1973–74), pp. 1–16; vol. XV (1974–75), pp. 6–17. Reference here *Abr-Nahrain* vol. IX, p. 23. The article in vol. XV, pp. 6–17 is devoted to the Tibetan plateau. I owe this reference to Anthony O'Mahony, Heythrop College, University of London.
52 The French archaeologist, Paul Pelliot, (1878–1945) discovered a large number of manuscripts in the Cave of the Thousand Buddhas at Tuen-huang in China.
53 Cf. J. Dauvillier, 'L'Evangelisation du Tibet au Moyen Age par l'Eglise Chaldéenne: le probleme des Rapports du Bouddhisme

et du Christianisme' in *Histoire et Institutions des Églises Orientales au moyen Age*, 1983, III, 110–11.
54 Marcelle Lalou, 'Influences Chrétiennes (au Tibet)' in Dauvillier, *Histoire et Institutions des Églises Orientales au moyen Age*, V, 15–19.
55 Ibid., p. 19.
56 Tucci Guiseppe (tr. Samuel, G.), *The Religions of Tibet*, London, Routledge and Kegan Paul, 1970, p. 196.
57 Ian Gillman and Hans-Joachim Klimkeit, *Christians in Asia before 1500*, Richmond, Curzon, 1998, pp. 258–62; cf. also p. 223 and plate 24 for a description and reconstruction of what may be a representation of Christ in the pose and garb of a *Bodhisattva*.
58 G. M. Young, 'A Journey to Toling and Tsaparang in Western Tibet' in *Journal of the Punjab Historical Society*. vol. VII, no. 2, pp. 177–98.
59 Hugues Didier, 'As fontes e o Tibete' in A *Companhia de Jesus e a Missionação no Oriente*, Lisbon, Brotéria/Fundação Oriente, 2000, pp. 451–58.
60 For the distinction cf. A. A .B. Crollius, 'What is so new about Inculturation' in *Gregorianum*, Rome, 1978, pp. 721–33.
61 Cf. M. J. Buckley, 'The Suppression of the Chinese Rites' in *Monumenta Serica Monograph* XXXIII, p. 282.
62 *Nostra Aetate* 2.
63 Unlike Ricci whose name is still widely recognized in China. Cf. Spence J. D., 'Claims and Counter-claims ...' in *Monumenta Serica Monograph XXXIII*, p. 16.
64 Esteves Pereira, p. 8.

Notes on Contributors

Archbishop Michael L. Fitzgerald, M.afr, Prefect of the Pontifical Council for Interreligious Dialogue was born in Walsall (UK) in 1937. Ordained priest as a member of the Society of Missionaries of Africa (White Fathers) in 1961, he obtained his doctorate in theology from the Pontifical Gregorian University (1965) and a BA Hons in Arabic from the School of Oriental and African Studies, London University (1968). After teaching at Makerere University, Kampala, Uganda and at the Pontifical Institute of Arabic and Islamic Studies, Rome, there followed two years of pastoral work in Sudan. After a period on the General Council of the Missionaries of Africa 1980–1986, there came in 1987 an appointment as Secretary of the Secretariat for Non-Christians, now Pontifical Council for Interreligious Dialogue. In 1991 Fr Fitzgerald was appointed titular bishop of Nepte and was ordained by Pope John Paul II on 6 January 1992. On 1 October 2002 he was appointed President of the Pontifical Council for Interreligious Dialogue and was raised to the rank of archbishop. He is author (with R. Caspar) of *Signs of Dialogue. Christian Encounter with Muslims* (1992) and of numerous articles in *Concilium, Islamochristiana, Pro Dialogo*, and *Spiritus*.

Peter Bowe, OSB, is a monk of Douai Abbey, and after a year in India has been much involved with monastic dialogue since the early 1980s. He is the convenor of

Monastic Interfaith Dialogue in Britain & Ireland, which is affiliated to DIM (Dialogue Interreligieux Monastique) and which animates interreligious dialogue throughout the monastic world. He is a member of the European DIM committee and is the author of a number of articles. He was one of the founding fathers of a renewed foundation of Douai Abbey in Douai in 2005.

Pierre de Béthune, OSB, International Secretary of The Monastic Interfaith Dialogue (MID) was born in 1936 at Merke in Belgium. Since 1955 he has been a Benedictine monk at the Monastery of St André de Clerlande, Ottignies, Belgium. He studied theology in Rome, lived in Zaire for eight years, and discovered Zen Buddhism in 1971. In 1977 he travelled to Japan to live in a Zen monastery and learn 'The Way of Tea' and has, since then, maintained numerous contacts with Japanese Buddhists. He is President of the Commission for Monastic Interreligious Dialogue (MID) and a Consultant to the Pontifical Council for Interreligious Dialogue. He has published over fifty articles on the encounter of cultures and religions.

Eoin de Bhaldraithe, OSCO, was born in Co. Mayo; the family name is a Hiberno–Norman version of 'Waldron'. He joined the Cistercians at Roscrea in 1956 and came to the new foundation at Bolton, Co. Kildare in 1965, becoming abbot in 2000. He studied theology with the Benedictines in Sant' Anselmo and since then has written on monastic spirituality, liturgy, christology and ecumenism.

Agnes Wilkins, OSB, is a nun of Stanbrook Abbey. She has always believed that the hidden, contemplative aspect of monastic life has a vital contribution to make in interfaith dialogue. Since acquiring a BA (Divinity) in Catholic Theology at the Maryvale Institute, Birmingham, she has become particularly interested in the spiritual and theological aspects of the dialogue with Islam.

Ian Latham, **LBJ** (Little Brothers of Jesus), has studied in

France and lived for many years in Asia and the Middle East. He now lives in a community of followers of Charles de Foucauld in Peckham, London. He has made a number of special studies on Catholic encounters with Islam, including Louis Massignon in Iraq, and recently published, 'Christian Prayer' in *Catholics and Shi'a in Dialogue: Studies in Theology and Spirituality* (2004).

Jean-Owen Maynard works at CAFOD in London and has recently published two studies on José Vaz and Christian de Chergé with the Catholic Truth Society.

Steven Saxby is an Anglican priest working in East London, where he is Vicar of St Peter's-in-the-Forest, Walthamstow and Secretary of the Waltham Forest Faiths Forum. Steven trained at Westcott House, Cambridge and studied postgraduate theology on Christianity and interreligious dialogue at Heythrop College, University of London.

Anthony O'Mahony, Heythrop College, University of London, Director of Research at the Centre for Christianity and Interreligious Dialogue, with a specialist interest in contemporary Christian theology and politics and Christian-Muslim relations. His publications include *Palestinian Christians: Religion, Politics and Society in the Holy Land* (1999); *Christians and Muslims in the Commonwealth,* (2001); *The Christians communities in Jerusalem and the Holy Land: Studies in History, Religion and Politics,* (2003); *Eastern Christianity: Studies in Modern History, Religion and Politics* (2003); *World Christianity: Theology, Politics, Dialogues* (2003), *Catholics and Shi'a in Dialogue: Studies in Theology and Spirituality* (2004), *Christianity in the Middle East: Studies in Modern History, Theology and Politics* (2005).

Judson Trapnell is a graduate of the Catholic University of America where his doctoral research was on English Benedictine monk Bede Griffiths' theory of religious symbol and practice of dialogue. He published widely on Christian theological encounter with other faiths – *Bede Griffiths: A Life in Dialogue,* 2001; 'Bede Griffiths as Culture

Bearer: An Exploration of the Relationship between Spiritual Transformation and Cultural Change', *American Benedictine Review*, (1996). He died in 2003.

John Flannery undertook postgraduate studies in Catholic theology and other religious traditions and has recently undertaken a research project on the Jesuit encounter with Islam and Buddhism in Asia at the Centre for Christianity and Interreligious Dialogue, Heythrop College, University of London. At present he is working on the history of Catholic relations with Eastern Christianity and Shia Islam in Iran, India and Georgia, and has recently published an account in *Sobornost* (vol. 27:1, 2005) of the martyrdom of the Georgian Queen Ketevan in seventeenth-century Iran, and 'The Syrian Catholic Church', in *Christianity in the Middle East: Studies in Modern History, Theology and Politics* (2005).

Index

Abhishiktananda, Swami (Le Saux) 4, 13
  and *advaita* 8, 13, 19, 199–200, 201–2, 206
  Ascent to the Depth of the Human Heart 215 n.28
  and Bede Griffiths 195–200, 205–6, 215 n.29
  and fulfilment theology 203
  Hindu–Christian Meeting Point 201–2
  Saccidananda: A Christian Approach to Advaitic Experience 201–2, 214 n.18
  and *sannayasa* 208–10
  and Shantivanam Ashram 195–6, 200–1
  spiritual awakening 205–8
  and suspension of judgement 19
Abraham 40, 102–3, 146
  and Massignon 102–3, 155, 158–9, 164, 170, 172–5, 176–7, 181
  and Merton 112, 115
acculturation 220, 236
Acquaviva, Rodolfo 226
adoration of God, and de Foucauld 49–51, 64
advaita: and Abhishiktananda 8, 13, 19, 199–200, 201–2, 206
  and Griffiths 207
Aide al'Implantation Monastique (AIM) 4
AIM *see* Alliance for International Monasticism
Algeria: and de Chergé 13–14, 71–80, 82–93
  and de Foucauld 47–9, 52–65
  Groupe Islamique Armée 83–6, 90–3
  and Massignon 161, 177–8
  Ribat es-Salam 77, 84, 86, 91–2
Alliance for International Monasticism 4–6
  North American Board for East-West Dialogue 6
  see also Monastic Interreligious Dialogue
Almeida, Diogo de 227
Alverny, A. de 152
'Amr al-Makki 105
Andrade, António de: and archetype of lost brother 223–7
  and evangelization from within 227–9, 237
  as Jesuit 217–18, 221–2, 223
  knowledge of other religions 222–3

life 217–19
psychological profile 221–3
theological profile 219–20
Armstrong, R., Hellmann, W. and Short, W. 128
ascetism 11, 14
  Buddhist 33, 228
  in early Church 33, 36
  Sufi 107
ashrams: Christian 195–6
  Hindu 196
Asia: and hidden Christianities 224
  and monastic dialogue vii
  see also Tibetan Buddhism
Asian Mass, silent 17–18
Assisi interfaith meetings: 1986 15, 82
  2002 16
Atisha 228
The Attitude of the Church towards the Followers of Other Religions viii
Attiyah, Sayah 84–6, 91
Augustine of Hippo, St: and the Church 220
  and war and peace 26, 27–8
Avranches, Henri d', *Versified Life of Saint Francis* 131, 135
Aziz, Abdul 97, 104, 108, 113, 114

Al-Badaliyyah movement 101, 102, 146, 162, 163, 177, 179–81
Bainton, R. H. 27–8
Bangkok, pan-Asiatic congress (1968) 5, 15
Barros, João de 225
Basetti-Sani, G. 123, 135, 142, 146
belonging, double 34
Ben Muhalhil (geographer) 234
Benedictine Order: and hospitality 8
  and interreligious dialogue vii, 4–5

see also Abhishiktananda; Griffiths, Bede
Bernard of Clairvaux 36, 41, 122, 137
Bhagavad Gita 211 n.4
Bonaventure, St, *Major Legend of St Francis* 127, 131–2, 135, 136, 139
Bondy, Marie de 59
Boniscambi, Ugolino, *Deeds of Blessed Francis and His Companions* 134
A Book of Exemplary Stories 132, 135
Britain, and interfaith dialogue 16
Buddhism: and asceticism 33, 228
  and Christianity 16, 17, 21, 229–33, 237
  and compassion 21
  and enlightenment 34
  and Islam 223, 226–7, 229–33, 237
  and John Paul II 16
  and Merton 34–6, 112
  and monastic dialogue viii, 3, 5–7, 12, 14, 17, 21–2, 36
  Tibetan 14, 217–38
  Western knowledge of 222–3, 224–5
Burrell, David 22–3, 145

Cannuyer, C. 127
caritas and compassion 21
Carr, Anne 33–4
Caspar, Robert 163, 181
Cassian, John 14, 34
Castries, Henry de 49–51, 53
Cathay, and lost Christians 224–7
Celano *see* Thomas of Celano
celibacy: in Buddhism 33, 225, 226–7
  in early Church 33, 36
  in Hinduism 33
Chaduc, Marc 215 n.29

The Challenge of Peace (US bishops) 30
Charles-Barzel, R. 165, 177
Chergé, Christian de 13–14, 71–95
  abduction and death 14, 92–5
  and Islam 71–81, 94–5
  as prior 78–9, 82–5, 91–2
Chidananda, Swami 215 n.29
Chittick, William C. 107–8
Christianity: and Buddhism 16, 17, 21, 229–33, 237
  and Islam 37–41, 166–8, 228–9
  lost 223, 224–6, 233
  Nestorian 37, 40, 219
Christology: and Islam 38–41, 42
  and Tibetan Buddhism 219
Chronicle of Bernard the Treasurer 130, 135
Chronicle of Ernoul 125, 129–30, 135
Chronicle of Jordan of Giano 142
Church of the East 225, 233–4
Cicero, and war and peace 26, 27–8
Cistercian Order: and interreligious dialogue 4
  and Our Lady of Atlas 71–95
Clement of Alexandria 34–5, 237
Clement VII, Pope 221
communicatio in sacris 4
compassion: and *caritas* 21
  in Islam 155, 159
  in Massignon 101, 151, 160–1, 164, 176, 180
contemplation, in Islam 111–12, 115; *see also* monasticism
Contemplation and Interfaith Dialogue – the Monastic Context 20
Corless, R. 17, 24 n.18, 34
Cragg, K. 127, 145
criteria for dialogue 20
Crusades 28, 41, 122–3, 224

Fifth Crusade 124–7, 130–1, 135–8, 145

Danielou, J. 152
Dauvillier, Jean 234–5
De Beer, F. 136–8, 142–3
De Vitry, Jacques, *Historica Occidentalis* 125, 128–9, 135, 137, 141
desert, and monasticism 35–6, 106, 112–13
Desert Fathers 20, 35, 36
detachment, and monasticism 10, 14
dhikr (remembrance) 113
dhyana (meditation) 200
Dialogue and Proclamation viii
Didier, Hughes 49, 64, 231, 236, 239 nn.31,41, 240 n.44
discernment 20
divinization 13, 34
Dunn, J. 44 n.33
Dupu, J. 19

East-West Spiritual Encounters 7
Eckhart, Meister 32–3, 34, 36
ecumenism 22, 26, 30, 32, 41
Ernoul (chronicler) 125, 129–30, 135
eschatology, Christian 38
Esteves Pereira, Francisco Maria 237
evangelization: and Andrade 220, 227–9, 237
  and de Foucauld 58–60
  from within 158, 224, 227–9, 237
exclusivism 120, 144
experience, spiritual: and dialogue 6–9, 17–18, 22, 34, 51
  as fragmented 18–19

Fakr-El-Din-Farsi 134

Fitzgerald, Michael L. 99, 102
Ford, John 28–9
Foucauld, Charles de 47–67, 77
   conversion 50–1
   death 62–3
   as friend 55–63, 65–6
   and Islam 48–67, 164
   linguistic work 52, 58, 64
   loss of faith 47–8
   and Massignon 47, 54, 62, 66, 99–100, 156–7
   as a monk 52–65
   ordination 52
   as universal brother 54–6, 60, 63–6
Fox, James 29–30
Francis of Assisi, St 120–46
   accounts of encounter with Sultan 128–34
   and Christian witness 140–4, 145
   and Christian–Muslim enmity 122–4
   Earlier Rule 137, 139–40
   and Fifth Crusade 124–7, 130–1, 135–8, 143, 145
   Later Rule 139
   life 121–2
   and mission of peace 138–40, 143, 145
   and stigmata 130, 143
Franciscan Order 121–2, 146
Francke, A. H. 234
Frois, Luis 223

Gandhi, Mahatma 161–2, 164, 175
Al-Ghâzali, Abu Hamid Muhammad al-Tusi 156
Gillet, Ignace 29
Gillman, Ian 236
Goddard, Hugh 122
Goís, Bento de 226–7
Greek Catholic Melkite Church 101, 154, 156, 162, 175

Green, J. 126
Gregory IX, Pope 126, 131, 137
Gregory VIII, Pope 122
Griffith, Sydney 40
Griffiths, Bede 4, 13, 31–2
   and Abhishiktananda 195–200, 205–6, 215 n.29
   and fulfilment theology 203–4
   The Golden String 196
   and inculturation 197–8
   and Kurisumala Ashram 196–7, 201
   The Marriage of East and West 193–5
   'The Meeting of Religions' 203–4
   and *sannyasin* 193–5, 208
   and Shantivanam Ashram 201, 203, 205, 207
   spiritual awakening 205–6, 207–8
Groupe Islamique Armée (Algeria) 83–6, 90–3

Hagar and Ishmael 102, 112–13
Al-Hallâj, Abu 'Abdallah al-Husayn b. Mansur
   and Massignon 98–104, 114–15, 151, 153, 156–9, 164
   and Merton 98–9
   and monasticism 105–12
   and substitution 155, 159, 161
Harpigny, G. 154, 164
Henri d'Avranches, *Versified Life of Saint Francis* 131, 135
Hinduism: and Abhishiktananda 195–6, 198–203, 208
   and Christianity 31–3, 197–8
   and Griffiths 193–5, 196–8, 203–4, 208
   and monastic dialogue viii, 6, 12–13
   and *sannyasa* 193–5
   spirituality 12–13, 197

Vendanta 8, 13, 19, 199
history: in Andrade 219–20
  in Massignon 162
The History of the Emperor Eracles 130
Hoeberichts, J. 124, 136–7, 138–40, 141–2
Honorius III, Pope 123, 126
hospitality: and Massignon 160
  Muslim 100
  in religious dialogue 8–9, 13, 15, 53, 78
Hours, Joseph 59, 61
Hugolino, Cardinal *see* Gregory IX, Pope
Husserl, Edmund 19
Huvelin, Henri 47, 50
Huysmans, Joris-Karl 101, 156

Iacopozzi, 125
Ibn al-Torjoman (Anselmo Turmeda) 166–7
Ibn al-Zayyat 134
Ignatius of Antioch 39
Illuminato, Br 127–8, 131, 132, 135
inbibliation 219
Incarnation 89, 107
  and Buddhism 219, 220
  and Islam 38, 103, 158, 176
inclusivism 120, 144
inculturation 5, 35–6, 54, 197–8, 200
India *see* Abhishktananda, Swami (Le Saux); Griffiths, Bede; Hinduism
Innocent III, Pope, and Crusades 123, 137
Interfaith Network 16
Ishmael: and Massignon 102, 155, 158, 170, 172–5, 179, 181
  and Merton 112–13
  and Second Vatican Council 189 n.54

Islam: and Andrade 222, 223
  and Buddhism 226–7, 229–33, 237
  and Christianity 37–41, 166–8, 228–9
  and de Chergé 13–14, 71–95
  and de Foucauld 47–67, 164
  and Francis of Assisi 120–46
  and Jesus 39–40, 42
  and Massignon 14, 99–104, 145–6, 151–82
  and Merton 26, 37–8, 97–8, 104, 107–10, 112–16
  mission 172–3
  and monastic dialogue viii, 13–14
  as natural religion 167–71, 172–3, 181
  prophetic role 171
  and Second Vatican Council 31, 41
  see also Al-Hallâj; Muhammad; Sufism

Jahangir Khan 218, 229
Jesuits: and evangelization from within 227–9
  and lost Christians 226–7, 229–33
  and Tibetan Buddhism 217–38
Jesus Christ: divinity 38–40, 156, 176
  and fulfilment theology 204
  humanity 50–1, 54
  in Islam 37–8, 39–41, 42, 97, 104, 156, 166, 176
  and self-disclosure of God 19
  in Sufism 106
  see also Christology
John Damascene, St 41
John Paul II, Pope: *Crossing the Threshold of Hope* 16
  and interreligious dialogue 16, 81, 163

John XXIII, Pope, *Pacem in Terris* 29
Jolliet, Jehan 3
Jomier, Jacques 188 n.51
Jubilee interfaith gathering 16
Judaism, and Massignon 184 n.17
judgement, suspension 18, 19–20
Julian of Speyer, *Life of Saint Francis* 125, 130, 135
Al-Junayd, Abu 'l-Qasim al-Baghdadi 105, 106
Justin Martyr 39, 237

Kahil, Mary 101, 145–6, 179
karman, in Tibetan Buddhism 235–6
Kilcourse, George 34
König, Franz 29

La Croix, Jean de 74–7
Lalou, Marcelle 235–6
language, religious 106, 208, 210
Lateran Council, Fourth (1215) 123, 137
Lavigerie, Charles Martial Allemand 48
Le Saux, Henri *see* Abhishiktananda, Swami
Leclercq, Fr Jean 5, 11–12, 115
Lehmann, L. 143
Leloir, Louis 112
Lemarchand, Bruno 91
Lemmens, L. 125–6
liberation, in monasticism 18
The Little Flowers of Saint Francis 134
liturgy: and *advaita* 213 n.12
 and inculturation 197–8, 200
Löhrer, Magnus 30
Loyola, St Ignatius 222
Lubac, Henri de 214 n.17
Lumen Gentium 189 n.54
Lustiger, Jean-Marie 93

Madkour, Ibrahim 187 n.36
Mahieu, Francis 196
Maier, C. 132, 135–6, 141
Malik al-Kamil, Sultan of Egypt:
 and Fifth Crusade 123–7
 and Francis of Assisi 120, 125–6, 128–44
 knowledge of Christianity 127
 as peacemaker 126–7
Maritain, Jacques 69 n.32, 104
marriage, interchurch 30, 34
Martin, K. John 32–3, 36
martyrdom: and de Chergé 13–14, 86, 90, 93–5
 and de Foucauld 62
 and Francis of Assisi 121, 130, 132, 136, 141–4, 145
 and Al-Hallâj 100, 151, 157
 and Massignon 146
Mason, Hubert 98, 100
Massignon, Louis vii, 4
 conversion 99–101, 157
 and De Foucauld 47, 54, 62, 66, 99–100, 156–7
 and al-Hallâj 99–102, 114–15, 151, 153, 156–9
 and Islam 14, 99–104, 107, 145–6, 151–82
 and Judaism 184 n.17
 life 99–102, 154–7
 and Merton 98–104, 108, 112, 114–15, 156
 and St Francis 134, 145–6
 as scholar 154–5, 157–63, 164
 theological reflection 163–82
 writings 164, 165–6, 185–6 n.22
 'Le signe marial' 165, 175–7
 letters 165, 177–81
 'L'Examen du "Présent de l'homme lettré"' 166–71
 L'Hégire d'Ismaël 171–5
meditation: Buddhist 21
 Christian 21–2
 coinherent 17

Hindu 199–200
Menasce, J.-P. de 151–2
Merad, Ali 63, 64, 66–7
Merton, Thomas vii, 4, 5, 14–15, 22, 26–42
  Asian Journal 30
  and Buddhism 14, 34–6, 112
  and Christology 26, 38–41
  Conjectures of a Guilty Bystander 113–14
  conservatism 27
  and Islam 26, 37–8, 97–116
  and issues in dialogue 33–6
  and Massignon 98–104, 108, 112, 114–15, 156
  as peacemaker 27–30
  Seeds of Contemplation 108
  Seeds of Destruction 29
  and Sufism 37, 97–8, 104, 107–10, 113, 115
Meyer, Albert 29
Michon, Bishop Hubert 79
Mico, J. 123, 127–8, 140, 141
MID *see* Monastic Interreligious Dialogue
Monastic Interreligious Dialogue (MID) vii–ix
  criteria for dialogue 20
  future prospects 17–22
  history 3–9
  present status 10–12, 15–17
  seminal figures 12–15
  unobtrusive dialogue 21
monasticism: as archetype 10–11, 14, 111, 153, 209–10
  and asceticism 36
  Buddhist viii, 3, 5–7, 12, 15, 17, 21–2
  Christian vii–viii
  Hindu viii, 6, 15
  as paradigm 11
  and Sufism 97–8, 106–7, 109–12
Monchanin, Jules vii, 12–13, 195–6, 199, 212 n.8, 213 n.13, 214 n.17
Mongol Empire, and lost Christians 224–5
Montserrat, Antonio de 226
Morocco, and de Chergé 73, 79–80
Muhammad: and Abraham 155
  and Jews and Christians 31, 37, 40, 155
  and Massignon 103, 158, 168–71, 173–5, 176, 179, 181
  as negative prophet 103, 173, 175, 181
  night journey 174–5
Munir, F. 126–7, 144
Murray, John Courtenay 28
mysticism
  and Abhishiktananda 13, 208
  and Griffiths 201, 208
  and Massignon 151, 153, 159
  and Merton 33–4
  Sufi 37, 101–2, 106–7, 154, 155, 157

neo-Platonism, influence 33–4, 41
Nestorian Christianity 37, 40, 219
Nicholas of Cusa 37, 39–40
Nobili, Roberto de 196, 219, 227, 237
nonduality *see advaita*
Nostra Aetate vii, 102

Olivera, Bernardo 90
O'Mahony, A. 38, 145, 146
Origen: and Christology 39, 42
  and neo-Platonism 33, 34–5, 41, 237
  and war and peace 26, 28, 41
Our Lady of Atlas Abbey 71–80, 82–90

Pacem in Terris (John XXIII) 29
pacifism, and Merton 28, 30, 41

Palacios, M. A. de 155
pan-Asiatic congress: 1968 5, 15
1973 5
Panikkar, Raimundo 7, 11, 194, 196, 209
Paul III, Pope 221
Paul VI, Pope: and interreligious dialogue vii, 163
and Massignon 101, 102, 163
and Merton 29–30
peace, and Merton 26, 27, 41–2
Pelliot, Paul 234, 235
Peter the Venerable 41, 137
Pieris, Aloysius 17
Pignedoli, Sergio vii–viii, 5
Plotinus, *Enneads* 35–6
pluralism 120, 144
pointe vierge 113–15, 163
Pontifical Council for Interreligious Dialogue vii
and monasticism viii, 5
Pontifical Institute of Arabic and Islamic Studies 74, 80, 167
presence, as dialogue 65
Prester John legend 224–6
Psichari, E. 156

Quran 37–8, 39
and de Foucauld 49
and Massignon 102–4, 158, 167–71, 173–4, 176–7, 181

Rahner, Karl 111
Rajan, Jesu 210 n.1
reason, and Massignon 152–3, 167, 171
reciprocity 57–9, 61–2, 66
religions, fulfilment theology 203–4
renunciation *see sannyasa*
resurrection of Jesus 38–9
Ribat es-Salam, Algeria 76–7, 84, 86, 91–2
Ricci, Matteo 219, 227, 229, 237

Richard I 'The Lionheart' 122
Riley Smith, J. 123
Rocalve, P. 164
Rogers, Murray 206
Roncaglia, M. 124, 125, 127
Rossano, Piero 5
Rubrouck, Guillaume de 224–5, 227, 229, 235

Sabanegh, E. S. 165, 181
sacramentalism: in Christianity 194, 200
in Hinduism 197–8
Said, Edward 184 n.15
Salah al din (Saladin) 122, 127
Salmân Pâk 156
salvation: and Buddhism 235
in Griffiths 203–4
and Hinduism 32–3
in Massignon 179–80, 182
sannyasa (renunciation) 13, 193, 208
sannyasin (renouncers) viii
and Abhishiktananda 196, 208–10
and Griffiths 193–5, 196, 208
Saracens, and Francis of Assisi 124–5, 128–40
Schuon, Frithjof 111–12
Second Vatican Council *see* Vatican II
Serpette, Maurice 64
Shankara 32–3, 36
Shantivanam Ashram 195–6, 200–1, 203, 205, 207
Shawe, and Toussaint, 234
silence, and monasticism 9, 11, 12, 13
Six, Jean-François 49, 64–5
Sortain, Gabriel 28–9
Spellman, Francis 27, 29–30
Stuart, J. 205
Suarez, Francisco 42 n.9
substitution: and Al-Hallâj 155,

159, 161
  and Massignon 101, 146, 162, 176, 180–1
suffering, in Massignon 101, 151, 161, 164
Sufism viii
  Christian 109
  and De Foucauld 77–8, 84
  and *dhikr* 113
  and Massignon 107, 154
  and Merton 37, 97–8, 104, 107–10, 113, 115
  and monasticism 97–8, 106–7
  see also Al-Hallâj
Suyskenus 125
Sykes–Picot agreement 161
symbols, in Hinduism 12, 197–8

Teissier, Henri 85, 87–8, 92
Theisen, Jerome 6
theology: Alexandrian 39, 40
  Antiochene 37, 39
  and dialogue 6, 9
Tholens, Cornelius 5
Thomas of Celano: *First Life of St Francis* 125, 130–1, 135, 141
  Second Life of St Francis 130–1, 137
Tibet: and Christian influence 233–6
  and Church of the East 233–4
  and evangelization from within 227–9, 237
  and Jesuit mission 218–19, 223–4, 226–7, 228, 230–3
  and lost Christians 225–7, 230
Tibetan Buddhism 14, 217–38
Touareg nomads, and de Foucauld 55–62, 64
Tracey, David xi, xii n.1
transformation, and monasticism 14–15, 17–18, 206–7

Trapnell, Judson B. 13
Trent, Council (1545-63) 221
Trinity: and Abhishiktananda 19, 202
  and de Foucauld 48
  and Griffiths 198, 203
  and Islam 38, 103, 158, 176
Tsong Khapa 228
Tucci, Guiseppe 235

Urban II, Pope 122

Vajrayana Buddhism *see* Tibetan Buddhism
Van Rollenhen, Dominique 196
Vatican II: and de Chergé 72–3, 78–9
  and inculturation 197, 200
  and interreligious dialogue vii, 4, 200, 203, 237
  and Islam 31, 41, 102, 189 n.54
  and Massignon 102, 163
  see also Nostra Aetate
Vergès, Henri 86
Vietnam War 27, 29
Visitation of Mary to Elizabeth 60
vocation, in Islam 159

war, Christian teachings 26, 27–8
Weakland, Rembert vii, 5
Wolf, Notker 21
Word of God, and Andrade 219–20

Xavier, Jerome 226
Xavier, St Francis 220, 222–3, 226

Young, G. M. 236

Zahn, G. 42 n.6
*zaouïa*s 53–5
Zen Buddhism 14, 34, 112, 222

Index of Biblical Citations

Old Testament
Genesis
   16:10–12 159
   16:11 113
   17:18–20 102, 155
   18 100
   21:11–13, 18 159

New Testament
Matthew
   10:16 131
   13:11 240 n.47

Luke
   18:9–14 82

John
   3.8 82
   10:30 199
   13:1 ff. 82
   14:6 201

Romans
   1:3 38

1 Corinthians
   15 39

2 Corinthians
   3:17 40
   11:14 4

Ephesians
   2:10 81
   4:3 77

1 Thessalonians
   5:17 113

2 Timothy
   4:7 163

www.ingramcontent.com/pod-product-compliance
Lightning Source LLC
Chambersburg PA
CBHW032020230426
43671CB00005B/150